An Introduction to Social Justice Education in the UK

Also Available from Bloomsbury

Justice Matters, Gloria Ladson-Billings

Race, Politics, and Pandemic Pedagogy: Education in a Time of Crisis, Henry A. Giroux

Insurrections: Education in an Age of Counter-Revolutionary Politics, Henry A. Giroux

Education, Equality and Justice in the New Normal: Global Responses to the Pandemic, edited by Inny Accioly and Donaldo Macedo

Transnational Feminist Politics, Education, and Social Justice: Post Democracy and Post Truth, edited by Silvia Edling and Sheila Macrine

Capitalism, Pedagogy, and the Politics of Being, Noah De Lissovoy

Education and Historical Justice, James Miles and Matthew R. Keynes

An Introduction to Social Justice Education in the UK

Key Challenges and Opportunities

Edited by Sheine Peart

BLOOMSBURY ACADEMIC
LONDON • NEW YORK • OXFORD • NEW DELHI • SYDNEY

BLOOMSBURY ACADEMIC
Bloomsbury Publishing Plc, 50 Bedford Square, London, WC1B 3DP, UK
Bloomsbury Publishing Inc, 1359 Broadway, New York, NY 10018, USA
Bloomsbury Publishing Ireland, 29 Earlsfort Terrace, Dublin 2, D02 AY28, Ireland

BLOOMSBURY, BLOOMSBURY ACADEMIC and the Diana logo
are trademarks of Bloomsbury Publishing Plc

First published in Great Britain 2026

Copyright © Sheine Peart 2026

Sheine Peart has asserted her right under the Copyright,
Designs and Patents Act, 1988, to be identified as Editor of this work.

For legal purposes the Acknowledgements on p. xviii constitute an extension of this copyright page.

Cover Design by Megan Wilson
Cover image © Tinashe Chipawe

All rights reserved. No part of this publication may be: i) reproduced or transmitted in any form, electronic or mechanical, including photocopying, recording or by means of any information storage or retrieval system without prior permission in writing from the publishers; or ii) used or reproduced in any way for the training, development or operation of artificial intelligence (AI) technologies, including generative AI technologies. The rights holders expressly reserve this publication from the text and data mining exception as per Article 4(3) of the Digital Single Market Directive (EU) 2019/790.

Bloomsbury Publishing Plc does not have any control over, or responsibility for, any third-party websites referred to or in this book. All internet addresses given in this book were correct at the time of going to press. The author and publisher regret any inconvenience caused if addresses have changed or sites have ceased to exist, but can accept no responsibility for any such changes.

A catalogue record for this book is available from the British Library.

A catalog record for this book is available from the Library of Congress.

ISBN: HB: 978-1-3504-3810-1
PB: 978-1-3504-3809-5
ePDF: 978-1-3504-3811-8
eBook: 978-1-3504-3812-5

Typeset by Integra Software Services Pvt. Ltd.
Printed and bound in Great Britain

For product safety related questions contact productsafety@bloomsbury.com.

To find out more about our authors and books visit www.bloomsbury.com
and sign up for our newsletters.

Contents

List of Illustrations — vii
List of Contributors — viii
Foreword *Paul Miller* — xiv
Acknowledgements — xviii

1 **Socially Just Education in a Socially Unjust World: Challenges, Issues and Opportunities for the Teachers and Educators** *Sheine Peart* — 1

2 **Bringing Motherhood into the Classroom: Why Parenting Can Build Careers** *Jane Chambers* — 9

3 **Who Benefits from the Great Outdoors: Accessing Nature-Based Learning Opportunities in Prevailing Socio-Economic Inequalities?** *Rachael Fell-Chambers* — 23

4 **Men Becoming Teaching Assistants in an Inclusive Primary School Workforce** *Caroline Meredith* — 37

5 **Making Higher Education More Care-Full: The Complexities of Being a Student Carer** *Sacha Mason and Leanne Leverton* — 49

6 **Capturing the Struggle of Mature Learners in HE** *Sacha Mason* — 63

7 **Is Ebenezer Scrooge Jewish? Countering Antisemitism and Considering Social Justice in the Teaching of *A Christmas Carol*** *Ed Collyer* — 77

8   Drama and Mathematics Educators Working Together: Working at Social Justice with Teachers *Tony Cotton and Helen Toft* 91

9   Meeting Our Responsibilities to All: Re-Cripping Classroom Texts *Clare Lawrence and Clare Mahon* 105

10 'Rethinking Childhood Development: Critiquing Norm-Referenced Approaches in Early Years Education' *Nyree Nicholson* 119

11 Lived Experiences of Black, Asian and Minority Ethnic Students on White Majority Higher Education Campuses in the UK: Can You See Me? *Sheine Peart and Hadiza Kere Abdulrahman* 135

12 Is This Going to Hurt? Engaging in Structural Cultural Change through Implementing Black History Month (BHM) as an Institutional Endeavour in a Small UK University *Sheine Peart and Rachael Fell-Chambers* 149

13 Safe and Accessible Use of Social Media Is a Matter of Social Justice *Katya Bozukova* 163

14 The Expansion of Digital Technology in the Post-Compulsory Sector and Factors Which Influence Students' Engagement with Using Technologies: Are We Swimming or Sinking in Today's Information Age? *Theresa Marriott* 181

15 Conclusions and Key Messages for Educators *Sheine Peart* 197

Index 202

Illustrations

Figure

1	ACROS Fukuoka Prefectural International Hall	28

Tables

1	Refugees Recorded in Different Countries	97
2	Generation Categories and Digital Capabilities (Prensky, 2001; Wolstencroft, and Zhou, 2020)	186
3	Generation Categories and Digital Capabilities (King's College London, 2022: 1)	187
4	Key Indicators of Imposter Syndrome (Phenomenon) Based on Clance's Imposter Phenomenon (IP) Scale (Clance, 1985: 20–2)	188
5	List of Common Issues and Behaviours Arising from Individuals Being Asked to Carry Out Digital Tasks	190

Contributors

Hadiza Kere Abdulrahman is a senior lecturer in Inclusive and Special Education at the University of Lincoln, UK. She is a mother to three sons with the youngest one just coming into adulthood, a daughter, wife, sister, aunt and friend – a really proud Black Muslim woman who taps into those three identifiers all the time. Not only do they inform her, they constantly remind her of her purpose, of who she is and how to move through time and space. After finishing undergraduate studies in Nigeria, she gained a doctorate and other postgraduate qualifications from various universities within the UK. Before becoming an academic, she worked in secondary schools and in further education. She now researches around broader issues of knowledge and identity, and the Almajiranci system of Qur'anic education in Northern Nigeria; she also advocates for the practitioners of Almajiranci and works within the community and with other stakeholders to bring about reforms. She is the founder and the coordinator of the 'Adopt an Almajiri School Initiative', a non-profit organization that engages with the system in a holistic way. For over half of her life, she has officially lived in Lincolnshire and is involved with her local community in various ways and the UK has begun to feel like home. She co-owns a nursery/primary school with her sister in their hometown of Minna, Niger State, Nigeria, and remains deeply invested in Nigeria and all that concerns her.

Katya Bozukova was born in Bulgaria. She gained a bachelor's degree in business from the University of Bath, a master's degree in security from the University of Bath, and a doctorate in criminology and sociology from Royal Holloway, University of London. She began her career in research in 2014, investigating social media-mediated aggression as part of her master's degree, before turning her attention to the role of risk and trust in family perceptions of social media technologies for her doctorate. Throughout her career, she has worked with a number of charities and community interest companies, first as Open Research Fellow and then as Project Manager at the Lincolnshire

Open Research and Innovation Centre. Katya currently pursues her research projects independently.

Jane Chambers is an associate professor and head of the School of Education at St Mary's University. Jane began her career in education as a secondary teacher of chemistry and biology and then worked as a Primary Care Trust schools' advisor and as a national public health advisor. Jane is an ardent advocate of equality and chaired the University's Athena SWAN Self Assessment Team; she is also an active member of the University Equality, Diversity and Inclusion Working Group and co-chair of the University's Parents and Carers Network. Jane was a joint winner of the St Henry Walpole Prize for Teaching and Learning, awarded by St Mary's, in 2022 for her contribution to work on inclusion within the secondary initial teacher education curriculum, and previously in 2022 and again in 2024 was awarded the University Inspirational Leader Award. Jane teaches on the Professional Doctorate in Education programme and is a doctoral research supervisor. She is currently Chief University External Examiner for Post Graduate Taught programmes in education. Jane is a member of the British Educational Research Association and the Chartered College of Teaching. Jane is Chair of the Cathedrals' Group Education Sub-Committee. After completing her MA in Health Promotion and Health Education from the Institute of Education, University of London, Jane completed her MA in Education (Leading Innovation and Change) in 2008 at the University of Surrey, researching the academic value of fourteen to nineteen vocational subjects. She achieved her doctorate in 2017 focussing on the professional identity of teacher educators.

Ed Collyer is a secondary phase English teacher based in East Anglia. He studied towards an English Literature degree at the University of Lincoln before embarking on a PGCE at Lincoln Bishop University in 2016. Ed has worked in secondary education since qualifying, taking roles in subject leadership, school leadership and in the coordination of teacher training and early career induction. He has published and researched in a number of areas including English Education – for which he was awarded the National Association for the Teaching of English's Terry Furlong Award – special educational needs and pedagogy. He has worked for Lincoln Bishop University as a PGCE and PGDE lecturer, alongside being recognized as an honorary research fellow. Ed is currently studying towards his PhD in the field of English Education with Lincoln Bishop University, where he is exploring how trainee English teachers' identities develop in relation to the core aspects of the English curriculum. As an English teacher, Ed views social justice and the exploration of difficult issues through literature as central to his work and always strives to find sensitive and meaningful ways to address these issues in his teaching.

Tony Cotton is an independent education consultant and author and has published many texts on inclusion, equality and mathematics education which are used here in the UK and globally. He is the editor of *Mathematics Teaching*, the journal of The Association of Teachers of Mathematics, and has worked with Ministries of Education around the world, including Belize, Jamaica and Oman. Tony started his career teaching mathematics in secondary schools in Sheffield, England. He then worked as an advisory teacher for anti-racist and multicultural education, completing a master's degree in multicultural education. After gaining his PhD in 1999, he became a lecturer in secondary mathematics education at the University of Nottingham and has taught secondary and primary teacher education in Nottingham and Leeds, becoming the head of the School of Education and Childhood at Leeds Metropolitan University. In 2012, he left the university sector to work full time as a writer and freelance education.

Rachael Fell-Chambers was born in Beverley, East Yorkshire, and has studied at universities in Lincoln, Leicester, Nottingham and Hull gaining a bachelor's degree in criminology, a postgraduate in youth and community work and a master's degree and doctorate in education. Rachael is currently working towards a master's in psychology at Leeds Beckett University with British Psychological Society accreditation. She began her career in social work in 1999 working in residential children's homes, followed by an extensive period in alternative curriculum provision spending ten years as a senior leader. She transferred to higher education in 2010 engaging in a wide range of teaching activity across the university. She has a deep commitment to social justice volunteering for numerous projects and organizations involving young people, including school governor roles and an active charity trustee. In her current role at The University of Hull, she is a lecturer on education and youth work programmes. Rachael lives in East Yorkshire with her husband and two children, dog and cat. Passionate about the natural environment, the family prioritize being in nature wherever possible.

Clare Lawrence is Associate Professor of Participatory Autism Research at Lincoln Bishop University in Lincoln, as well as the English subject lead for the postgraduate teaching course. She is a graduate of York, Oxford, Northumbria and Sheffield Hallam universities and has a twenty-year interest in the ways that disabilities are presented and discussed, both in the classroom and in literature.

Leanne Leverton has studied at universities in Nottingham, Lincoln and Sheffield, gaining a Nursing Diploma (specialism: children) working as a children's nurse on a general ward, paediatric intensive care and community. She continues her nursing education by attaining a Degree as a Specialist

Community Public Health Nurse (Health Visitor). She specializes again as Practice Educator, leading to a combination of her specialist interests of nursing and education studying for a master's in healthcare and education. Working as Practice Educator enabled her to ensure the students working towards the qualification of a health visitor were supported to work towards the standards of best practice. Beginning her university career as a lecturer in health and social care in 2019 afforded her the opportunity to consider the broader remit of health and social care education. She became a senior lecturer three years later. As an unpaid carer, she is invested in weaving her life story as a carer into higher education through her teaching delivery and differing platforms that become available to help shape carers' experiences of higher education both students and staff.

Clare Mahon studied at the University of Warwick before completing her PGCE and a Masters in Education in Critical Approaches to Children's Literature. She is now working as a Latin and Classics teacher while undertaking a PhD at Cambridge University exploring the representation of invisible disability and neurodiversity in myth.

Theresa Marriott comes from a small seaside town on the North East Lincolnshire coast. After travelling across the UK as a forces wife, in her late twenties she resettled back in her hometown and started training to become a teacher in post-compulsory education with an English specialism. In the space of twenty years, while teaching across various sectors, she has achieved a Certificate in Education and a First Class BA Hons in Education and Training from the University of Huddersfield and gained Qualified Teaching and Learning Status (QTLS) from The Society of Education and Training. Additionally, she is a senior fellow of The Higher Education Academy (now Advance HE). Postgraduate education followed immediately afterwards with a PhD in Education awarded in 2020 from the University of Lincoln, with research specializing in professional identities of post-compulsory education teachers and the emergence of Imposter Syndrome as a result of being a trainee teacher. Initially Theresa focused on teaching English in the compulsory, further education and third sector but after completing her honours degree she moved onto teaching the Post Graduate Certificate in Education and worked closely with staff to develop their pedagogies and practice for teaching enhancement. Latterly, she has been working in various universities to develop both staff and student digital capabilities utilizing her extensive knowledge and experience of Imposter Syndrome and her developing theory of Digital Imposter Syndrome particularly during the Covid pandemic. Away from education and academia, Theresa enjoys travelling with her husband, mixed media art and sea glass collecting. She is also currently training to become an Integral Eye Movement Therapy therapist.

Contributors

Sacha Mason has a Bachelor of Education (Hons) with Qualified Teacher Status from Brighton University, a master's degree in Education and a Doctor of Philosophy. She taught in the primary education sector before working in Further Education and has been in Higher Education for over twenty years. Sacha's research background is in education. She has conducted research and published in the fields of Relationships and Sex Education, academic literacies and work-based learners. She is a postgraduate supervisor for master's and doctoral students. Sacha is deeply interested in and committed to widening participation and, in particular, mature learner groups. She seeks to raise awareness of the need for education programmes in Higher Education to acknowledge all aspects of the learner to understand and consider the multifaceted, interconnected and complex lives that they may manage and learn within.

Caroline Meredith grew up on Dartmoor, Devon, and attended school in Plymouth. Following eight years' service in the Women's Royal Air Force, Caroline retrained as an Early Childhood Practitioner in 1993. Alongside a full and varied career in education, Caroline gained a Bachelor of Science degree, a master's degree in Early Childhood Education and a professional doctorate in education. Having worked in playgroups, nursery and playwork, Caroline became a development officer and trainer with the Pre-school Learning Alliance (latterly the Early Years Alliance), visiting and working with over 100 early years settings in the eastern region. She spent seven years as a specialist early years Teaching Assistant for Peterborough City Council, in the field of children's speech, language and communication development. Caroline is a qualified teacher in Further Education, Training and Skills. She worked full time as a curriculum manager at Huntingdonshire Regional College (latterly Cambridge Regional College), teaching vocational programmes and foundation degrees, in partnership with Anglia Ruskin University, for five years. Here, Caroline developed her interest in professional development, sustained by a passion for and belief in the power of lifelong learning to change lives. She joined Lincoln Bishop University in 2012 and lives nearby in Lincoln.

Nyree Nicholson grew up in Poole in Bournemouth and moved to Hull in her teens. Nyree began her career as a childminder and foster carer, going on to do a Foundation Degree in Young Children's Learning and Development through Leeds Beckett University, a BA in Childhood Education and Care and an MA in Education (Early Childhood) at the University of Hull, a Post Graduate Certificate of Education at the University of Huddersfield and a PhD in Education at the University of Lincoln. Nyree is a programme leader at Lincoln Bishop University in Lincoln, UK, specializing in Education and Early Childhood Education. Nyree's research focuses on the critical evaluation of normative development within early years' education frameworks. Her work contributes to the understanding of the complexities and challenges faced by children from diverse backgrounds, including those with Special Educational Needs and Disabilities (SEND). Nyree is a passionate advocate for educational equity and social justice through adding to a dialogue about the equity of assessment methods to accommodate the varied developmental trajectories of young learners. Her research and collaborations with early childhood practitioners provide a foundation for her advocacy of more inclusive and flexible educational strategies.

Sheine Peart was born in Reading Berkshire and has studied at universities in London, Leicester, Sheffield and Nottingham gaining a bachelor's degree in biology, and a master's degree and doctorate in education. She began her career in education in 1986 working first in secondary schools, followed by a period in advisory and youth and community work and then spent fifteen years as a manager in further education. While in FE she also taught numeracy to learners on a wide variety of vocational programmes and managed the college's teacher education programmes. She transferred to higher education in 2006 and through her external examiner work with a range of universities has developed a deep appreciation of quality assurance and strategies to enhance programmes. She has a deep commitment to justice and equality and has led a number of projects designed to enhance and broaden student experience, including an innovative peer support programme, *Black on Track*, in FE for Black male students. In her current role at Lincoln Bishop University she is an associate professor for Access, Equality and Inclusion and the programme leader for the Education Doctorates and is supporting the university to create a more inclusive, welcoming learning environment. Sheine lives in Nottingham with her family.

Helen Toft has taught for many years in primary and secondary schools in England as a teacher of drama and literacy support from primary to adult learners, as well as a brief spell as a visual impairment support teacher which led to her working as inclusively as possible with teacher groups around the world. More recently Helen has used these skills to work with older learners on education degree courses as a way of helping them to deepen their personal understanding as an educator in England. She is currently teaching on the PGCEi at the University of Nottingham with master's level student cohorts in South-East Asia. Helen is a passionate advocate of social justice and works creatively in her local Yorkshire community supporting the elderly as well as asylum-seeking educators escaping regimes and customs which threaten their lives as women or members of the LGBTQ+ global community.

Foreword

An Introduction to Social Justice Education in the UK: Key Challenges and Opportunities is a welcome addition to our understanding of social justice in the context of teacher education and teaching. Hitherto, many publications have focused on social justice in education, in educational/school leadership, although less so on teaching and teacher education. This is an important development, and one which presents a real opportunity for advancing understanding and practice in teacher education and teaching. The four sections of this edited volume – 'Sociological Pressures in the Sector', 'Curriculum Challenges', 'The Impact of Race' and 'Digital Issues for Educators' – reflect the changing nature of social justice issues, and are skilfully and carefully woven together to tell a compelling story of challenges and opportunities in 'doing' and achieving social justice in different educational contexts.

By focusing on these issues in a single volume, Sheine Peart has given effect to Brooks's point that 'Justice is both an abstract "big" idea and also a concrete "little idea"' (Brooks, 2008: 8). This paradox is crucial to our understanding of social justice as a practice. What is it? Can it be felt? Can it be touched? How can it be realized? Through Brooks's statement we deduce that social justice is connected to systems and structures, and to individuals' lived experiences, often negotiated in and through institutions and organizations. This interplay is reinforced by Turhan (2010) who asserts that justice '[I]s not a thing or specific structure to be reified, defined, reduced, observed and replicated'. Rather, it may be understood more usefully as a process, or a way of 'ethical living' in a diverse society (Furman and Shields, 2003: 1358). The events, stories and experiences reported in this volume are therefore uniquely important, each providing insights into the interaction between individuals and institutions, in a specific social, cultural, national and political context, at a particular time.

In Section 1, 'Sociological Pressures in the Sector', the authors provide a critique of challenges simultaneously influencing and shaping education in the UK. The chapter on 'Motherhood' in the classroom is a thoughtful counternarrative to the ways in which motherhood can, in fact, strengthen the professional identity of teacher educators. Teaching 'is an ethic of care' (Smith, 2003), and this chapter is a welcome reminder of the role of 'nurture' in teaching and teacher education. It would be important to understand the extent to which being a father, or a parent, or a carer influences one's professional identity as a teacher or teacher educator, an opportunity for future research.

The chapter on *Nature Based Learning Opportunities* is a refreshing antidote to how education is conceptualized and delivered in highly health- and safety-regulated educational environments. When calls across society are loudest for citizens to protect their environment, why not start by connecting people with nature? The call to embed nature-based pedagogy in teaching is understood and should be made by policy makers who have the power to dictate current content. What an opportunity to link environmental protection to schooling in practical way?

The chapter on *Male Teaching Assistants* highlights critical issues on gender in education and sits against the backdrop of longer-term debates about the absence of male role models at all stages of education. How do we attract males into teaching? How do we retain them? How do we ensure they are not put at undue reputational risks by children? How do we ensure they do not put children at risk? Attracting men in teaching or as teaching assistants must be understood against the experiences of men in teaching, and of those who are teachers, and sustainable ways of building trust while also ensuring safety and security for all are widely implemented. Both have to be considered hand in hand. Otherwise, the relative absence of men in teaching and as teaching assistants will remain an opportunity cost to the educator, to learners and to society.

The chapter on *Being a Carer for Those Working or Studying in HE* surfaces personal, financial and structural tensions within a dynamic of caring for loved ones. While acknowledging the Carers Award as a symbol of recognition, more difficult questions are also asked in relation to the nature and necessity of the carer's role, and about caring for the carer. This complex intersection provides a context within which Rebore (2001) points that social justice is a principle and a guide underlining how humans should live and treat each other as members of a society.

The chapter on *the struggle of adult learners in HE* is an important reminder that learners are different, and age profile is one such measure or indicator. It is true that majority of learners in universities will be recent school leavers; however, a significant minority comprises people who are older, and perhaps with less (or less up to date) experience of education norms (e.g. for referencing). The interplay between university support structures and systems, learner self-efficacy and a form of pedagogy that accepts and understands differences in learner profiles based on age provides a complex yet hopeful background for learners and staff. Development for university staff (lecturers, tutors, professional services staff) that combines knowledge of systems and pedagogy with cultural competence appears an obvious starting point in making university less of a struggle for this learner group.

The above are mere illustrations of a content in a volume that covers *Antisemitism in Canonical Texts, Drama and mathematics teacher-educators working together for social justice, Challenging Ableist Narratives in Classroom Texts, Normalization of Early Childhood Education, Lived Experiences of BAME Students on White Majority Higher Education Campuses in the UK, Safe and accessible use of social media is a matter of social justice, and Digital Technology in the Post-Compulsory Sector.*

Each chapter questions the status quo – whether in education and/or in society – some asking for, and others demanding, more from leaders. As Speight and Vera (2004) note, social justice is a negotiation about process and relationships and not only about outcomes. These chapters present elements as critical tools for change or reifying of the status quo. In other words, social justice cannot be achieved without people in various relationships negotiating about process and outcomes. This is what colleagues and I mean when we describe social justice as 'activism' (Miller et al., 2019). Yet, the oppositive is also true – people and relationships can undermine the attainments of social justice through processes and structures.

This dialogic is foundational to our understanding of social justice. In one word, social justice is fairness. Fairness for each person regardless of any particular ascription. Unfortunately, education, as a tool for social transformation, and educational institutions have often reinforced inequalities observed and experienced in society. Therefore, the tools (education content) and the institutions providing the tool have come to symbolize socially and educationally accepted oppressive forces and spaces. While these outcomes are no doubt unintentional, especially of educational institutions, the contradictions are clear, and these must be carefully examined in order that education (content/tool), learners and educational institutions achieve the best outcomes and returns for all. Put differently, we must not also ask why education (content/tool) is or can be seen as an oppressive force, but we should ask what can be done about it, and we should also do it. Social justice therefore requires much more than ruminations and/or the surfacing of contradictions and tensions. Surface justice in education calls for and demands 'activism: pedagogic, emancipatory and regulatory' (Miller et al., 2019).

Many publications on education and teacher education frame these areas a 'pure sciences' with social justice sitting somewhere in a corner or to the side. That is partly why this volume is so important, for in addition to its expansive coverage, it brings social justice to bear in teaching and teacher education.

This is a welcome opportunity for adding to our understanding of a range of social justice concerns, while simultaneously learning about a range of opportunities for social justice in different educational contexts. This duality is worth noting since many publications on social justice in education do not go far enough, to include opportunities and/or case studies of individuals, leaders, institutions or systems engaging in or leading change, but are instead squarely focused on amplifying 'what's wrong' or gaps in practice or conceptual tensions and deficiencies. While such gaps and deficiencies are important opportunities, it is also important to strike a meaningful balance between what can help move forward understandings and practice, and what can keep us in a space of conceptual and perspectival mistrust. This book offers us a way forward from this potential perspectival and conceptual mistrust by combining challenges and opportunities and by combining theoretical with perspectival and descriptive – leading to authentic visions of optimism and hope, despite the ever-present reminders of the precarious and perilous nature of educational institutions and of society.

Sheine Peart should be congratulated for her bravery in thinking outside the proverbial box in pulling together this edited volume. Furthermore, all the authors involved should also be congratulated for the innovation shown around topic choices and for how they have properly located social justice work as a duality of challenges and opportunities, where one can be greater, or lesser, depending on context, individual agency, and social and political structures.

Paul Miller, PhD
Professor of Educational Leadership & Social Justice
Director, Institute for Educational & Social Equity
Huddersfield, UK
27 August 2024

Acknowledgements

The team of authors are truly grateful to everyone who has worked to make this publication possible. While you are too numerous to name individually, you each know who you are and the contributions you have made. Please accept our sincere and deep appreciation.

Particular thanks are extended to many participants who engaged in primary research and who freely and generously shared their stories and the data which form the core of this volume.

We also want to thank all the staff at Bloomsbury including Mark Richardson and Elissa Burns for their kindness and concern they have shown and the careful way they have guided the authors through the publication process.

We are extremely grateful to Professor Paul Miller for his unique insights and making the time in his hectic working life to write a foreword for us which succinctly synthesizes the core underpinning messages of the text.

Socially Just Education in a Socially Unjust World: Challenges, Issues and Opportunities for the Teachers and Educators

Sheine Peart

Introduction

Education provision in the UK is a rapidly changing landscape which is both impacted by central government and influenced at a grass-roots level by those who work in the diverse settings. Education has become disputed territory where many people from government ministers to religious leaders, sports people and the parents and carers of children and young people have asserted their opinions. While many may hold strong views, the challenges faced in settings are primarily managed by educators and their colleagues. Although politicians have the authority to impose policies, it is the educators who work within settings who are required to create solutions to support policy implementation and to navigate the shifting terrain of legislative obligation and personal ethical commitment.

This chapter explains why this book has been written and its significance for readers. This book adopts a curated approach, bringing together the work of multiple educators, each an expert in their own field and with a successful track history of working in education and making a positive difference to the lives of learners. The text uses both primary research and the reflexive lived experiences of practitioner/educators to provide a rich, multifaceted account of the real-life daily dilemmas faced in education. The text inspires and promotes active engagement with the situations described and through focussed prompts supports the reader to develop their own situated approaches to similar challenges. As such the text provides a model for building and supporting success.

Teachers and educators in all sectors are contractually and legally obliged to provide the best possible educational experiences for all students they work with, including children, young people and adults. Educators are expected to provide moral guidance, support the promotion of government policy and help others navigate increasingly complex social landscapes. They are required to make sense of politically driven educational reforms while simultaneously developing a morally just vision for the future, often with little guidance from central government. As new challenges arise, educators need to be well-informed, academically agile and able to employ creative solutions as they confront ever-increasing complex situations while continuing to provide educationally meaningful learning opportunities for all students in an increasingly fragmented system. This UK-focused text alerts educators from across sectors to a range of persistent curriculum, policy and social issues which require innovative approaches in working towards a just and fair resolution.

The need for clear-sighted, rational education professionals who can work effectively with students, peers and other stakeholders to see beyond headline knee-jerk, quick-fix responses and to interrogate situations in reaching informed, balanced conclusions has increased over time. This edited collection is configured as a socially just response to this tumult and drawing on original innovative research and reflections on lived experience from established and emerging, new scholars present a series of case studies and scenarios which invite the reader to consider how they would manage these situations to secure socially just outcomes for all participants. By utilizing an interdisciplinary approach, this text highlights the interconnectivity across education sectors.

This textbook is based on a philosophy of social justice and draws on contemporary research completed by established and emergent practitioner researchers from a variety of disciplines. The author team embody equality and the team are differently abled, drawn from varying ethnic groups, are of differing ages and genders who are currently working across or who have recently worked in UK and international universities, further education colleges, state and independent primary and secondary schools, early years settings and independent education businesses. As such, the text gives direct voice to individuals who intimately know and understand the scenarios discussed from both personal and professional perspectives. The text therefore provides the awareness of insiders who have direct lived experience and the authority of a research community and gives voice to those at the forefront working in the field and who are ideally placed to represent the issues encountered, pose thought-provoking questions and support practitioners to develop their own unique situated responses.

Structure and organization of this book

Using four key themes that are integral to education to organize the debate – (1) Sociological Pressures in the Sector; (2) Curriculum Challenges; (3) The Impact of Race; and (4) Digital Issues for Educators – this text directly confronts the multiple conundrums regularly faced by practitioners and probes the ambiguities and uncertainties in education. The text has been written for educators by educators working in diverse settings, including informal education, primary classrooms and higher education. By drawing on research from across different sectors, the text highlights how each sector is implicitly connected to all the other sectors and how actions in one area can ripple outwards to impact on the other area.

The book offers a topical and challenging approach to social justice which acknowledges the persistent messiness of education and explores these challenges in depth through giving voice to those working at the forefront of the field and who are ideally placed to represent the issues encountered, pose thought-provoking questions and support practitioners to develop their own unique situated responses. In doing so the book sets out to inspire readers' engagement and support practitioners in building successful outcomes for the children, young people and families they work with and meet.

The different content foci of the four sections support a greater understanding of different themes relevant to all educators and the specific chapters enable readers to explore issues in greater depth by bringing together both theory and practice. Through robust debate, this text:

- Provides insights into different situations which are immediately relevant to the setting specified in the chapter and which have implications for other educational environments;
- Encourages greater understanding of the interconnectivity of different education settings and in so doing provides opportunities for learning across and between sectors;
- Supports reflection on localized and wider issues;
- Offers suggestions on how to approach and work with challenging issues;
- Invites readers to identify personal strategies for the challenges they face in their settings.

Book sections and chapters

Each chapter in this book is organized in the same way. To assist you in developing and growing your skills and understanding, in each chapter there is a 'pause for thought' activity, which presents a scenario and encourages you to consider how you might respond to a comparable situation. At the end of each chapter, there are a set of critically reflexive questions; using the information from the chapter, these questions are designed to help you consider how you might manage a situation like the one described.

The first section of the book, 'Sociological Pressures in the Sector', comprises five chapters and paints a broader picture of different sociological aspects within education. Each chapter examines a key sociological issue which influences the way learning and teaching occur. The section opens with a chapter on motherhood and, rather than taking a child as the starting point of an educational journey, considers how parenthood can be configured as a prequel to learners' engagement with education and how becoming a parent, specifically a mother, enhances the skill set of educators and therefore promotes the achievement of learners, particularly in the field of teacher training. Chapter 3 explores how accessing external green and blue spaces can promote general well-being and improve learners' engagement with learning. The chapter raises the challenge of how educators can help learners to access nature to help support their emotional, physical and mental health and to protect access to outdoor spaces, ensuring that the opportunity to be in and experience nature does not become the sole privilege of those who have sufficient financial assets. Chapter 4 discusses under-researched areas of gender in education. While heteronormative masculine toxicity has been identified as a cause for concern in education, there is a popular perception that increasing the number of male educators would help to challenge continuing gendered disparities in attainment. Although recruiting more males has been offered as a potential solution to attainment, recruitment of men into education remains low, particularly in the primary sector, raising further questions on how male entrants navigate this space. The challenges of providing childcare while studying have been broadly studied. As longevity increases and mental health issues have become widespread in the population, a growing number of students are needing to provide continuous care for relatives while studying at university. Chapter 5 explores the effect of the Carers Charter Quality Award on students' capacity to engage with study and highlights the need for a strategy to provide greater support for student carers which more readily recognizes and accommodates their ongoing needs. Chapter 6, the final chapter in this section, looks at how one group, mature adult learners, often struggle to fully engage with university study as a consequence of multiple competing demands on their time and emotional and physical energies. The chapter asserts that the affective aspects of a students' life should be more fully appreciated and recognized.

The second section of the book has four chapters and covers the familiar territory of the curriculum. Chapter 7 considers how Ebenezer Scrooge is portrayed in Dickens's 'A Christmas Carol' and how his redemption aligned to prevailing Victorian attitudes which positioned Jews as suspicious outsiders. Educators need to be alert to this antisemitic bias when teaching the text and have a clear strategy to contextualize the work and demonstrate how such attitudes are not consistent with the values of contemporary democratic societies. Chapter 8 explores the ways in which drama and mathematics education can be synthesized to explore issues of social justice, with a focus on classroom practice. The chapter demonstrates how two practical workshops, a refugee's journey and modelling the spread of Covid-19, provide opportunities to humanize and bring compassion into the curriculum to help learners appreciate real world impacts on communities and individuals, and ways in which we, as educators, can reconfigure teaching so that social justice is at the centre of all our work. In Chapter 9, educators are asked to examine the ways in which ableist perspectives dominate literature and how disabled people are commonly portrayed as deficit or may be silenced, denied the opportunity to express views in their chosen language. Crip theory is used to move debates away from charity to entitlement and inclusion and readers are directed to consider what this may mean for them, their teaching and their students. Chapter 10 concludes this section and examines how the pressure on early years educators to adopt a normative approach to assessing child development using a narrow, pre-determined set of outcomes provides only a partial picture of a child's capabilities and directs educators to look beyond simple metrics which encourage standardization in every aspect of child development. The chapter concludes by encouraging practitioners to take a broader perspective and adopt a more individualized way of working with children which captures the full range of their abilities.

The third section of the book provides a situated examination of issues associated with race, the experiences of minoritized populations and how organizations can work to develop more inclusive practices using data from one UK university. Chapter 11 examines the life, the daily practices and the prevailing culture. Using a critical race lens, the chapter explores how students of colour may experience university differently from their white counterparts and how these events can be overlooked or ignored when placed in the context of a majority white organization. The chapter encourages a racially literate approach which seeks to provide all students with relevant and appropriate support. Chapter 12 examines how Black History Month (BHM) can be used as a vehicle to raise debates and celebrate achievements of people from the Black diaspora. Rather than taking an ad-hoc, marginalized approach to BHM, the chapter explores how the significance of this occasion can be raised through using a centralized embedded strategy which encompasses all areas of the organization benefiting the whole university community.

The final section of the book looks at the different ways digital technologies impact on our lives and the imperative for everyone to be digitally competent and confident in the twentieth-first century. Chapter 13 examines how gaps in education on social media use from the perspective of parents and children can raise concerns for safety and how some individuals may, due to lack of proper support, be at risk of social disenfranchisement. Chapter 14, the final research-based chapter in the book, explores how technology may be overtaking some communities and individuals' capacity to develop the skills needed to use technology effectively to support and promote learning, creating alienation and exclusion, leading to imposter syndrome. The chapter considers strategies for educators to support learners to enable them to develop the skills they need to successfully navigate the constantly evolving digital terrain.

Conclusion

This book has been written primarily from a UK perspective and details the challenges, frustrations and issues faced in UK education contexts. However, many of the chapters are about larger universal issues such as digital access and racism which transcend international boundaries. As such the text has global relevance and the experiences will be relatable to many different contexts. In an increasingly fractured world where issues of identity and belonging appear to have become even more significant, this text will through its practical approach support readers to identify parallels with their own situations. The book enables the reader to work through and work out contextually relevant responses to the issues they face; how they may identify and challenge social injustice in their own settings; to wrestle with bigger, complex issues; and to produce customized responses to the issues they regularly confront.

The purpose of this chapter was to explain how this book has been organized and to provide you with a tool to navigate the book effectively. While this book will not give you an answer to every situation you will meet, it offers a considered view of how social justice issues are encountered and conceptualized, together with suggestions on the ways you can challenge injustice and how these issues may be managed and positively progressed in educational settings. Like oxygen is essential for human life, social justice is essential for the well-being of everyone in education, including workers in all areas and learners who engage with education. Social justice is not an optional extra, an aspect which is considered at the end; it is the foundation and bedrock of a fair and equitable system of education which strives and adjusts to meet the needs of all staff and all learners at all times. It is situated and contextual and achieving social justice demands active engagement, commitment and vision.

Bringing Motherhood into the Classroom: Why Parenting Can Build Careers

2

Jane Chambers

Introduction

This chapter is about motherhood and teaching, the importance of which focuses on the personal and professional experiences of being a teacher educator and a mother. It explores how motherhood might shape the professional identity of teacher educators and in doing so examines notions of professional identity and understandings of motherhood. A narrative will be constructed about how much women's professional identities are shaped by being a mother and how motherhood weaves into the professional life tapestry of being a teacher educator. My research addresses whether a woman's life as a mother, as Gavron writes, '*complemented rather than restricted [her] performance of other contemporary roles*' (1966: 148). Furthermore, it will explore the extent to which the experience of motherhood allows the teacher educator to be an 'agent' (Bandura, 2006: 164) of their own professional identity. Bandura defines agency as the ability to 'influence one's functioning and life circumstances' (ibid) and it is this notion of self-determination rather than notions of power relations which I suggest drives at deeper understandings of professional identity. The question is of significance because professional women today are still the main carer of children (EIGE, 2021) and the demands of family and home still tend to be the task of women (Wolf, 2013). Furthermore, the recruitment and retention crisis in teaching in England shows no signs for abating (McLean, Worth and Smith, 2024) and therefore how we can retain great teachers continues to be a significant feature of school and academy improvement plans, and not least the country's Department for Education (DfE, 2024).

Of particular significance in the writing of this chapter has been Gavron's landmark work, which, although over fifty years old, remains pertinent today. Conducted in the first half of the 1960s, Gavron's study focused on women and their position within their married familial-economic spheres of existence. It considered the ways in which women's lives were prescribed by marriage and having children which would be at '*the expense of their prior paid employment*' (1966: 154). These observations are to an extent still seen today with women being more likely to take a career break to look after children than their male counterparts (Wolf, 2013). A woman who has children will therefore most likely encounter interruptions to her professional work which needs to be managed if she is to continue with her professional practice.

Drawing on Miller's (2005) work, motherhood is described and explained in terms of a woman having the main responsibility for the growth, nurturing and development of a child in her care. In her writing on women's experiences of motherhood, Miller interchanges between the terms motherhood and being a mother and acknowledges that motherhood is '*not a universally standard experience*' (2005:15). Lyotard writes that our histories are made up of '*wisps of narratives*' and '*little stories*' (1977:36), which for this chapter will be concerned with the experiences of motherhood and being a teacher educator and will be voiced by those who contributed to the underpinning research. Rather than presenting a '*grand narrative*' (Pring, 2006: 32) of the impact of motherhood on professional identity, this writing seeks to share women's personal accounts about the influence of motherhood on their professional identity as a teacher educator, and in doing so will draw upon each woman's situated experience.

In summary, this chapter explores the formation of women's professional identities as teacher educators. It examines the construction of professional identity. A construction which is complex and changing and intricately woven into daily experiences (Hokka, Vahasantanen and Mahlakaarto, 2017), and in light of women's experiences, considers how motherhood influences the formation of their professional identity, and therein their commitment to teacher education.

Teacher educators and professional identity

In developing an understanding of professional identity, Lunenberg, Dengerink and Korthagen differentiate between identity and a professional role. They attest to professional identity being a construct of '*personal views and self-images*' (2014: 6) as compared to the professional role of the teacher educator mainly focusing '*on positions and expectations from the environment'* (ibid). While Hokka, Vahasantanen and Mahlakaarto agree teacher educators are influenced by how they are perceived by others, they do not separate out the notion of professional identity from professional role. They highlight how a teacher educator's perception of self-efficacy, or '*agency*' (2017: 37) in their role is mediated by their professional identity. Identity, they assert, is informed by a collective of self-perception, by '*individual and social/collective issues*' and '*how one presents that "self" to others'* (ibid: 38), a position also held by Thiele, Pope, Singleton, Snape and Stanistreet (2017). In keeping with this theme, Day's (2012) research signals the connection between a teacher's perception of their professional identity and the extent to which they report high levels of self-efficacy. A stable professional identity, Day reports, is '*so important to their [the teacher's] sense of self-efficacy and agency*' (2012: 11). Hokka, Vahasantanen and Mahlakaarto attest to identity being informed by how the person '*feels others perceive and react to them*' (2017: 55). Identity and role are therefore intricately linked and are mediated by a sense of agency, that being the ability to '*make choices and act deliberately in ways that make a significant difference'* (ibid: 37).

Ruohotie-Lyhty and Moate's (2016) research further explores the weave of professional identity. In keeping with Hokka, Vahasantanen and Mahlakaarto (2017), they affirm the importance of making sense of personal experience and history in forming a professional identity. Buchanan writes that professional identity is a '*reconstruction of stuff over time*' (2015: 724). Day goes onto note there is an '*unavoidable interrelationships between the personal and professional'* (2012: 15), because, and with reference to Kelchtermans, teaching is a '*human endeavour*' (2009: 15).

In sharing new understandings of professional identity in terms of the experiences of motherhood and individual agency, this chapter offers an illuminative understanding of women's experiences. This discourse is not, however, concerned with producing a '*higher order*' (Bruce et al., 2016: 4) explanation of women's professional identity nor serves to contribute to '*a feminist perspective on the position of women in society'* (Grbich, 2013: 95). It does not consider motherhood to be an agent of '*limitation ... suffering ... and dependence*' (Benhabib, 1992: 161) while recognizing that women who have children, in mean terms, incur '*a significant wage penalty*' (EIGE, 2021's) when compared to those who do not take career breaks to parent. However, this piece is not principally concerned with whether one's gender drives professional inequality, and neither does it affiliate with a position that a woman's professional identity is in some way inferior to men because (some) women have a biological capacity to give birth to children. This writing acknowledges motherhood assumes '*huge responsibilities*' (Fox and Neiterman, 2015: 671), and it appreciates motherhood as a life-changing event. The phenomenon of motherhood is experiential and gradually develops over time (Miller, 2005). It becomes the frame within which all other figured worlds (Holland, Cain, Lachiotte and Skinner, 2008) come to be contextualized, including that of being a teacher educator. Noddings attests to the complementary roles in being both a mother and a teacher educator when she writes of the '*caring relationship*' (2011: 372) that she has with both her own children and with her students. Being a mother and a teacher educator has a shared endeavour of developing meaningful human relationships, which as Belenky et al. express is no less than a '*complicated human achievement*' (1997:178).

This chapter positions that motherhood has a positive influence on a woman's professional identity. Motherhood can be an agent for development and empowerment rather than an inconvenient episode in a woman's career, and therefore it can contribute to a woman's professional identity or what Lovejoy and Stone (2012: 649) refer to as an '*expanded sense of the self*'.

Pause for thought: Vignette

A trigger for me researching the influence of motherhood on professional identity is the experience I had when returning home from work as a teacher educator. When at work, my purpose was to be a teacher educator; when I returned to the house which I shared with my children and my partner, my role was principally to be a mother. I was frequently late home after a heavy workload and long commute and often when I returned my children were near their bedtime. I was to all purposes an absent parent who returned to the leftovers of my family's endeavours. At work, my office space offered no signal that I was a mother – there were no family pictures in my space, nor children's drawings on the walls. My experience of being was a separation of teacher educator and then mother.

Reflection

With an ever-growing awareness that these two parts of my identity were both spaces of discontent, I began the process of asking that in a context of having to work for financial means, how might being a mother influence who I am at work? My challenge was own motherhood by exploring how it was shaping my professional identity. In doing so, deep questions of self-understanding were examined and in that was the generation of a notion that motherhood serve strength and not be seen as an act of career denial. I therefore invite you to consider how the experience of being a parent or a carer for a loved one has influenced your professional identity and whether this is a question which you have previously encountered.

Methodology: Gathering data and exploring the impact of motherhood

This chapter subscribes to an epistemological understanding that knowing is generated by the individual and their unique phenomena, and which is *'constructed over time and context'* (Uprichard, 2011: 104). The phenomenon of experience is not only therefore temporal but also positional and mediated by history. Women contributing to this chapter were therefore equally valued for their individuality of experience and as being informants to the research (Powney and Watts, 1987). They were invited to offer their stories Clandinin and Connolly (2004) of being a mother and teacher educator. It was these narratives which were used to make new meanings and generate better understandings of the teacher educator's professional identity in relation to the phenomenon of motherhood. What is shared by way of findings is women's idiographic experiences of being mothers and teacher educators and captures their subjective and unique interpretations of their identities. Through the course of an open narrative approach, the women spoke freely; they were invited to *'slacken the intentional threads which attach us to the world'* (Merleau-Ponty, 2013: XIV) and tell their stories. In doing so a pseudonym is used for each woman. Data was collected via a single in-depth face-to-face semi-structured interview with eight women; all interviews lasted a minimum of forty-five minutes.

The influence of motherhood on professional identity

Women who offered their stories universally described how motherhood had changed their professional identity. Maeve, whose child was one year old and who, at the time of interview, had recently returned from maternity leave. She indicated that while she had been up until very recently defined by her professional identity, she anticipated it would be *greatly* affected since recently becoming a mother. This Maeve reasoned would be down to a change of *priorities* and *responsibilities*, and that her professional identity would *become less important* to her. Fiona wrote that motherhood had *shaped how I am*, Alison stated that *it has shaped and pulled and changed who I am and how I work with others* and Ruth noted that *my professional identity has changed in many ways since becoming a mother.* Returning to Maeve she spoke of how her professional identity was being repositioned as a consequence of becoming a mother:

> Before being a mother the importance of being a professional was everything to me and was more important than anything else but that didn't mean family wasn't important but my professional identity was who I was. (Maeve)

Similarly, but from the perspective of a participant who had adult children, Karen indicated her professional identity had changed as a result of being a mother. She summarized this change in terms of motherhood having offered a much broader perspective on her personal and professional life.

For some, such as Maeve, the experience of motherhood had softened their career ambitions as teacher educators. Karen, who had been a mother for twenty-four years, reported that work was no longer at the top of her *priority list* after having children, and Una indicated the needs of her children took precedence over the need for an ambitious career:

> When they were growing up and at home, their needs always came before my professional work. Having been very ambitious as an early career teacher (I completed an MEd whilst working full time in school and became a Head of Department very quickly), this ambition disappeared as they were growing up. (Una)

Brunton, Wiggins and Oakley refer to this transition as being a period in which there is '*a general shift in prioritizing motherhood over paid work*' (2011: 25). Maeve stated while her identity as a teacher educator was changing since having become a mother, she still focused on the need to constantly develop her professional practice:

> Being a mother has affected my identity as a teacher educator that is what I do but my thoughts are very often on trying to do the other role better. (Maeve)

Becoming a mother had for most of the women resulted in them becoming more empathetic, relational and more adaptable. Sarah, a mother of eighteen years, referred to this as a process of:

> 'growing up' and acting more mature in my role as a teacher and feel this is possibly the stage when I had children. (Sarah)

Equally, Alison, a mother of nine years, focused on the reciprocity of a mother-child relationships and the change that brings:

> In shaping my professional identity, I feel he keeps me grounded: sometimes work can be overwhelming but I go home and help him with his homework, and it gives me a necessary perspective. (Alison)

The theme of becoming more empathetic with students and with parents and carers was mentioned by a number of the women, including Alison who said:

> *Having my own children has given me a greater awareness of children's development socially and academically as well as foster a great empathy for those with children and the joys and difficulty that role brings.*
> (Alison)

With an eldest child of six years, Amanda also considered that being a mother had given her *a 360 degree approach to teacher education as opposed to a 270 degree* (Amanda).

Similarly, and drawing upon her experience of being a schoolteacher, Sarah, whose eldest child was eighteen years in age, came to understand her professional role through the eyes of the families whose children she taught. As a result, she had come to question the assumptions she once held about the impact of her professional opinion:

> *I remember speaking to parents at curriculum evenings and happily assuming the position of power and knowledge … Yet I now realize that I had no understanding of this parental identity.* (Sarah)

Consequently, the women had come to adapt their practice and take an even greater account of their learners' needs. This required a reflexive approach which is summarized by Sarah, and then Bella:

> *I do think I spend more time thinking about my possible actions before responding nowadays, taking into account my changed ways of knowing and being and hoping to access more understanding of the person/s I engage with.* (Sarah)

> *You learn very quickly as a mother that what works for one does not work for another you learn the importance of listening and watching and learning from people around you (parents, friends, professionals etc.). You learn to amend and change in light of experience.* (Bella)

Navigating new perspectives – What's changed?

Karen, a mother with adult children, stated that being a mother had offered her a *different perspective* which enabled her to have a *better understanding* of student teachers because she was able to nurture those she taught. This was particularly so when teacher educators were teaching student-teachers similar in age to their own children. Bella summarized this point when she stated:

> *Because I am a mother I realise what some of the students are going through and in fact because I have come from junior school all the way up to HEI and my children are following that route ... I can identify the issues as a mother that I am having as teacher as well.* (Bella)

Maeve, who had ten years' experience of working as a teacher educator, noted that she looked to her role as developing students who she would want to teach her own child. Since becoming a mother, this shift in approach she noted had *become more important – it is more than teacher education.* (Maeve).

Being a mother and appreciating students' needs was further expressed in terms of personal experiences. Amanda noted that the process of learning became more concrete and *real* when she saw her own child developing language and reading skills:

> *Developing language, developing reading skills those things become much more real to me now that I see my own son doing them but I think as a teacher I saw children doing them but I wasn't always aware of my role.* (Amanda)

Lisa, whose eldest child was thirteen years, and Alison, a mother of nine years, made a similar point about how the experience of being a mother informed their practice. Lisa mentioned having children allowed her to see education from a *different angle*, which was in keeping with Alison's opinion that *I consider very particularly what I do because I have a child.* Equally Amy described the influence of motherhood on her professional practice as giving *a particular perspective on children's learning and education,* and Karen, the mother with adult children and twenty-three years' experience of being a teacher educator, stated:

> *I don't just see the student in the class, I try and see them as part of a whole.* (Karen)

Amy, a mother of seventeen years, indicated being a mother had given her cause to look to the long term and make a *very concrete investment in the future, and the community*. The experience of motherhood would seem to have threaded itself into the professional identity, a point affirmed by Mead when she suggested there is '*no hard and fast line*' (1934: 164) in the roles women do. In being so, the stakes are raised for what is expected of being a teacher educator.

The importance and value of education and being a teacher educator is closely associated with being a mother. Fiona stated it was important to her to have a working relationship with student teachers in the same way that she values the relationships she has with her family:

> *It is important to me that they feel their [her children] life is meaningful, whether this be through their work, play or families. I sort of hope I extend this message to the children I have taught and to the students I teach now and I think I always have.* (Fiona)

This notion of motherhood and teacher educators sharing similar values is highlighted in the work of Healy (1999), as too is having high expectations in the classroom. Alison highlighted that as a teacher educator she expected the same high standards from her student teachers as she would from her own children – *I would ask the same of my child what I do of a student in my class.* Amy too spoke of how *passionate* she was to offer a high-quality educational experience which, as she stated, was no different from that she *would hope for [her] own children.* This notion of overlapping identities of being a mother and a teacher educator is evidenced by Jan when she wrote:

> *the roles are possibly not separate on the grounds that a lot of the time you think that while you are with the students would you want them teaching my kids.* (Jan)

Motherhood – What really matters?

Being a mother and teacher educator therefore appears to have a common purpose – the notion of working with integrity:

> *I try to approach motherhood with integrity, aiming to be a good role model, sharing my values and beliefs, and with commitment. I love being a mother, so there's passion there, too! These are some of the same ways that I approached teaching (even before becoming a mother) and my subsequent role as a teacher educator.* (Kath)

Motivating and inspiring people to become a teacher is something which Ruth describes as a profession she *loves and* has *something to do with being a mother* and *about nurturing.* Alison articulates the influence of motherhood on professional identity when she expresses how one's personality comes to *inhabit [and] informs the professional teacher you are.* However, while Karen, Una and Maeve identify with more distinct identity-roles, it appears that motherhood offers them a perspective on the relative importance of the various identities. Maeve, for example, reported motherhood has helped *me not to see my professional identity as my only or most important identity,* and Una, whose children had left home, wrote:

> I now a full time professional and part-time mother (still dropping everything if they need me to). (Una)

Being a teacher educator and a mother involved being sentient, values-led and empathetic and for some women their career ambitions had softened. Sarah conveyed the essence of overlapping values in being both a mother and being a teacher educator when she said:

> who am I as a person and how I treat them [student teachers] is about how I value people, and that comes more from my own identity which precedes being a mother or a teacher educator. (Sarah)

Amy stated her identity prior to having children was defined by being a teacher and it was when she became a mother that her professional identity *radically changed*. She was no longer *defined* by her professional role but *more so by being a mother* (Amy). In relation to motherhood, professional identity therefore appears to evolve with children, and while personal identity begins with the self – *I am me and that is how I see myself first* (Lisa) – the importance of children and professional roles affects how the participants made sense of their own identities. Karen captured the connection between the two identities when she simply stated the identities *influence one another* (Karen), yet the priority maxim is always given to the women's children; *my children always come first and my job a very close second* (Sarah). This applies even when children are older as noted by Karen:

> I am still really concerned about them and still really involved with them and their lives, and so I find getting that balance really difficult if I am honest and so the mother bit is always going to be the most important. (Karen)

It has been discussed how being a teacher educator and mother share similar values and the identity of being a teacher educator is something to take pride in. However, despite these commonalities, the women did report being both a mother and a teacher educator could at times be challenging. Amy said managing a full-time position and being a mother left her *stressed* and often feeling she was not being *a good mother*. She knew she was a *very good teacher* but sometimes she *averaged out feeling like rubbish* (Amy). Similarly, Jan indicated it was at times difficult *to keep both [roles] equally balanced,* and Amy also addressed this point when cautioning against being *defined by one's job* at the expense of caring for your own children. Managing workload for all teachers is a critical contemporary issue for teacher retention (MacLean, Worth and Smith, 2024), and therefore the recommendation here must be how educational systems and structures purposefully retain women who experience career breaks because of motherhood and caring.

Conclusion

Motherhood influences the professional identity of teacher educators. Over time and through social learning experience motherhood informs an enhanced self-understanding of identity which in turn enables a better understanding of professional and personal priorities. It does so in a manner which is positive and affirming and threads together empathetic and relational values and beliefs that are evident in the identity of a teacher and a mother. Ruth summarized this enhancing interrelationship when she stated:

> *my daughter, I didn't realise it but she is absolutely the most important thing that I have ever done in my life, she is my legacy.* (Ruth)

This chapter has highlighted a group of signifiers, concerned with values and personal constructions, which thread through a teacher educator's professional identity. These are integrity and appreciation, and an idiosyncratic, changing and multifaceted understanding of identity. The professional identity of a teacher educator is underscored by an empathetic and relational personality (Buchanan, 2015), driven by a moral quest of betterment (Noddings, 2015). In arriving at this conclusion women spoke of the teacher educator being purposeful in their role, championed by a vocational identity (Wolf, 2013) and belonging to a community of learners (Hokka, Vahasantanen and Mahlakaarto, 2017).

Common to being a teacher educator and a mother are shared values and a purposeful intent for a common good, a conclusion which is affirmed by the work of Gavron (1966). She signalled motherhood would complement other roles women held. Similarly Lovejoy and Stone (2012) gave light to a shared purpose between being a mother and a teacher, and Emslie and Hunt (2009) indicated women with children readily identify the overlap involved in caring work, such as teaching and being a mother. By way of contrast, Kim and Lang (2001) considered motherhood to be a limiting agent on careers, and Butler in 1990 reported on how the label of mother oppressed women. For the women in this enquiry, however, motherhood is an agent of self-efficacy; teacher educators draw upon their personal experiences of being a mother to inform their teaching and recognize their identity of being a mother and a teacher educator are intricately weaved together.

The experience of motherhood is a cause for celebration; it brings opportunities for teacher educators to reflect upon teaching and motherhood as being mutually reinforcing and beneficial, and in doing so offers a richness to professional identity. The experience of motherhood appeared to confer a sense of greater confidence and agency in their professional role and mediated a deeper understanding of the connection between pedagogical theory and pedagogical relationships. The outcomes of this enquiry have indicated being a mother shapes professional identity in a manner which enhances the agency of being a teacher educator. There is a striking concordat between the identity of being a teacher and of being a mother, and of significance, motherhood seems to strengthen professional self-efficacy because it happens at a personal level. There is an enhanced sense of professional self-efficacy and heightened agency comes from within. Given therefore the positive influence motherhood has had on professional identity, teacher educators returning to work following maternity/adoption leave, during keeping in touch days and professional learning events, should be encouraged through dialogue to consider the benefits of being a mother and dissuade discourse away from it being career limiting or inhibiting professional progress. Those with managerial responsibilities should consider the scheduling of meetings to enable teacher educators to fully participate in their multiple roles, and as Gavron back in 1966 recommended, workplaces need to be child-friendly so women can readily work and not seek alternative employment which has closer proximity to childcare facilities (Wolf, 2013). Furthermore, career promotion opportunities and policies should be assessed for the extent to which mothers encounter barriers to progression, and evaluated in terms of whether there is a contextual assumption women will abandon their career plans when they have children.

This chapter positions teaching is a commitment and vocation which is reinforced and enhanced by the experience of motherhood. Being a mother is professionally enabling and enriches the identity and agency of being a teacher educator; it engenders a deeper sense of empathy and appreciation and heightened sustenance to enable and facilitate learning and personal achievement. While being a mother can be exhausting children are their priority and the deeper understanding of the phenomenon of motherhood is it brings strength to the professional identity of teacher educators.

Critical reflective questions

1. How would you describe your professional identity?
2. When you consider your professional identity, what do you consider to be its defining features?
3. To what extent has your professional identity changed over the course of your career?
4. If you are a parent or a carer for a loved one, have you considered how this aspect of your life has influenced your professional identity and if so, how has it?

5   As a parent of carer of a loved one, what advice and guidance would have benefited you when developing your career in education?

References

Bandura, A. (2006). Toward a psychology of human agency. *Perspectives on Psychological Science*, *1*, 164–80.

Belenky, M. F., McVicker Clinchy, B., Goldberger, N. R., and Tarule, J. M. (1997). *Women's Ways of Knowing*. New York: Basicbooks.

Benhabib, S. (1992). *Situating the Self: Gender, Community and Postmodernism in Contemporary Ethics*. Cambridge: Polity Press.

Bruce, A., Beuthin, R., Sheilds, L., Molzahn, A., and Schick-Makaroff, K. (2016). Narrative research evolving: Evolving through narrative research. *International Journal of Qualitative Methods*, *15*(1), 1–6.

Brunton, G., Wiggins, M., and Oakley, A. (2011). *Becoming a Mother: A Research Synthesis of Women's Views on the Experience of First-Time Motherhood*. London: EPPI Centre, Social Science Research Unit, Institute of Education, University of London.

Buchanan, R. (2015). Teacher identity and agency in an era of accountability. *Teachers and Teaching*, *21*(6), 700–19.

Butler, J. (1990). *Gender Trouble: Feminism and the Subversion of Identity*. New York: Routledge.

Clandinin, J. D., and Connelly, M. F. (2004). *Narrative Inquiry: Experience and Story in Qualitative Research*. Oxford: Wiley.

Day, C. (2012). New lives of teachers. *Teacher Education Quarterly*, *39*(1) Winter, 7–26.

Department for Education (2024). *Measures Announced to Boost Teacher Recruitment and Retention*. https://www.gov.uk/government/news/measures-announced-to-boost-teacher-recruitment-and-retention (accessed on 29 April 2024).

Emslie, C., and Hunt, K. (2009). '*Live to work*' or '*Work to live*'? A qualitative study of gender and work-live balance among men and women in mid-life. *Gender, Work and Organization*, *16*(1), 151–72.

European Institute for Gender Equality (2021). *Gender Equality Indies 2021: Health*. https://eige.europa.eu/publications-resources/toolkits-guides/gender-equality-index-2021-report/domain-work?language_content_entity=en (accessed on 1 April 2024).

Fox, B., and Neiterman, E. (2015). Embodied motherhood: Women's feelings about their postpartum bodies. *Gender and Society*, *29*(5), 670–93.

Gavron, H. (1966). *The Captive Wife: Conflicts of Housebound Mothers*. London: Routledge and Kegan Paul.

Grbich, C. (2013). *Qualitative Data Analysis*. London: Sage.

Healy, G. (1999) Structuring commitments in interrupted careers: Career breaks, commitment and the life cycle in teaching. *Gender, Work and Organization*, *6*(4), 185–210.

Hokka, P. Vahasantanen, K., and Mahlakaarto, S. (2017) Teacher educators' collective professional agency and identity – Transforming marginality to strength. *Teaching and Teacher Education, 63,* 36–46. Available at http://www.sciencedirect.com/science/article/pii/S0742051X16308150.

Holland, D., Cain, C., Lachicotte, W., and Skinner Jr, D. (2008). *Identity and Agency in Cultural Worlds.* Cambs, MA: Harvard University.

Kelchtermans, G. (2009). Who I am in how I teach is the message: Self-understanding, vulnerability and reflection. *Teachers and Teaching: Theory and Practice, 15*(2), 257–72.

Kim, J. L. S., and Ling, C. S. (2001). Work-family conflict of women entrepreneurs in Singapore. *Women in Management Review, 16*(5), 204–21.

Lovejoy, M., and Stone, P. (2012). Opting back in: The influence of time at home on professional women's career redirection after opting out. *Gender, Work and Organization, 19*(6), 631–53.

Lunenberg, M., Dengerink, J., and Korthagen, F. (2014). *The Professional Teacher Educator: Roles, Behaviour, and Professional Development of Teacher Educators.* Rotterdam/Boston, MA/Taipei: Sense Publishers.

Lyotard, J. F. (1977). *Instructions Paiennes.* Paris: Galilee.

McLean, D., Worth, J., and Smith, A. (2024). *Teacher Labour Market in England: Annual Report 2024.* Slough: NFER.

Mead, G. H. (1934). *Mind, Self and Society.* Chicago, IL: University of Chicago Press.

Merleau-Ponty, M. (2013). *Phenomenology of Perception.* London: Routledge.

Miller, T. (2005). *Making Sense of Motherhood: A Narrative Approach.* Cambridge: Cambridge University Press.

Noddings, N. (2011). Women and war, in *Peace Education: How We Come to Love and Hate War,* 111–24, Cambridge: Cambridge University Press.

Noddings, N. (2015). A richer, broader view of education. *Society, 52*(3), 232–6.

Powney, J., and Watts, M. (1987). *Interviewing in Educational Research.* London: Routledge and Kegan Paul.

Pring, R. (2006). *Philosophy of Educ*ation. London: Continuum.

Regulator of Social Housing (2024). *Ethnicity Pay Gap Report as at March 2023.* https://assets.publishing.service.gov.uk/media/662a5351e8c75df17da7e4fc/Combined_Pay_Gap_Report_March_2023__2_.pdf (accessed on 5 April 2024).

Ruohotie-Lyhty, M., and Moate, J. (2016). Who and how? Preservice teachers as active agents developing professional identities. *Teaching and Teacher Education, 55,* 318–27.

Thiele, T., Pope, D., Singleton, A., Snape, D., and Stanistreet, D. (2017). Experience of disadvantage: The influence of identity on engagement in working class students' educational trajectories to an elite university. *British Educational Research Journal, 43*(1), 49–67.

Uprichard, E. (2011). Chapter 5, Narratives of the future : complexity, time and temporality, in M. Williams and W. P. Vogt (eds.), *The Sage Handbook of Innovation in Social Research Methods,* 103–18, London: Sage.

Wolf, A. (2013). *The XX Factor: How Working Women Are Creating a New Society.* London: Profile.

Who Benefits from the Great Outdoors: Accessing Nature-Based Learning Opportunities in Prevailing Socio-Economic Inequalities?

Rachael Fell-Chambers

Introduction

The aim of this chapter is to review the evidence and explore strategies and policies to enhance access to nature-based learning opportunities in all guises amid socio-economic disparities. Over the last twenty years, the evidence documenting the benefits of engagement with the natural environment has burgeoned. Many authors have provided evidence to confirm that access to nature-based learning opportunities in the outdoors can have a range of positive impacts on individuals and communities, especially in the context of prevailing socio-economic inequalities (Waite, 2017; Constable, 2017; Roslund et al., 2020).

The majority of research around access to nature draws on the benefits of green spaces such as woodlands, parks, trees and vegetation cover. More recently, however, there has been an emerging interest in the under-explored role of blue spaces such as the sea, lakes and rivers (Georgiou et al., 2021). Acknowledging the diversity of natural settings across blue and green landscapes, and the limited amount of research around blue spaces, this chapter captures both when using the term 'nature'. Only by examining both simultaneously will we gain a clearer understanding of their respective potential advantages for the UK population.

As a consequence of the English Environment Act (2021), an Environmental Improvement Plan (DEFRA, 2023) was published. Acknowledging inequalities in access to nature, within the plan a commitment was made by the government that every household will be within a fifteen-minute walk of a green or blue space. Fields in Trust (2024) investigated the scale of the initiative reporting that over 2.8 million people live more than ten minutes away from green spaces. Since publication in 2023, this commitment has been heavily criticized due to the lack of funding allocated to the initiative and evidence generated to suggest that by not making the pledge legally binding, the government had no intention of meeting the target (Right to Roam, 2024). However, more recently the Department for Environment, Food & Rural Affairs (DEFRA) (2024) confirmed funding of up to 7 million has been secured to 'boost access to nature and support rural communities across England to become more green-fingered'. Reporting that the funding supports the government's ambition that no-one should live more than a fifteen-minute walk from a green space, examples of projects include the expansion of natural play spaces, outdoor kitchens and community orchards. Should this initiative come to fruition, the benefits of learning in nature will be experienced by many more people therefore reducing the inequality in accessibility gap.

Understanding socio-economic inequality

Socio-economic inequality refers to disparities or differences in economic resources, opportunities and outcomes among individuals or groups within society (Warwick-Booth, 2013). These disparities can manifest in various aspects of life, including income, wealth, education, employment, healthcare and housing. Despite a lack of consensus in the field about how to measure socio-economic inequality, there is a general agreement that there are several contributing factors including income, neighbourhood, education and health. This chapter focusses on the factors surrounding inequality in neighbourhoods and their related amenities with a particular focus on access to green spaces.

Inequality perpetuated through socio-economic resources can have significant consequences for individuals, communities and societies as a whole. It can maintain cycles of poverty and disadvantage, limit social mobility and contribute to social tensions and unrest. Addressing socio-economic inequality often requires comprehensive policy interventions aimed at promoting equitable access to education, employment, healthcare, housing, and other essential resources and opportunities.

The National Statistics Socio-Economic Classification (NS-SEC) is a mechanism maintained by the government that indicates an individual's socio-economic position based on their employment. This therefore gives an indicator of areas of deprivation and income poverty. However, this is just one of the contributing factors towards socio-economic status; the overall concept is a complex interplay between cultural, economic and social features. In their geographical analysis of inequality, Hamilton suggests that families experiencing poverty are more likely to reside in communities that have 'substandard housing' and 'poor access to safe open play spaces' (2021: 57). This therefore often leads to a number of health conditions such as respiratory problems and escalating food poverty (Hamilton, 2021). A further consequence of belonging to a lower socio-economic group is the increased likelihood of poor mental health and overall well-being resulting in an unfair distribution of risk. This complex and multifaceted issue is well-documented, and the Mental Health Foundation (MHF) (2020) even go so far to state 'People in the lowest socioeconomic groups have worse health' than those in the higher groups. In their report on inequalities, the MHF group mental health inequalities into four categories, one of which is environmental influences; noting that the 'adverse built environment' and the 'adverse natural environment' (2020: 36) are causative factors in increased mental health problems, they acknowledge the 'positive effects of green spaces on mental health and stress' (ibid).

On behalf of the National Health Service (NHS), Newlove-Delgado (2022) reported that the scale of probable mental health conditions amongst young people aged between eight and sixteen has risen by 12 per cent since 2017, with a notable 23 per cent of seventeen- to nineteen-year-olds reporting a probable condition in 2023. Worthy of note is the discovery that among individuals aged 17–22 with a 'probable mental disorder', 14.8 per cent reported residing in a household that had encountered difficulties in purchasing sufficient food or relied on a food bank in the previous year (Newlove-Delgado, 2022). In contrast, only 2.1 per cent of young people unlikely to have a mental disorder reported similar experiences. Friends of the Earth reported that 'investment in accessible quality green space, especially in areas that have been overlooked or neglected, would certainly be a sound investment in people's physical and mental health and in the nation's natural and semi-natural assets' (2020: 5). Describing green spaces as 'escape resources', the Mental Health Foundation (2020: 38) recommend that to reduce levels of poor mental health, increased green and blue spaces within deprived areas should be made available. With the concerning increase of reported poor mental health, in line with the pending implementation of the Environmental Improvement Plan (DEFRA, 2023), this requirement is seemingly more urgent. The importance of place is documented by Friends of the Earth (2020) who report that over 10 million people live in green-deprived areas. In their national campaign to end green-space deprivation, Friends of the Earth highlight the correlation between income and green-space availability, they provide clear recommendations to both central and local government to overcome the 'significant problem' (2020: 62) of green-space inequality recognizing the impact on health, climate change and biodiversity.

Access to nature

Government data identified that 38 per cent of people live more than a fifteen-minute walk from a green or blue space (DEFRA, 2023: 251). Furthermore, reviewing the geography of space inequality, the Office for National Statistics (ONS) reported that within the 200 most disadvantaged urban areas, 97 per cent do not have access to green space within fifteen minutes' walk from home (ONS, 2021). Examining this issue further, the National Trust, a conservation charity with an urgent priority to protect green spaces across Europe, was commissioned to generate evidence on the disparity in access to green spaces alongside related public demand. Exploring the views of 1,000 children and 1,000 parents, findings suggest that more than 76 per cent of children aged 7–14 desired to spend more time in nature with 31 per cent of parents reporting accessibility and cost as the main barrier (Grierson, 2024). Similarly, in their study Hinkley et al. (2011) explored parents' perspectives on socio-environmental influences with regard to outdoor physical activity amongst pre-school children. They concluded that environmental influences including gaining access to spaces and the quality of outdoor facilities combined with time spent outdoors were two of the main contributing factors associated with children's physical activity.

Another obstacle to children and young people accessing nature is the digital revolution. Innovative, stimulating and engaging technological devices with games that promote addiction are potentially deviating from natural play opportunities. Over thirty years ago Moore reviewed nature-based experiences in the daily lives of children and concluded that 'secondary, vicarious, often distorted, dual sensory' (1993) electronic media are replacing the primary experience of nature. Moore's research is now outdated however since then there has been an exponential digital advancement, particularly since the Covid-19 pandemic when a reliance on technology for communication burgeoned, therefore it could be suggested that the situation has worsened, and children's experience of nature has reduced even more. Burns and Gottschalk (2020) confirm that young people now spend more time in the digital environment than ever before, highlighting that children as young as two years old are mastering basic digital skills such as swiping screens. Whilst the necessity to develop digital competence is acknowledged, many education settings do not offer respite from digital technology therefore young people are deeply immersed on screens daily. Educational settings are responding to rapid developments in educational technology (EdTech) and artificial intelligence to support teaching, learning and management processes across institutions. Tobin (2023) reported that over 900 million was spent on EdTech last year with expenditure likely to grow significantly in coming years. The rapid rise in digital engagement coupled with increasing poor mental health amongst our young people supports the urgent need to leverage nature-based learning opportunities. Progressively, there are educational settings that have responded innovatively to the existing tension between digitization and nature-based pedagogy; an example is provided below by Burlington Junior School in East Yorkshire.

As part of the government's short-lived Nature-Friendly Schools initiative, which aimed to support schools to increase the amount of time spent learning outdoors using nature as the third teacher, Burlington Junior School created a sheltered outdoor classroom to facilitate alfresco learning an established a relaxation area in the form of a wildflower meadow. The nature friendly schools education officer, Andrew Steele (2021), reported,

> *It's been clear to see when we've been running sessions at the school whether working with pupils to make and locate bumblebee nests or taking poetic inspiration from nature as part of a literacy lesson how some pupils who struggle in a classroom setting really thrive when given the opportunity to step outside and engage all of their senses to work kinaesthetically.*

The school were praised during their latest Ofsted inspection on the benefits of the nature-based provision for pupils' physical and mental health. Since 2019, nature friendly schools have assisted the outdoor learning experience of over 48,000 students and 720 educators in more than 180 primary secondary special and alternative provision settings located in areas of social disadvantage.

Evidence generated through the Nature Friendly Schools initiative further endorses the view that access to nature-based learning can provide children and young people from low-income families with enriching experiences, fostering their cognitive, emotional and social development. The initiative however concluded earlier than expected due to competing government financial priorities, leaving schools with reduced resources to provide outdoor educational experiences. In his seminal text, 'Last Child in the Woods', Louv coined the phrase 'Nature Deficit Disorder' (2009) suggesting that children across the globe are suffering from a lack of engagement with nature. He suggests that the culture of performativity pervading the education system is detaching schooling from the physical world, causing 'de-naturing of childhood' (2009) and attributes the rise in childhood obesity to an increase in sedentary lifestyles. Acknowledging that environment-based education is only one antidote to remedying nature deficit disorder, he encourages education providers to view the outdoors and natural environment as the preferred classroom. Bearing resemblance to the renowned McMillan quotation: 'The best classroom and the richest cupboard is roofed only by the sky' (1914: 5), the call to action amongst educators is certainly persuasive.

The biophilia hypothesis advocates that as human beings, we have a deeply engrained genetic disposition to be near natural environments (Wilson, 1993). Awareness of biophilia has gained momentum in the last century with some organizations designing office spaces and schools in line with biophilic design, for example, in Zurich, schools were redesigned including replacing concrete areas with trees and grass. Supporters of this movement report that children and adults concentrate and are more productive in the more natural setting.

Pause for thought: Living the green

A further example of integrating green spaces within an urban area is the ACROS Fukuoka Prefectural International Hall in Japan which is situated in the centre of Fukuoka City (Figure 1). Pioneering green architect, Emilio Ambasz transposed a park in the city centre onto fifteen stepped terraces of the hall. Through the creation of an innovative agro-urban model, the design provides an innovative response to a common urban problem: balancing the private interest in utilizing a property for profit with the community's requirement for accessible green areas.

Figure 1 ACROS Fukuoka Prefectural International Hall.

Reflection

The example above was introduced to overcome the systemic social and environmental injustices evident throughout many urban areas. Supporting the concept of biophilia, such projects are leveraging access to nature in densely populated areas that typically experience more urban air pollution. Recognizing that air pollution affects human health as well as the climate of an area, as educators, particularly those working in urban settings, it becomes necessary to reflect on the possibility of integrating such features in the education domain. It is widely accepted that being outdoors in the fresh air, where trees absorb carbon dioxide and release oxygen, is healthier than being indoors or in congested areas. What could be questioned is whether communities would engage with the innovative projects aimed at reversing the decline of nearby nature. Acknowledging wider factors such as financial implications and planning protocols, decision makers need to give serious consideration to the emergence of urban biophilic creations and the potential to ease the nature divide. Prioritizing the development of community landscapes as areas for restoration, creativity and joy is a political imperative. If educational settings embrace the concept of biophilic design could children, families and communities unconsciously benefit during daily life experiences?

Whilst the biophilia hypothesis has gained considerable attention and has influenced various disciplines, it has attracted criticism. One critique is the lack of empirical evidence directly supporting the biophilia hypothesis. While studies have demonstrated the benefits of nature exposure on human well-being, the hypothesis itself is difficult to test empirically due to its broad and abstract nature. Nevertheless, embracing biophilia, the concept of green roofs, flower walls and living architecture is gaining popularity across the globe with some countries providing financial incentives for installing living roofs (Mihalakakou et al., 2023).

Nature-based learning opportunities

Residents of urban areas, particularly those in underserved communities with limited green spaces, can benefit from increased access to nature. In their study exploring access to nature play in urban parks across fifteen sites, Beery (2020) concluded being close to nature in urban parks can bolster personal resilience and promote sustainability within communities. Nature-based learning opportunities offer a break from urban stressors, promote mental and physical well-being and provide educational experiences.

Urban stressors are one factor Kaplan's Attention Restoration Theory (ART) aimed to overcome. Kaplan (1995) suggested that urban environments overwhelm our senses, constantly generating multiple assaults and demands on an individual's attention. Kaplan (1995) proposes that spending time in nature allows the brain to rest and replenish cognitive functioning aiding recovery from the multiple assaults. They argue that specific features unique to nature, such as clouds, trees, water and expansive landscapes, are restorative by engaging in more effortless involuntary attention. According to Kaplan (1995), the natural environment plays a crucial role in human functioning, encompassing both cognitive and physical aspects. Their research on restorative experiences in nature reinforces the idea that nature contributes positively to health and wellbeing. Kaplan's work points to those communities and individuals not located on a green corridor or close to natural spaces, missing out on the opportunities for mental restoration. Kaplan (1995) asserts that nature is not merely pleasant; it is not solely about uplifting one's mood, instead, it is an essential component of optimal human functioning.

Building on the work of Kaplan, more recent research by two University of Utah psychologists demonstrates that a peaceful walk through a natural setting enhances attention. Using sophisticated electroencephalography (EEG), McDonnell and Strayer (2024) recorded electrical activity in the brain, to measure participants' attentional capacity whilst walking in nature. Contributing to the growing body of empirical evidence on how natural settings contribute to a person's physical and mental health, the EEG data offers a more robust alternative to the surveys and questionnaires used more frequently in the field. A limitation of the study was the limited sample size of ninety-two participants, therefore further research is required in this area. In an alternative study carried out in Belgium, Sleurs et al. (2024) examined the link between green spaces and bone density. They concluded that physical activity is higher amongst children who live near parks, suggesting that access to green space encouraged the physical activity needed to support bone growth. The research 'emphasizes the importance of early-life exposure to green space on children's bone health during crucial periods of growth and development' (Sleurs et al., 2024: 1) therefore suggesting that those without access during the early years are disadvantaged. The authors urge policy makers to consider the 'importance of conserving and expanding residential green spaces to maximize bone mineral density during crucial periods of growth and development' (10) and therefore promote preventative strategies for bone health in later life aiding mutual beneficial outcomes for the individual and health services.

In a further study examining physical benefits of access to nature emerged from Finland in 2020, researchers investigated the impact of urban surroundings on children's microbiome. Roslund et al. (2020) studied seventy-five children aged between three and five years across two genres of pre-school settings. First, standard urban settings with very limited or no access to green space, and second, nature-based settings with access to diverse vegetation and rich soil. The standard urban pre-school settings' outdoor provision consisted typically of inorganic man-made landscaping materials. Over a 28-day period, researchers carried out stool, blood and skin sampling from the children before and after the experience. A subsequent analysis of changes in skin, gut microbiota and blood immunity was undertaken in laboratory conditions. Data analysis confirmed the study hypotheses that, indeed, the biodiversity experienced by the children in the nature-based settings enhanced their immunoregulatory pathways. Roslund et al, acknowledged limitations such as the extraneous variable of the home environment which could impact on the data; however, they concluded that 'low biodiversity in the modern living environment may lead to an uneducated immune system and consequently increase the prevalence of immune-mediated diseases' (2020: 7). Recognizing that correlation does not necessarily mean causation, the causal effects of access to nature-based environments and immunity need to be verified through further research around the globe.

In addition to physical benefits, it has been well documented that access to nature-based learning can offer an impactful way to supplement traditional classroom education. Numerous early pioneers placed great emphasis on outdoor learning environments as an alternative to traditional educational approaches, fostering creativity, problem-solving skills and a sense of curiosity (Froebel 1782–1852, Montessori 1870–1952, Steiner 1861–1925). Their philosophies are based on the understanding that the natural world is one of the best resources for educating children and for nurturing a sense of wonder. Recognizing the value of contact with nature and the importance of the outdoors for learning, aspects of their legacies can be observed in contemporary practice for example Froebel House School in Hull. Signalling caution that outdoor learning must not be romanticized or viewed as an escape from curriculum-based activities, Waite warns that if 'outdoor learning remains an add-on, unembedded in what schools do on a daily basis', an opportunity for 'sustained and sustainable practice' (2017: 266) would be missed. Furthermore, she suggests that by viewing outdoor learning as separate educational resource, an 'anthropocentric view of the world that is counterproductive to education for sustainability' is being reinforced amongst future generations.

The generic nature of the UK statutory schooling system makes a number of assumptions including that all children thrive in a school environment; all children respond well to a timetabled curriculum structure and all children engage with examination as a means of assessment. These assumptions are heavily generalized and for some children, overtly oppressive. A review of school exclusion statistics demonstrates just how many young people do not thrive in the mainstream school system. A Department for Education (2019) study reviewed literature surrounding the disproportionate levels of school exclusion amongst particular groups of children. The detailed literature review revealed that multiple factors contribute to a higher risk of school exclusion including socio-economic deprivation and poor housing. Reasons for school exclusion are multifaceted however, one of which is pupil's needs not being met by the learning environment. Constable supports this notion and suggests that 'children who find classrooms threatening and scary are the same children who take charge outside and as a result they discover new skills and begin to excel' (2017: 7). Recognizing the inexhaustible new discoveries children and young people can make in the outdoor environment, Constable (2017) reports that the outdoor space offers a secure and frequently distinctive environment where children can explore the world. This notion of safety and freedom is one documented by Fell-Chambers (2020) in her doctoral research working alongside young people in a care farm environment.

Care farming is a developing concept that is offered throughout the UK and across the world. Under the umbrella of green care, care farming has many facets such as social farming, therapeutic horticulture and multi-functional agriculture. However, the philosophy of each enterprise is the utilization of natural agricultural landscapes to nurture health and well-being amongst a variety of participant groups (Social Farms and Gardens, 2024). One of these groups is young people who are attending the farm as an alternative curriculum activity due to the statutory school system not meeting their needs. Denys Fell, proprietor of Densholme Farm, remarked that on a care farm young people: 'learn how to play their part and once they become accepted and they feel they have a role to play, bringing their particular talents and experience to bear, I think on a care farm they can thrive very well, a lot better than they can at school'. In her research Fell-Chambers (2020: 140) worked alongside thirteen young people across three differing care farm sites revealing 'care farms provide a nurturing and enabling learning environment for young people to self-discover and freedom from the humiliation and frustration experienced by some in the traditional schooling system' (2020: 140).

Another group who access the farm environment are school children visiting the farm for a day excursion. Recognizing that many urban schools have limited green spaces, schools schedule visits to ensure children who may experience green space deprivation are supported to access nature-based opportunities. With a key role facilitating school visits, Linking Environment and Farming (LEAF) is a charitable organization that strives to involve, inspire and encourage young people through nature-based experiential learning, with the aim of providing future generations with a well-rounded and sound understanding of food production and the environment. Although the work of LEAF is not targeted specifically at those schools located in deprived areas, specialist regional Education Officers ensure that every school has access to the opportunities available, leaving no school or pupil behind.

Expanding nature-based learning opportunities helps support and enhance children's understanding of environmental justice issues, providing equitable access to outdoor education and recreational activities. A further example of nature-based learning in action is the Beach School Network established in 2017, which was drawn together so educators could contribute to addressing educational, social and health inequalities with accessing nature-based spaces. Acknowledging that 'engagement with blue and green space is often lacking in areas of socioeconomic deprivation', the network supports and encourages schools themselves to provide opportunities to subvert this (Talbot-Landers and Garrett, 2024).

Implications for policy

What can be ascertained from the research documented above is persuasive encouragement for outdoor resources and nature-based learning to support public health initiatives such as increasing physical activity levels, reducing sedentary lifestyles and improving the mental and physical health of the nation. Narrowing disparities in health and well-being through embracing the potential of engagement with nature requires a policy imperative. Some researchers and organizations even go so far as suggesting access to nature is enshrined in law (The Wildlife Trusts, 2024). Data demonstrates that the most impoverished communities face greater challenges, as they are twice as likely to reside in areas lacking abundant natural spaces (ONS, 2021).

Worthy of note for policy makers is the wider contribution of nature-based learning to the economy, the longevity of the natural world and care of our people. Education in the outdoors can cultivate a sense of environmental stewardship, encouraging informed decision-making and responsible behaviour towards the natural world. Furthermore, increasing opportunities for nature-based education can aid in generating employment in outdoor education, environmental science and allied sectors. This is particularly important for individuals residing in communities grappling with economic hardship. In their study examining green space and health equity, Rigolon et al. confirmed that enhancing access to green spaces 'could be used as a tool to promote health equity' (2021: 1) identifying that prioritization amongst 'urban planners, park managers, and public health professionals to address health disparities' (ibid) should be given to developing green spaces in low socio-economic communities over other areas, with a particular focus on the consideration of natural spaces beyond the immediate surrounding of their home. The abundance of previously documented empirical evidence such as the immunology study (Roslund et al., 2020) and bone density study (Sleurs et al., 2024) emphasize that reducing green space deprivation can lessen sedentary lifestyles, contribute to positive physical health and potentially decrease the prevalence of health issues associated with a lack of outdoor activity.

Conclusion

This chapter has provided an insight into how socio-economic inequality impacts on access to nature-rich spaces. The impact of green space deprivation has been examined in the context of physical and mental health, education and opportunity. The documented risks associated with nature deficit are not equally distributed; therefore, opportunities for individuals to develop nature capital should be a fundamental priority for policy makers. In a socially just society, access to blue and green spaces should not be a privilege, rather it needs to be an integral aspect of daily existence; however, this opportunity remains out of reach for numerous communities. Further research is required to examine social, economic, cultural and environmental inequalities with a focus on particular populations at risk and their intersections; however, it will take time to achieve this goal. Moreover, research is required to disentangle the relationship between exposure, connectedness to nature and health, in order to delineate their distinct roles.

In summary, expanding access to nature-based learning opportunities in the great outdoors can benefit a wide range of individuals and communities, particularly those facing socio-economic inequalities who are, evidently, disproportionately affected. Replacing nature deficit with nature abundance through the creation of innovative architecture or investment in biodiversity within urban areas has the potential to address disparities in education, health and well-being while fostering a deeper connection to the environment.

Critical reflective questions

1 What are your own experiences and feelings about nature? How might these influence your professional practice?

2 Is a country where everyone is only fifteen minutes from a green or blue space realistic or purely utopian?

3 Are there any times when accessing nearby nature would not be appropriate? Consider why and how this could be overcome.

4 Thinking about your own organization, how can you ensure young people experiencing social inequality are supported to engage in nature-based learning to foster their naturalistic intelligence?

References

Beery, T. (2020). Exploring access to nature play in urban parks: Resilience, sustainability, and early childhood. *Sustainability*, *12*, 1–17.

Burns, T., and Gottschalk, F., eds. (2020), Education in the digital age: Healthy and happy children, *Educational Research and Innovation*. Paris: OECD Publishing.

Constable, K. (2017). *The Outdoor Classroom*. London: Routledge.

Department for Education (2019). *School Exclusion: A Literature Review on the Continued Disproportionate Exclusion of Certain Children*. Available at: https://assets.publishing.service.gov.uk/government/uploads/system/uploads/attachment_data/file/800028/Timpson_review_of_school_exclusion_literature_review.pdf (accessed 10 March 2024).

Department for Environment, Food & Rural Affairs (2023). *Environmental Improvement Plan*. Available at: https://assets.publishing.service.gov.uk/media/64a6d9c1c531eb000c64fffa/environmental-improvement-plan-2023.pdf (accessed 13 March 2024).

Department for Environment, Food & Rural Affairs (2024). *Rural Community Green Spaces to be Rejuvenated through New Government Investment*. Available at: https://www.gov.uk/government/news/rural-community-green-spaces-to-be-rejuvenated-through-new-government-investment (accessed 11 March 2024).

Fell-Chambers, R. (2020). *Care Farming, Learning and Young People*. Available at: https://educationstudies.org.uk/wp-content/uploads/2022/12/BESA-Journal-EF-13-2-09-Fell-Chambers.pdf (accessed 12 February 2024).

Fields in Trust. (2024). *Green Space Index*. Available at: https://fieldsintrust.org/insights/green-space-index (accessed 12 February 2024).

Friends of the Earth. (2020). *England's Green Space Gap*. Available at: https://policy.friendsoftheearth.uk/sites/default/files/documents/2020-10/Green_space_gap_full_report_1.pdf (accessed 15 February 2024).

Georgiou, M., Morison, G., Smith, N., Tieges, Z., and Chastin, S. (2021). Mechanisms of impact of blue spaces on human health: A systematic literature review and meta-analysis. *International Journal of Environmental Research and Public Health*, *18*(5), 24–86.

Grierson, J. (2024). *Three-quarters of Children Want More Time in Nature, Says National Trust*. Available at: https://www.theguardian.com/environment/2024/apr/01/over-three-quarters-children-want-more-time-nature-national-trust?mc_cid=6553a87b99&mc_eid=4d03f9efc6 (accessed 17 February 2024).

Hamiliton, P. (2021). *Diversity and Marginalisation*. London: Sage.

Hinkley, T., Salmon, J., Okely, A. D., Crawford, D., and Hesketh, K. (2011). Influences on preschool children's physical activity. *Family Community Health*, *34*(1), 39–50.

Kaplan, S. (1995). The restorative benefits of nature: Toward an integrative framework. *Journal of Environmental Psychology*, *15*(3), 169–82.

Louv, R. (2009). *Last Child in the Woods*. London: Atlantic Books.

McDonnell, A. S., and Strayer, D. L. (2024). Immersion in nature enhances neural indices of executive attention. *Scientific Reports*, *14*, 18–45.

McMillan, M., 1919. *The Nursery School*. London: J. M. Dent and Sons.

Mental Health Foundation. (2020). *Tackling Social Inequalities to Reduce Mental Health Problems*. Available at: https://www.mentalhealth.org.uk/sites/default/files/2022-04/MHF-tackling-inequalities-report.pdf (accessed 12 February 2024).

Mihalakakou, G., Souliotis, M., Papadaki, M., Menounou, P., Dimopoulos, P., Kolokotsa, D., Paravantis, J., Tsangrassoulis, A., Panaras, G., Giannakopoulos, E., and Papaefthimiou, S. (2023). Green roofs as a nature-based solution for improving urban sustainability: Progress and perspectives. *Renewable and Sustainable Energy Reviews*, *180*, 113–306.

Moore, R. (1993). *Plants for Play: A Plant Selection Guide for Children's Outdoor Environments*. London: Atlantic Books.

Newlove-Delgado, T., Marcheselli, F., Williams, T., Mandalia, D., Davis, J., McManus, S., Savic, M., Treloar, W., and Ford, T. (2022). *Mental Health of Children and Young People in England*. Leeds: NHS Digital.

Office for National Statistics (2021). *Access to Public Green Space in Great Britain*. Available at: https://www.ons.gov.uk/economy/environmentalaccounts/datasets/accesstopublicgreenspaceingreatbritain (accessed 12 April 2024).

Right to Roam (2024). *The Right to Roam Is the Right to Reconnect*. Available at: https://www.righttoroam.org.uk/ (accessed 10 February 2024).

Rigolon, A., Browning, M. H. E. M., McAnirlin, O., and Yoon, H. (2021). Green space and health equity: A systematic review on the potential of green space to reduce health disparities, *Journal of Environmental and Public Health*, *18*, 1–27.

Roslund, M., Puhakka, R., Grönroos, M., Nurminen, N., Oikarinen, S., Gazali, A., Cinek, O., Kramná, L., Siter, N., Vari, H., Soininen, L., Parajuli, A., Rajaniemi, J., Kinnunen, T., Laitinen, O., Hyöty, H., and Sinkkonen, A. (2020). Biodiversity intervention enhances immune regulation and health-associated commensal microbiota among daycare children. *Science Advances*, *6*, 25–78.

Sleurs, H., Inês Silva, A., Bijnens, E. M., Dockx Y., Peusens, M., Rasking, L., Plusquin, M., and Nawrot, T. (2024). Exposure to residential green space and bone mineral density in young children. *JAMA Network Open*, *7*(1), e2350214.

Social Farms & Gardens (2024). *Care Farming Knowledge Base*. Available at: https://www.farmgarden.org.uk/knowledge-base/homepage (accessed 1 April 2024).

Steele, A. (2021), *Nature Friendly Schools*. Available at: https://www.naturefriendlyschools.co.uk/ (accessed 12 April 2024).

Talbot-Landers, C., and Garrett, B. (2024), *Teachers Are Doing It for Themselves: Developing Beach School Approaches to Support an Effective Climate Change Curriculum*. Available at: https://www.bera.ac.uk/blog/teachers-are-doing-it-for-themselves-developing-beach-school-approaches-to-support-an-effective-climate-change-curriculum?fbclid=IwAR08yxyHpGeeHK-hL8dPUHcn77SVmCY-0r6t2oxtUY (accessed 12 February 2024).

The National Trust (2024). *About Us*. Available at: https://www.nationaltrust.org.uk/who-we-are/about-us (accessed 12 February 2024).

The Wildlife Trusts (2024). *About Us*. Available at: https://www.wildlifetrusts.org/about-us (accessed 12 February 2024).

Tobin, J. (2023). *Educational Technology: Digital Innovation and AI in Schools*. House of Lords Library. Available at: https://lordslibrary.parliament.uk/educational-technology-digital-innovation-and-ai-in-schools/#:~:text=During%20this%20period%2C%20research%20cited,mix%20of%20new%20and%20old (accessed 9 March 2024).

Waite, S. (2017). *Children Learning Outside the Classroom*. London: Sage.

Warwick-Booth, L. (2013). *Social Inequality*. London: Sage.

Wilson, E. O. (1993), Biophilia and the conservation ethic, in S. Kellert and E. O. Wilson (eds.), *The Biophilia Hypothesis*, 31–40, Washington, DC: Shearwater Books.

Men Becoming Teaching Assistants in an Inclusive Primary School Workforce

4

Caroline Meredith

Introduction

Over the past thirty years, as performativity and accountability have tightened their grip on England's education policy and practice, the schools' workforce has been transformed. The 'Schools Workforce in England' review reveals a three-fold increase in the number of Teaching Assistants (TAs) in England since 2003 (National Statistics, 2003, 2023). Now occupying one-third of the school workforce, TAs work alongside qualified teachers to deliver the curriculum, and support pupils' learning and well-being. In 2021–22, 93 per cent of the 274,235 TAs in English primary and nursery education were women, adding to the female-concentrated primary school workforce, in which 85 per cent of qualified teachers are women (National Statistics, 2023).

A pervasive debate about gendered, attainment inequality in primary education emerged through the shift to data-driven education policy from the late 1990s (Pepperell and Smedley, 1998). Conflated with a long-standing discourse that problematizes gender within the primary education workforce, political perspectives have tended to make causal associations between a perceived, negative attainment gap between girls and boys, boys' apparent under-achievement, and the female-concentrated teaching workforce in primary schools (Brownhill et al., 2021). Public and political voices have demanded action to increase recruitment of men as teachers. As argued by Arnot and Mac an Ghaill (2006: 6), this seems paradoxical 'given the huge number of female teaching assistants recruited into schools to sustain the performance culture'. Nevertheless, the popular press continues to decry the female-concentrated primary school workforce (*ITV News*, 2023), and demands for men to be recruited into primary teaching endure within contemporary political discourse (UK Parliament, 2022).

Competing voices dispute the issues of children's (particularly boys') under-achievement, alleged lack of role models in the home and qualitative assumptions about men and women's teaching styles (Warin and Wernersson, 2016). Adding fresh voices to this long-standing debate, this chapter utilizes evidence from primary research, which examined the motivations, aspirations and experiences of men becoming primary school TAs. Men TAs' voices have rarely been captured in research about the TA role, and they remain relatively silent within popular and political commentary that demands more men teachers in primary education. Therefore, the research asked two principal questions: What motivates men to become TAs? What are their experiences and aspirations?

The past decade has seen a paradigmatic shift in language surrounding gender identities (Paechter, 2021). A complex set of alternatives has emerged, which challenges established, binarized perspectives of masculinity, femininity and gender roles. Increasingly, gender-identity is presented as variable and spectral. Expressions such as non-binary, a-gender and gender-fluid have entered the lexicon of policy and practice (Paechter, 2021). This paradigm shift has exerted pressure on taken-for-granted gender norms and boundaries, placing the spotlight on gender awareness in education contexts. This presents a timely moment within a persistent debate, to re-examine normative understandings of a gender inclusive workforce in primary education, and implications for practice.

This chapter acknowledges the plurality of gender identity which has percolated in social consciousness and political discourse in the past decade and recognizes how these have influenced education practice. Popular and political debates surrounding the gendered workforce in primary education remain essentially binarized, and the research and its discussion reflect the sometimes-reductive language of surrounding discourse. Nevertheless, this discussion recognizes that contemporary interpretations of masculinity, femininity and gender itself are plural and variable.

Gender inclusivity and the TA role

Whilst some authors suggest wide acceptance of the need for a more equal number of men and women in primary teaching (Mistry and Sood, 2014), others dispute the existence of a robust, research-informed evidence-base with which to support this notion (Francis, 2008). Whilst outcomes in terms of attainment remain speculative, it might be reasonably supposed that increasing the male presence in primary schools will change primary schools' culture and pupils' perceptions of gender. However, it cannot be assumed that this will be a positive change, if the way men are enculturated into the workforce perpetuates gender stereotypes and undermines multiple configurations of masculinity and femininity, across a broad and increasing spectrum of gender identity. The social world of the primary school is more than a mere reflection of social structures and norms; it is one of the principal sites of social construction (Tait, 2016), in which life templates are established, re-enforced and normalized. Multiple interpretations of gender (Paechter, 2021) have long-term implications for education and wider society. This raises the urgency to confront rigid, binarized assumptions that typify contemporary debates about men and women as teachers and TAs in primary education, as part of a knowledge-informed drive to promote a gender-inclusive workforce.

TA work displays the characteristics of a feminized occupation, such as low status and low pay and subordination (Seeley, 2018). The TA role is deferential to the superior status of qualified teachers. It lacks a clear career progression structure, or professional identity of its own. Opportunities for TAs' advancement within the role are characteristically few. Contracts are precariously dependent upon funding streams, school cohort size and school-based staff deployment decisions (Blatchford, Russell and Webster, 2012). Combined, these factors present the TA role as a job with relatively limited scope or reward. As a context for employment, TA work remains insecure and vulnerable to external and internal pressures on school budgets and staff deployment needs. In keeping with other feminized occupations, these pressures render TA work as a potentially risky source of family income.

Against this unappealing backdrop, the question of what motivates men to become TAs concedes the low material benefits and status of the role. Men becoming TAs are unlikely to be motivated singularly by the wage or any prospect of job-security. Even in the presence of vocational rewards, such a scenario might be intolerable for extended periods for men, who frequently encounter social pressures to be primary household earners (Torre, 2018). The research therefore explored what had motivated some of the men who are already working as TAs, what had attracted them to the role, and their aspirations.

Gendered discourses of damage and repair

A discourse of boys' failure that focuses on a perceived gender gap in achievement, attainment and behaviour pervades internationally, for example, in Australia, New Zealand and Canada (Brownhill et al., 2021). Commonly, as in England this discourse is characterized by policymakers' pre-occupation with comparing pupils' outcomes, accompanied by claims that the school curriculum has become excessively 'feminised' by the prevalence of women teachers (Brownhill et al., 2021: 645). In response, a discourse of male repair rests on the premise that employing more men teachers in primary schools will provide a panacea to a generation of troubled, fatherless boys who are failing at school through a lack of male role-models (Warin and Wernersson, 2016). Prevailing arguments therefore tend to be predicated in normative claims about men's absence from, rather than their presence in children's lives in and outside of education. Far from countering gendered stereotypes this perspective further entrenches normative, gendered constructs of men and women by suggesting that certain challenges in education (and in family life) can only be overcome by men. It perpetuates the stereotype of women as less competent in certain areas of teaching and learning and suggests the need for a superordinate male to redress a problematic deficit. Hence, an implied rarity value privileges men teachers over women teachers and further relegates the TA role.

For men becoming TAs, the conflation of TA work with caring and mothering (Barkham, 2008) intensifies the assumed maternality of the role, alongside normative discourses, and rhetorical claims about the separate and distinctive contribution that men are assumed to bring to an otherwise feminized work sector. This can manifest as sexist stereotyping, in which certain workplace tasks or specialisms such as sports or teaching older children may be presented as requiring a specialist, masculine approach. Men teachers tend to be perceived as disciplinarian, which Burn and Pratt-Adams (2015) attribute to a patriarchal social script of male discipline in school and the home. Whilst it might enable men to legitimize their position in a female-concentrated employment sector, gendered role appropriation carries a disadvantageous tendency to assume that men are innately unsuited to other roles, such as nurturing very young children in Early Years education (Cruikshank, Kerby and Baguley, 2022).

Pause for thought: Role models

The expression 'role model' has become ubiquitous in popular and political discourses that argue for more male educators in primary education. Research by Brownhill et al. (2021) investigated male educators' understanding of the concept of 'role modelling' as applied to their professional roles, as teachers or trainee teachers. Emerging themes included the *sources of role models* ('far off' sources such as sports personalities and 'real world' sources in the child's direct experience); *behaviours* (negative and positive); what *being a role model* means in learning and teaching, and *tensions* that exist around role modelling (whether the role model is 'something' or 'someone'). The researchers warn that the notion of 'role modelling' remains ambiguous and they encourage educators to critically question the validity of the 'role model' argument, as a key driver of male recruitment. Instead, they argue for greater clarity, and professional development opportunities to deepen educators' understanding of role-modelling, its meanings and interpretations in practice.

Reflection

Dominant discourses promote the concept of gender-matched role models in primary school, particularly for boys. This relies on the dual assumption that some boys lack suitable or sufficient models elsewhere in their lives and that boys readily accept men teachers as models. If this is the case, is the male teacher required to model a particular interpretation of 'masculinity'? Is this equitable with the expectations of women teachers? Brownhill et al. (2021) challenge the assumption that role modelling is gender specific and argue that children select models of different genders. Reflecting on your own professional role, can you identify yourself as a model for children's behaviour, learning and self-concept? How can educators help children to identify their own, chosen role models, and the behaviours and attitudes they value? What support might school staff need, to gain deeper understanding of positive role-modelling and develop a collective approach to role-modelling?

Saviour or threat?

Further tensions occur between the perceived 'need' for male practitioners and contemporary, normative discourses which question the motives of men who choose to work with young children. Burn and Pratt-Adams (2015) discuss sexualized stereotypes which routinely cast men who work with children as sexual deviants or predators. They note the reality of sexualized suspicion about men working with children, as an ever-present threat of false accusation. They suggest that this 'silent discourse' (2015: 123) is rarely voiced, yet widely acknowledged in professional contexts. Whilst unspoken, this discourse can manifest in institutional 'gender regimes' which separate men from children's care needs (Cruickshank, Kerby and Baguley, 2022: 979). Although well-intended and perhaps invoked to shield men from false accusation, arbitrary 'no-touch' policies which do not establish safe boundaries for all practitioners also carry the risk of perpetuating the stereotype of the dangerous male in primary education contexts and run counter to the notion of a gender-inclusive workforce.

Contradictory discourses therefore present a confused landscape for men practitioners, who are expected to perform as role models (Brownhill et al., 2021) and rescue the primary education sector from its own feminization, whilst on the other hand being constituted as a potential threat to children's well-being. This dichotomy presents a persistent dilemma in the context of a gender-inclusive workforce that is characterized by full and equal participation of its members. Fresh, compelling reasons to champion a more diverse workforce for the primary education sector are based in models of social diversity and inclusion rather than male repair. Any profession, which resists equal participation in all of its activities through negativity and bias, deprives itself and wider society of the richness of contribution by all members. Rather than emphasizing difference, the 'social-equity hypothesis' (Francis, 2008: 325) proposes that a more gender-inclusive schools workforce might present primary education as a desirable and worthwhile vocation for all.

Methodology: Capturing unheard voices

A narrative approach was adopted, which invited nine men who had become TAs in primary education settings to share their personal career stories. The sample group was drawn from a field of men who were studying for degrees in education alongside their regular work as TAs. The degree programmes they had chosen offered professional development routes into teaching for experienced TAs. It was recognized at the outset that this sample group was therefore limited to TAs who demonstrated desire to develop personally and professionally, within the TA role. This defining characteristic was relevant to the questions of what had motivated the participants to enter the TA role, in the context of their future career aspirations.

The study acknowledged that personal and career identities are constituted through various, subjective and relative actions and interactions, depending on individual circumstances, influences and resources (Savickas et al., 2009). Nevertheless, although they are highly personalized, individual career stories offer potential insight into wider social influences on working lives (Meijers and Lengelle, 2012). The narrative approach provided a valid means to explore and understand individual experience, in the context of wider social influences, and socially constructed norms. The study valued individual participants' recollections and interpretations of their own career paths, as authentic and relevant data, to better understand men's experiences of becoming primary school TAs. Data was captured through one semi-structured interview with each participant, using a life-grid to scaffold the emerging narratives through significant events and key moments in their personal lives, education and work. Narrative data was presented and developed using graphic timelines and chronicled career stories. Four opportunities for participant verification (one at each stage of the methodology) enabled participants share further reflections, which contributed to the analysis. Hence, the research sought to capture faithfully the participants' intended meanings and provide an authentic representation of their voices as men becoming primary school TAs.

The men participating in the study provided a diverse range of career narratives. Their occupations and experiences prior to becoming TAs included uniformed services, funeral services, travel and tourism, sports, childcare, telecommunications, logistics and haulage, hospitality, retail and unskilled factory work. Participants had entered the role of TA, either directly through paid employment including apprenticeships, or indirectly through regular volunteering as students or parents.

Men becoming TAs

The findings of the research indicate that the motivations, experiences and aspirations of men becoming TAs were interwoven and holistic. The narratives did not suggest that any participant was directly influenced or inspired to enter the primary education work sector by rhetorical discourses of boys' failure or excessively feminized curricula, or to re-dress the numerical gender balance in the TA workforce. The participants in this study were motivated to become TAs by intrinsic drivers such as a vocation to help people, to listen to and inspire children, and a desire for meaningful work that made a positive difference to other people's lives. Personal, vocational satisfaction was augmented by the opportunity for professional development within longer-term career plans. Motivation was frequently associated with aspiration to teach, with Ben stating: *I just really wanted to make the most of it ... and now I'm at a point where my future plans are to get into teaching.* In some cases, this was part of an ambitious career trajectory in which the TA role was considered temporary, from an early stage. Mark explained: '*Being a teaching assistant isn't something I'd want to do for the rest of my life. It was always a very short-term plan to get me into that position of being a teacher.*'

Participants' planned exit routes from the TA role affirmed a high rate of attrition in the sample group, which was frequently associated with limited earnings as a TA, or the opportunity to earn more as a teacher. By becoming primary teachers, the participants in this study had consciously chosen to transfer their careers to another female-dominated occupation, albeit a higher status one.

Gendered roles and the enactment of care

Narratives contained some references to gendered phenomena. Four narratives suggested some passing encounters with gender discrimination or a generalized sense of discomfiture about being a man in a female-dominated sector. Most of the participants mentioned their numerical minority. Luke commented that: *There are only two male teachers. There are four female teachers plus all the TAs ... and the office staff, they're female as well.* Moving into a primary school from the male-dominated social world of haulage and logistics, Roy disclosed that it felt very 'odd' to work somewhere that: *seemed so top-heavy with women ... there was only one other man there. So, I struggled a bit at first.*

Some participants believed their deployment was gendered, for example being sent on sports tours and other residential trips. Acknowledging the genuine need for men and women staff to accompany residential groups, Luke remarked that he knew he was chosen for such trips because: *they need a male ... but I like to think it's 'cause I'm good at my job, not just 'he's a man, send him'*. Deploying men TAs with older children might suggest a form of stereotyping, to meet the normative positioning of men as authoritative. Aaron had been deployed with ten- and eleven-year-olds, even though he was a qualified and experienced early childhood practitioner. He explained: *Because they see this male role model as more dominant ... the Head put me in with Years 5 and 6.*

Two participants had been directly questioned, by parents and children, about their sexuality. They felt that this would not happen to their women colleagues. Other participants expressed feelings of having been judged by their gender. Some had on occasion felt challenged to justify themselves, as legitimate practitioners working with children. Roy observed: *it was like they were thinking, 'why is he in there?' ... 'you're a bloke, why are you working with ... ?' No-one's ever said it to me, but I can feel that they are thinking like that.* This was supported by Aaron whose presence in the nursery had been challenged by a parent who believed it was inappropriate for men to provide personal care for young children. He reflected: *I felt bad. ... I never really thought, this is how people might see me, until that day. It put into perspective, ... the 'thing' that people might see me as.*

Nevertheless, the participants each made a personal connection with the TA role, as a medium through which to express themselves as caring and nurturing adults. Roy stated: *I found out, working in schools, I actually enjoy it ... I love the children, I like that interaction, and I like to watch them learn,* while Ben affirmed: *What I love about it is, it's a job where I can really help people every day.* These references to 'love' and 'helping people' in the participants' narratives underline the motivational opportunity to enact care for men becoming TAs. Mark and Aaron each recognized the implications of care, as an emotion that can be channelled as a skill for work. Mark's narrative suggests that he accommodated his desire to care for others more comfortably as a TA, than he had previously, as a special police constable. Aaron likened his care for families in funeral services to his care for children and their families at the nursery. Their narratives each showed how men had found ways to enact care for others in their work as TAs.

In summary, the narratives showed that despite some contradictory discourses, and gendered assumptions about what they might offer to the TA role and to primary school life, the men in this study were motivated to become TAs by intrinsic drivers such as a vocation to help people, to listen to and inspire children. Narratives demonstrated they viewed TA work as meaningful, providing job satisfaction and opportunities for personal and professional development, such as routes into teaching.

Conclusion

The research findings suggested that whilst TA work displays the defining social and economic characteristics of a feminized occupation, men TAs who enact care run counter to the perception of the TA role as inevitably female. On the contrary, their narratives accentuate the concept of multiple masculinities and femininities within the schools workforce. TA work provided a context for participants to develop and follow their own career directions. Accordingly, they tended not to view TA work as permanent, but they embraced it fully, as a stage in the journey towards a more sustainable career. For most, this meant a transition into teaching, through which they would remain in the primary school workforce, in the longer-term.

Established discourse has demonstrated a tendency to focus on the assumed damage and deficit of men's absence from primary education. However, there remain some gendered assumptions and barriers which affect men's experiences of becoming TAs, and challenge gender inclusivity. Based on this research, I argue that men becoming TAs ought to be able to experience an equitable position in the primary education sector, which consolidates and defends men's status and contribution as legitimate practitioners across the entire primary phase. Assumptions about men's status as authority figures, and the notion of care as an essentially female quality have been unhelpful to men entering the primary school workforce as TAs, highlighting gender difference rather than fostering inclusivity. Instead, the work sector might emphasize the potential rewards for men (and women) who become TAs, celebrate their presence in the classroom and the opportunities this might afford to children and adults, to perform, witness and interact with multiple masculinities and femininities across a broad spectrum of gender identity. Hence, the ambiguous, homogenous concept of 'male role-models' might be best replaced by opportunities for nurturing and caring relationships which are mutually enriching to the emerging self-concept and long-term self-worth of children and adults alike.

Critical reflective questions

1 Contemporary discourses have positioned men in Early Years and primary education as both a saviour and a threat. How might men TAs be supported to negotiate these opposing pressures?

2 Thinking about your own professional experience, can you recall examples of gender stereotyping and/or discrimination within staff deployment, which demand critical reflection?

3 Could or should anything be done to diversify TA recruitment?

References

Arnot, M., and Mac an Ghaill, M. (2006). (Re)contextualising gender studies in education: Schooling in late modernity, in M. Arnot and M. Mac an Ghaill (eds.), *The RoutledgeFalmer Reader in Gender and Education*, 1–14, Abingdon: Routledge.

Barkham, J. (2008). Suitable work for women? Roles, relationships and changing identities of 'other adults' in the early years classroom. *British Education Research Journal*, *34*(6), 839–53.

Blatchford, P., Russell, A., and Webster, R. (2012). *Re-assessing the Impact of Teaching Assistants; How Research Challenges Practice and Policy*. Abingdon: Routledge.

Brownhill, S., Warwick, P., Warwick, J., and Brown Hajdukova, E. (2021). 'Role model' or 'facilitator'? Exploring male teachers' ad male trainees' perceptions of the term 'role model' in England. *Gender and Education*, *33*(6), 645–60.

Burn, E., and Pratt-Adams, S. (2015). *Men Teaching Children 3–11: Dismantling Gender Barriers*. London: Bloomsbury.

Cruickshank, V., Kerby, M., and Baguley, M. (2022). How do male primary teachers cope with the fear and uncertainty they experience in relation to physical contact? *Education 3–13*, *50*(7), 979–92.

Francis, B. (2008). Teaching manfully? Exploring gendered subjectivities and power via analysis of men teachers' gender performance. *Gender and Education*, *20*(2), 109–22.

ITV News (2023). *Do Britain's Schools Need More Male Teachers?* 23 April. Available online: https://www.itv.com/news/2023-04-28/do-britains-schools-need-more-male-teachers.

Meijers, F., and Lengelle, R. (2012). Narratives at work: The development of career identity. *British Journal of Guidance and Counselling*, *40*(2), 157–76.

Mistry, M., and Sood, K. (2016). Busting the myth of gender bias: Views from men and women primary school trainees and teachers. *Education 3–13*, *44*(3), 283–96.

National Statistics (2003). *Schools Workforce in England 2003(updated)*. Available online: https://webarchive.nationalarchives.gov.uk/ukgwa/20120905035027mp_/http://media.education.gov.uk/assets/files/pdf/sfr232003pdf.pdf.

National Statistics (2023). *School Workforce in England: November 2022*. Available online: https://www.gov.uk/government/statistics/school-workforce-in-england-november-2022.

Paechter, C. (2021). Implications for gender and education research arising out of changing ideas about gender. *Gender and Education*, *33*(5), 610–24.

Pepperell, S., and Smedley, S. (1998). Calls for more men in primary teaching: Problematizing the issues. *International Journal of Inclusive Education*, *2*(4), 341–57.

Savickas, M. L., Nota, L., Rossier, J., Dauwalder, J., Duarte, M. E., Guichard, J., Soresi, S., van Esbroech, R., and van Vianen, A. E. M. (2009). Life designing: A paradigm for career construction in the 21st century. *Journal of Vocational Behaviour*, *75*, 239–50.

Seeley, J. L. (2018). 'Show us your frilly, pink underbelly': Men administrative assistants doing masculinities and femininity. *Gender, Work and Organization*, *25*, 418–36.

Tait, G. (2016). *Making Sense of Mass Education*. 2nd edition. Port Melbourne: Cambridge University Press.

Torre, M. (2018). Stop gappers? The occupational trajectories of men in female-dominated occupations. *Work and Occupations*, *45*(3), 283–312.

UK Parliament (2022). *Research Briefing: Increasing the Number of Male Primary School Teachers*. House of Commons Library. 11 November. Available online: https://commonslibrary.parliament.uk/research-briefings/cdp-2022-0197/.

Warin, J., and Wernersson, I. (2016). Introduction, in S. Brownhill, J. Warin and I. Wernersson (eds.), *Men, Masculinities and Teaching in Early Childhood Education: International Perspectives on Gender and Care*, 1–10, Abingdon: Routledge.

Making Higher Education More Care-Full: The Complexities of Being a Student Carer

5

Sacha Mason and Leanne Leverton

Introduction

In every country around the world, individuals with disabilities, chronic health issues or frailty rely on unpaid care from family and friends (International Alliance of Carer Organizations, 2021). According to International Alliance of Carer Organizations (2018), unpaid caregiving has become one of the most important social and economic policy issues worldwide and an estimated 26 per cent of the UK adult population is providing unpaid care (Carers UK, 2020), predominantly by women. This indicates that there are 6.5 million unpaid carers in the UK (Carers First). Khan-Shah highlights 'that almost two-thirds (65 per cent) of today's UK adults will care for family and friends at some point during their life' (2020: 144) and that carer needs should be identified and addressed sooner rather than later. The financial benefit to society of unpaid carers saves the economy £132 billion per year (Carers UK, 2020). However, there appears to be limited overarching support offered to carers as a comprehensive strategy. This chapter seeks to highlight the challenges faced by students studying in Higher Education (HE) who are also unpaid carers. It utilizes the concepts of care-full and care-free (Moreau and Galman, 2021) to discuss dominant narratives and structures.

Using evidence from a project in a small HEI located in the East Midlands, Lincoln Bishop University, the chapter explores student perspectives of the impact of the Carer's Charter Quality Award (CCQA). The Carer's Community

Project sought to better understand how impactful the Award was on student carers and whether they considered the Award had made a difference to them in supporting their particular needs as students and carers. The aim of the CCQA was to support institutions in the design of policies and processes for carers, along with raising the profile of the challenges that unpaid carers may face so that carers may be afforded a fulfilling life of their own, by using best practice through the implementation of quality markers. The CCQA is an umbrella term that had been developed locally to shine a light on unpaid carers. Unique to Lincolnshire, the CCQA ensures that the profile of unpaid carers is raised and that the invaluable and essential contribution they make is recognized, through pledging to Identify, Recognize and Value Carers (Every-One Charity, 2021). Businesses, schools and Universities can apply for the CCQA status. Adopting the CCQA has strengthened the University's collective vision around what a carer's community should look like. The Carer's Community project built on the work of the University's Carer's Steering Group which was formed to support the university in meeting the criteria to be awarded the CCQA. The project had a central theme of enhancing the experiences of students who have caring responsibilities within the University. It sought to recognize that although there may be invaluable emotional benefits to providing care, being an unpaid carer can be time-consuming and seriously impact on the carer's health and well-being (Global State of Caring, 2018).

Lindt, Jantien van Berkeland and Mulder suggest that 'the most important predictors of caregiver burden, or heavy toll, are the duration of caregiving and the patient's dependency level' (2020: 1) and this requires consideration when supporting unpaid carers. There requires further understandings of care and caring whilst a student is in HE, to capture the breadth of experiences (Larkin and Kubiak, 2021) which, in turn, are dependent on systems within HE required to identify students (NUS, 2013; Day, 2021; Kettell, 2020; Larkin and Kubiak, 2021). Baker and Burke (2023) argue that care is hard to define and as such this makes being a carer even more difficult to define. Therefore, disclosure as a carer is recognized as complex due to multiple factors and is frequently bound with a reticence by unpaid carers to be defined as such (Office for Students, 2023).

National Health Service (NHS) England (2021) defines carers as:

> … anyone, including children and adults who looks after a family member, partner or friend who needs help because of their illness, frailty, disability, a mental health problem or an addiction and cannot cope without their support.

The care they give is unpaid.

However, the charity Carers First states that 'there are no qualifications or criteria that stipulate who is or isn't a carer' which makes providing a definition challenging and the diversity of the population of carers means that they 'do not belong under one definitional umbrella' (Milne and Larkin, 2015: 7). Therefore, for the purposes of this chapter and the Carer's community project that underpins it, the NHS definition was used as the working definition.

The research team gained ethical clearance to survey all BGU students in May 2021 via the use of the student portal and social media feeds which produced eight responses. Despite the low response rate, which is revealing in itself, the data generated have supported the exploration of particular themes in one-to-one interviews with two student carers, Stef and Susanna. Themes from the survey and the interviews focussed on:

1. The multi-faced identity of carers;
2. The complexities of disclosure for carers;
3. A need for a higher profile of the Carers Award.

The identity of carers

Care and caring in their broadest meaning are frequently invisible in HE (Baker and Burke, 2023) and can be described as more care-free (Moreau and Galman, 2021: 41) than care-full. Care-free, in this context, describes an environment that has care-free norms where the needs of carers and this are understood as being instrumental in creating current barriers for student carers (Moreau and Galman, 2021: 41). In this chapter, care-full depicts an institution that demonstrates, within its values, cultures, systems and structures, care for all. Moreau and Galman, in their research, aimed to 'foster belonging' (2021: 40) to make care in HE potentially more visible and seeking to 'disrupt ... carefree academic norms' (2021: 41). Aylward (2009) argues that student carers are shown a lack of professional understanding within HE for the challenges they face, stating that they are often seen as problems or difficult, with caring responsibilities adversely impacting on studying (Gonzalez-Arnal and Kilkey, 2009; NUS, 2013) and also on student carer well-being. The often unpredictable, changing nature of the caring role can mean that gaps in studying or work are needed to attend to these and lead to a lowering of aspirations (Becker and Becker, 2008; Aylward, 2009). These challenges are identified, for example, as multi-tasking, on seeking time to study by finding replacement care for their responsibilities, financial hardship and having to study at unsociable hours (Gonzalez-Arnal and Kilkey, 2009; NUS, 2013; Moreau and Kerner, 2015). One of the student carer participants who was interviewed stated that they have to spend time '*re jigging my day, to study late into the night*'. Day describes 'time poverty' (2019: 6) as a reality for many student carers.

Positive experiences of student carers are usually dependant on taught sessions operating around school times and/or flexibility whilst studying (Becker and Becker, 2008; Marandet and Wainwright, 2010; Burton et al., 2011), alongside students finding additional informal caring structures to enable them to have study. These hidden individualized self-sustaining supporting factors of student carers require consideration by the academy and surrounding policies.

A significant challenge faced by HEIs is in the identification of carers. The identification of carers in the student community is equally hindered by student carers own difficulties in self-identification. This was evident in the data collected from the Carer's Community project where student participants shared that their caring responsibilities ranged from between three and seventy hours a week to undertake. When asked how she defined herself as a carer, Stef stated that it is '*very personal how you define it*' exemplifying the different complexity of personal recognition and disclosure. Caring remains hidden in society (Carers UK) so the university aimed to ensure carers had a safe space to explore their separate identity, as a student and carer. From the many conversations held with carers during the social events as part of the Carer's community project, it became apparent that carers position themselves within the situation of delivering care, and as such, they remain unseen. The multifaceted identities of the carer with the cared for are frequently overlapping and complex such as partner, mother, brother, daughter where a carer identity takes precedence in the relationship. However, State of Caring (2022) suggests that these interconnected identities are a barrier to identification of carer status.

The complexities of disclosure for student carers

Breaking down any barriers to self-identification and recognition of being a carer is essential. The significance of non-disclosure for carers is highlighted by Carers UK (2020) where recognizing carers and encouraging them to self-identify is a significant challenge. This was confirmed by Carers UK (2020), who reported that over half of carers (54 per cent) were taking over a year to recognize their role as a carer. Stef in her interview described how '*it's difficult to say as you probably do not realise you were a carer, and that could be why it took me four years to realise*'. Carers are usually family members positioning themselves as a partner, wife, daughter, son, mother, father, child who are often uneasy with a separate identity as a carer. Participants in the study reported 'carer' as an unfamiliar term and when asked what might prevent them from disclosing that they were an unpaid carer to the university, some commented that they did not really understand that they were a carer. Another shared '*not knowing how to explain the role I do as so informal and changes as health* [of the cared for] *goes up and down*'. The changing nature of the responsibilities for the student carer indicated that there was a challenge in not being able to explain the role as definitive or set leading to subsequent non-disclosure. Susanna's interview revealed that there appeared to be a blind spot in her recognition of herself as a student carer where despite being a teacher and having a professional responsibility to identify and support pupil carers, she states that she '*never applied this to myself, none of us applied this to ourselves, but we [family] do now*'. These comments provide a unique insight into her understandings of her student carer identity. Another participant commented that they would only disclose being an unpaid care if they thought that '*I could not handle or cope with the course and assignments*' suggesting a reactive strategy rather than proactive in seeking support prior to not being able to cope.

Day (2021) reports that many student carers feel unsatisfied with their performance in their studies, due to the pressures on their time, and the inability to fully engage with all aspects of the course such as completing pre-taught session reading or tasks. Maintaining focus on a programme of study is more challenging both physically and mentally when managing the different demands of caring. For many carers the constant worry of looking after someone else's needs, alongside their own, is ever-present and pervasive. The acknowledging of the disempowerment of the cared for was a triggering for disclosure from Stef who indicated that as her father deteriorated and he '*could not do it* [self-care tasks] *for themselves, that's when I figured out, I was a carer*'. One participant simply stated that they '*never thought it was relevant*' to disclose that they were a carer to the university.

When asked what might facilitate in disclosure of being a carer, one participant indicated that '*understanding* [by the university] *that being a carer doesn't necessarily mean being in receipt of carer's allowance*' and that better understanding of the support that may be available was needed. Another shared that '*being asked the question, advertising how/where to disclose*' would help. These hidden identities support the notion of the academy being 'care-free' (Moreau and Galman, 2021) rather than 'care-full' as indicated earlier. The CCQA seeks to raise awareness of unpaid carers in the university, to provide a community of carers for shared support and understanding, and practical institutional strategies that address the hidden inequalities and opportunities. A barrier that requires consideration was highlighted by Stef who stated that '*self-identification- if the person is unaware this* [disclosure] *will not happen*', evidence that as well as raising the profile of the CCQA there needs to be work alongside recognition of their additional role and self-disclosure.

Vignette: Changing approaches

In 2017, a Lincolnshire charity, Every-One, was commissioned by Lincolnshire County Council through the Lincolnshire Health and Wellbeing Board to develop and establish a CCQA. The award has become a recognized symbol of quality in the region. Through achieving the CCQA, an organization is given recognition for the valuable way in which it supports those carers. It ensures the continuing development of quality approaches for those with caring responsibilities across Lincolnshire and beyond. In this way, the CCQA enabled the university to demonstrate a commitment to providing high-quality support to students with a caring role and responsibility. The varied strategies are discussed throughout the chapter. Embarking on a journey to achieve the award provided focus and a particular lens on the university's approaches for providing agency for and with student carers. Through evidencing the Quality Standards associated with the award, the university was able to demonstrate to a select panel the quality of the support offered to carers. The quality assurance process through the steering group enabled an open dialogue across all key stakeholders, of students and staff, to hear the voices of carers to consider the lived experience of a carer whilst at university and was able to acknowledge their unique challenges. The overarching stance that 'caring looks different to everybody' was conceptualized by one of the students in the steering group, enabling different approaches to be taken. Findings from research conducted by Day (2021) indicated that student carers were reluctant to share the issues facing them in a desire to not be treated differently from other students. Breaking down barriers to self and peer identification was an enabler of the award, for example, through the launch of a student carer's passport as a mechanism that allowed the carers a platform to consider areas of their caring role which may require adjustments while at university. The carer's passport was a key strategy to enable student carers to have the opportunity to consider the holistic needs of both the cared for and carers by prompting questions around who could support them while at university. Carers UK state that 'A Carer Passport helps to improve and embed identification, recognition and support for carers in the day-to-day life of an organisation or community.' The steering group enabled growing understandings around student carers as the quality standards were explored and applied to current strategies the university had in place.

Reflection

It is worthy of note that the longevity of a quality assurance award such as the CCQA is subject to the vagaries of funding and becomes threatened when the association promoting and offering it, such as the Every-one charity, ceases to hold the tender for this. The CCQA is awarded for a fixed term of one year and following this, the university has to re-apply. Potentially, the focus on carers can diminish without the award in place and the enhanced focus on student carers that it brings. In turn, the Carer's Community project sought to evaluate whether holding the CCQA was impactful on student carers in the university.

A need for a higher profile of the CCQA

The visibility of the CCQA through the steering group is one way to raise the profile of carers within the institution alongside the institutional APP. However, having the CCQA in place does not always guarantee reach to the whole of the student carer body due to the issues of self-identification and subsequent disclosure. The Carer's Community project sought to understand the impact of the CCQA and the associated activity to support student carers and the participants commented that the award '*recognises the unpaid work and compassion of those looking after others*' and that it '*is a system that recognises the steps taken by the organisation to support carers among the student ... body*'. The notion and presence of a system are significant as they suggest an integrated approach that is embedded in practices throughout the institution. Other participants indicated that the CCQA was less impactful as it required time to find out about, to access and utilize the support mechanisms available. A student carer stated that they only '*find out when they need to. This is our survival strategy*' which indicates that the prominence and accessibility of support is critical. Another participant commented that the CCQA represents '*Institutional recognition of an unseen and unsung area*'. The use of the word '*unseen*' is powerful and articulates a lack of visibility and the need to have a 'care-full' university environment.

A care-full institution, using the CCQA as a benchmark for quality assurance can utilize mechanisms for disclosure alongside strategies for support in multiple ways; identification of carers, promotion of available support and social events to support the building of a collective presence and voice. Approaches taken as part of the CCQA for the individual identification of carers at BGU within the broader student and staff community were through the wearing of pin badges which shared the central messaging of individuals as 'Carer's Champion'. The prominent use of pull up large banners placed strategically at events such as enrolment, Welcome Week and a Carer's video. The purpose of the video was to gain the trust of carers to come and join the carer's community in an informal safe space. The personal focus of carers videos was a key consideration, which entailed students who were self-identified carers, speaking openly and welcoming new carers to organized social events.

A fun flip artefact was used as an eye-catching strategy to promote the carer's community and placed in social spaces on campus and shared with programme teams. The fun flip artefact is an interactive, tactile four-sided origami-inspired product. As the multi-sided product is manoeuvred, a presentation with different views can be seen which seeks to encapsulate and represent the many faces and sides of the carer. As the user starts to move the cardboard along the pre-folded sides, they can interact with the deliberately placed messages and top tips. Consideration as to what the messages would be was again co-produced with the carers steering group. On the front of the fun flip artefact was a clear definition of a carer and inside, a self-navigation tool kit for carers was provided to support self-identification and disclosure. The university's quiet spaces were advertised within the artefact so that carers were aware of safe spaces they could retreat to. The promotion of quiet spaces was a key feature as designated areas that a carer is able to use to support their caring role such as needing to communicate with health and social care services. In this way a carer does not need to stay at home to make the arrangements for care packages and is able to come to university and have time out within the quiet space to focus on specific caring tasks. Wider carer's support groups were also included. This small resource enabled the promotion of the university services already available, guiding students through being a carer.

A carer's newsletter was also established and circulated widely that advertised the regular social events such as the Carer's café, the virtual café and picnics. Social activities and the sustaining of peer relationships beyond taught sessions for the degree are frequently challenging to attend for student carers due to their caring responsibilities. Specific social events for carers can build a community of support with those who share similar circumstances. '*I feel carers are getting a bigger recognition at BGU and have found it good being able to talk about my experiences.*' This statement from a participant recognizes the value of the strategies implemented as part of the CCQA, specifically related to the profile and community of student carers. However, taking a collective ownership of building the carer's community has been recognized as the essential component to the success and longevity of the CCQA.

In the evaluation of the Carer's Community project, it was established that in part, the CCQA was able to disrupt the dominant narrative in the university where carers are not visible or heard in a care-free environment, although further focus can be explored from a different approach where the approaches are extended to the whole of the student body as a community of care.

Looking forward to a care-full university experience

There has been an increased focus on positive student experience whilst studying at university particularly related to widening participation. Baker and Burke advocate a radical shift in thinking by HEIs and the consideration of care, and therefore carers, by the HE sector to understand care as 'kindness', 'compassion' and 'empathy' (2023: 1). Overgaard and Mackaway (2022) suggest that flexible responsiveness by universities within a kindness principled pedagogy can support all students and particularly those with caring responsibilities and articulate this approach as embedding a kindness principled pedagogy. Baker and Burke suggest that care needs to go beyond the individual and a pedagogical approach to 'permeate the institution' (2023: 1) as a whole to visibly incorporate and underpinning care and caring within all aspects of university life. The process of permeating the institution may need to include processes and strategies that go beyond the CCQA.

As the UK HEI sector currently continues to seek and closely examine effective academic support systems, Maxwell and McVitty (2024) suggest aspirations for achieving this:

1. Support towards agency
2. A shared understanding of a student development trajectory
3. Scalability through differentiation
4. Connecting things up around the student
5. Absolute clarity about the role of academics
6. Data-driving proactive systems

These aspirations for support have resonance for student carers, alongside all diversity of the student body to meet their needs. The key principles for support needs to embed kindness through human connections in the academic community and encompasses people, processes and policies, technology working together effectively (Maxwell and McVitty, 2024). As such, the diversity of all students, including student carers, needs to take centre stage.

Increasingly universities are responding to the need for degree programmes to be offered in a range of accessible ways to suit the wider commitments of working alongside studying and caring for family such as through distance and online learning. This enables increased flexibility to study around other commitments, beyond the typical 9–5pm campus, where learners can manage their studies more successfully especially where caregiving is fluid and unpredictable. Day (2021) reports that student carers may suspend their studies, move between part- and full-time study which makes it difficult to sustain a learning community with their peers and staff and more likely that they will drop out. A more diverse programme offer supports agency for all learners to choose a mode of delivery and pace that works with, and not against, their needs and wider commitments. For example, the opportunity to engage with learning and group activities remotely through video meetings can allow for the maintenance of a community of learning and support. A well-designed asynchronous virtual learning environment can provide students with 24/7 access to the programme materials and wider academic services.

However, universities still need to be increasingly flexible in providing the synchronous human connections, that Maxwell and McVitty (2024) advocate, outside of normal working hours such as tutorial support from academics and wider university services both off and on campus. All students can benefit from this flexible approach to study for a degree which can, in some ways, assist with the reality of time poverty for student carers as discussed earlier, and therefore the aim to support students' self-belief, self-efficacy and ultimately their agency to complete their studies.

Conclusion

Increased flexibility and understanding of the student development trajectory (Maxwell and McVitty, 2024) is required for studying and to support for this to respond to growing student numbers and increasing diversity in universities. The university needs to not present the view of an overly simplistic, linear process to completing a degree, rather a more tailored approach that accommodates individuals' different trajectories through their studies is afforded, indeed, expected. HEIs need to consider a carefull learning community where all can benefit through careful design of programmes of study, particularly in relation to work-related opportunities and placements as part of the course. Working away from campus for a placement poses additional strain on those in relation to possibly increased travel and being further away from those they care for, greater inflexibility if unforeseen circumstances mean that a student carer cannot attend creates further tensions. Differentiation is needed to enable positive experiences for all students. Personal tutors can be pivotal in managing this, where placement opportunities, for example, can be adjusted to be closer to student carer's homes, or online.

However, the institution's policy infrastructure needs to be in place to support the Personal Tutor in being able to make these adjustments successfully whilst meeting the requirements of the programme of study; this relies on central points of joined up communication across the university. For example, Day (2021) describes a student carer participant in her research who felt unsupported by an unempathetic approach following the death of her father where assessment adjustments were not made during this difficult time. The role of the Personal Tutor is, therefore, central to a learning community that is care-full and as such, more equitable. The role of reliable data to drive policy and practices in the university is critical, especially in the shared knowledge of who and when particular strategies for support are needed across the whole of the student body. Maxwell and McVitty (2024) argue that although 'the job of connecting things up might look very practical and process-led, it can be grounded in a great deal of empathy and attention to students' lived experiences'. Baker and Burke state 'care is a fundamental component of human relations and connectedness' (2023: 3) and the Carer's Community project has shone a light on how dominant discourses can be disrupted.

Critical reflective questions

1. Considering the shared definition of an 'unpaid carer', how would you re-write this to align with your organization?
2. What would you prioritize, if you were considering establishing a carers network?
3. Why do you think that being a carer remains hidden in society?
4. Breaking down barriers to self-identification of carers has been discussed, moving forwards what could you implement to strengthen this?
5. In view of the discussion around the CCQA, what benefits do you feel this has?

References

Aylward, N. (2009). *Access to Education and Training for Young Adult Carers Project Summary Report*. National Institute of Adult Continuing Education (England and Wales).

Baker, S., and Burke, R. (2023). *Questioning Care in Higher Education*. Switzerland: Palgrave Macmillan.

Becker, F., and Becker, S. (2008). *Young Adult Carers in the UK: Experiences, Needs and Services for Carers Aged 16–24*. The Princess Royal Trust for Carers.

Burton, K., Lloyd, M. G., and Griffiths, C. (2011). Barriers to learning for mature students studying HE in an FE college. *Journal of Further and Higher Education*, 35(1), 25–36.

Carers First (2024). Available online: Carers First: Help and support for unpaid carers.

Carers UK (2020). *Carers week 2020 research report: The rise in the number of unpaid carers during the coronavirus (COVID 19) outbreak*. Carers UK. cw-2020-research-report-web.pdf (carersuk.org).

Carers UK (2022). State of Caring: A snapshot of unpaid care in the UK. cukstateofcaring2022report.pdf.

Day, C. (2021). An empirical case study of young adult carers' engagement and success in higher education. *International Journal of Inclusive Education*, 25(14), 1597–1615. https://doi.org/10.1080/13603116.2019.1624843.

Every-One Charity (2021). https://every-one.org.uk/.

Gonzalez-Arnal, S., and Kilkey, M. (2009). Contextualizing rationality: Mature student carers and higher education in England. *Feminist Economics*, 15(1), 85–111.

International Alliance of Carer Organisations (2018). *Global State of Care*, IACO. Available online:IACO-EC-GSoC-Report-FINAL-10-20-18-.pdf (internationalcarers.org).

International Alliance of Carer Organisations (2021). *Global State of Care*, IACO. Available online:IACO-Global-State-of-Caring-July-13.pdf (internationalcarers.org).

Kettell, L. (2020). Young adult carers in higher education: The motivations, barriers and challenges involved – a UK study. *Journal of Further and Higher Education*, 44(1), 100–12.

Khan-Shah, F. (2020). Support for unpaid carers: The working carers' passport. *British Journal of Community Nursing*, 25(3), 144–7. https://doi.org/10.12968/bjcn.2020.25.3.144.

Larkin, M., and Kubiak, C. (2021). Carers and higher education: Where next? *UK Widening Participation and Lifelong Learning*, 23(2), 130–51.

Lindt, N., Berkel van, J., and Mulder, B. C. (2020). Determinants of overburdening among informal carers: A systematic review. *BMC Geriatrics*, 20(1), 304. https://doi.org/10.1186/s12877-020-01708-3.

Marandet, E., and Wainwright, E. (2010). Invisible experiences: Understanding the choices and needs of university students with dependent children. *British Research Journal*, 36(5), 786–805.

Maxwell, R., and Vitty, D. (2024). Five aspirations for effective academic support systems. *WONKE/Solution Path Project*. 11 March. Available online:Five aspirations for effective academic support systems | Wonkhe.

Milne, A., and Larkin, M. (2015). Knowledge generation about care-giving in the UK: A critical review of research paradigms. *Health and Social Care in the Community*, 23(1), 4–13.

Moreau, M-P., and Galman, S. C. (2021). Writing/drawing care-based equity into practice: A research- and artbased collaboration about caring responsibilities in academia. *Access: Critical Explorations of Equity in Higher Education*, 9(1), 40–52.

Moreau, M-P., and Kerner, C. (2015). 'Care in academia: An exploration of student parents' experiences. *British Journal of Sociology of Education*, 36(2), 215–33. https://doi.org/10.1080/01425692.2013.814533.

NHS (2021). https://www.england.nhs.uk/commissioning/comm-carers/carers/.

NUS (2013). *Learning with Care: Experiences of Student Carers in the UK*. NUS. Available at: Layout 1 (learnworkcare.org.uk).

Office for Students (2023). *Access and Participation Plan*. Available online: https://www.officeforstudents.org.uk/advice-and-guidance/promoting-equal-opportunities/access-and-participation-plan-monitoring/.

Overgaard, C., and Mackaway, J. (2022). Kindness as a practice of Kittay's 'doulia' in higher education: Caring for student carers during COVID-19 and beyond. *International Journal of Care and Caring*, 6(1–2), 229–45.

Capturing the Struggle of Mature Learners in HE

Sacha Mason

6

Introduction

The Higher Education Statistics Agency (HESA) and the Office for Students (OfS) define a mature learner as a non-traditional student, and as someone who is twenty-one years of age, or over, when they start their programme of study at a university. In 2019/20 there were around 254,000 mature undergraduate entrants at UK universities which represents 37 per cent of all undergraduate entrants; a substantial proportion of the student population (Hubble and Bolton, 2021). In May 2021, the OfS released a media statement suggesting that a surge in applications from mature learners called for additional support to be offered in universities due to their specific characteristics stating that 'mature students often have more complex needs than younger students. They are more likely to be disabled, come from more deprived areas, or have family or caring responsibilities' (OfS Insight 9, 2021: 2). Mature learners may also be in paid full or part time work. These specific characteristics frequently position mature learners as distinctly different to other students in the University, or 'academy', in relation to inclusion and the accessibility of their degree programme. The term 'the academy' refers to the social and academic world of HE and represents the broad collective of places of study in the United Kingdom (UK) universities.

The introduction of the student loan system to support accessibility arguably provided greater opportunities for mature learners who would not typically have applied to university as school leavers. The most recent iteration of the Higher Education (HE) loan system was launched in September 2024 as the Lifelong Learning Entitlement (LLE) (Department for Education (DfE) 2023). The DfE are clear that the LLE is intended to provide 'additional flexibility ... as they [students] frequently study part-time while combining paid work and other family and financial commitments'. The LLE provides a loan structure for a modular approach to learning affording students the opportunity to effectively build credits to achieve a full undergraduate degree programme. In principle, learners will have the ability to engage with flexible and different modes of study; in person, blended, or online across a range of institutions and programmes to suit their needs. However, whilst this flexibility to build a degree may be beneficial for some, it also presents other potential challenges for mature learners who, for example, may find negotiating the funding system across various institutions difficult especially where additional access needs are required. As such, the aspiration to support widening participation through the LLE may just present further complexities.

The DfE (2023), along with the OfS, have reported that Universities are not always supportive of the needs of mature learners in scheduling taught sessions outside of typical working hours of 9am–5pm which makes the logistics of studying whilst working and having wider family commitments challenging. There is already some flexibility in the sector for mature learners with the aim to address this issue through the introduction of Foundation Degrees. Work-based Foundation Degrees (FdAs) were introduced in England and Wales by the Department for Education and Skills in 2000 (Quality Assurance Agency, 2015) and have an equivalence to the first two years of an undergraduate degree. According to the QAA, FdAs provide graduates who address perceived shortages of particular skills in the labour market by integrating academic and work-based learning hence equipping 'learners with the skills and knowledge relevant to employment' (2015: 2). FdAs are designed for those who may not hold the typical formal academic entry qualifications (A levels) to study an undergraduate degree such as mature learners who have left school and followed a vocation and undertaken work-related learning such as a National Vocational Qualification (NVQ) or Business and Technology Education Council (BTEC). Flexibility is considered a key aspect of FdAs where taught sessions are specifically timetabled for when it suits work-based learners, such as in the evenings or weekends to enable learners to navigate their working commitments. Despite the ambition of accessibility for mature learners into the academy, since the introduction of Foundation Degrees, HESA data (2017/18) show a declining profile of FdA learners. FdA learners represent only 1 per cent of students studying in university compared to 66 per cent of students studying a first degree in 2021/22 and many universities opting to return to a three-year degree for all learners which is potentially due to the increasing diversity and flexibility in delivery of courses as discussed.

This chapter explores the challenges of twelve mature learners studying a Foundation Degree and how the findings from a longitudinal project imply that universities need to adopt a pedagogy of transparency for adult learners within the context of widening participation. The notion of transparency advocates that learners' emotions should be welcomed and nurtured as these factors significantly impact mature learners' engagement and ultimate success in achieving their academic qualification within the academy. The findings are explored as four key themes: the positioning of the non-traditional mature learner; enculturation and socialization within the academy; notions of struggle; and finally self-efficacy, agency and the capacity of mature learners for transformational learning. The inclusion of specific vignettes from the data illustrates the personified struggles that were presented by the participants at different points during their FdA journey.

The non-traditional mature learner

The term 'non-traditional' implies a deviation from the norm of an eighteen-year-old school leaver and potentially positions the learner in a deficit position. A pedagogy of transparency seeks to disrupt this dominant narrative.

The characteristics and challenges already identified as faced by many mature students are representative of the learners within this study, the majority of whom were mature, female learners with some who were first-generation undergraduates in their social demographic. The life experiences that mature learners hold suggest a complex network of histories, demands and influences that are different from a traditional student. Non-traditional learners, such as mature students, are frequently excluded from undertaking studies at degree level because they typically lack the academic credentials, or present with vocational qualifications associated with their employment. Where Lea and Street (1998) suggest that the learner who has traditionally entered the academy with some academic qualifications is positioned as needing enculturation and socialization, then the non-traditional learner potentially faces greater challenge. An example from the data was Lucy who had returned to her studies after a substantial period after leaving school at 16. Lucy was aged 34 and her confidence was challenged by a mark on her assignment.

Pause for thought: Vignette

Lucy had a critical incident on the programme where her confidence was shaken by a low, or perceived low grade when she received 54 per cent for an essay in the first year on the programme, which was the lowest grade in her friendship group on the programme. Lucy shared her distress at the perceived low grade, although a secure pass (40 per cent or better). This may be due to her expectations in relation to her friendship group on the course. The low grade appeared to have impacted on Lucy's confidence and she reflected on the challenges she had experienced in the first semester when interviewed:

> *Well I think the first bump was in the first term when um, I'd, I didn't think I could actually do any writing and I struggled, cos I've not done it for so long, but I got there eventually, and then obviously I passed the second assignment.* (Lucy)

In discussion with Lucy about why she felt that she had found the first few modules challenging, she indicated that it was probably due to her having been so long out of education and in completing any formal assignments. Lucy received a low grade once again in the last module of the second year where she received a grade of 45 per cent and she commented on how she managed her feelings for this grade:

> *So I knew what I did wrong, I knew how I could show that I did know what I was talking about … but I just got on with it. I think, I thought: 'I can't sulk when I have a loan', I mean I suppose we all do- it can't just be me, but I can't keep sulking, I need to get on.* (Lucy)

Reflection

Lucy's determination to do well in her studies was commendable and the perceived or actual low grade supported her resilience to achieve her overall goal of achieving the degree. As Mason and Atkin argue 'the struggle that Lucy encountered in managing her confidence and emotions regarding the low grade she received, on both occasions, supported her self-efficacy and agency overall' (2020: 1057).

Relationships in HE

A further distinction of the non-traditional mature learner is the different type of relationship within formal education they hold and which is a key difference between young adults (eighteen to twenty-one years) and mature learners. Rogers (2003) suggests that the young adult-teacher relationship is fundamentally different to the mature learner-teacher relationship in the hierarchical relationships defined by age and maturity. These relationships can be discussed as concepts of hybridity which move beyond the dichotomies of powerless/powerful, self/other (2003) and this is particularly relevant for the mature learner and the mature teacher, and also equally complex in the different scenario of the mature learner and young adult-teacher. The mature learner challenges the traditional notion of 'studenthood' (Rogers, 2003: 58) and in defining the mature learner as student they are positioned differently and by default, I argue, are required to be taught differently. Rogers (2003) suggests that the relationship between young adult learner and teacher is a vertical one which indicates the hierarchical dynamic inherent in it, and the mature learner-teacher relationship is represented as a horizontal, adult-to-adult relationship. Learners in university are adults by default in being eighteen years old and over, however, for mature learners, as defined by OfS, I argue that the adult/adult relationship is more distinct as the closer the age gap. The horizontal relationship is more challenging within the academy as it is historically less ingrained and the challenges of the mature learner's positioning in HE are compounded with the academy's resistance to a reflexive pedagogy that may embrace other ways of thinking about learners (Bourdieu et al., 1994). The potential challenge in positioning mature learners differently is in the enculturation and socialization into the academy.

Enculturation and socialization

'Places of study are tangible, although the academy represents more than buildings and physical spaces' (Bourdieu, 1989: 19). Bourdieu uses the term 'social space' to describe a way of being that extends beyond a physical space and which 'tends to function as a symbolic space, a space of lifestyles and status groups characterised by different lifestyles' who are systematically linked together (Mason and Atkin, 2020: 1049). The academy is a social space which has its own body of knowledge, language and communication tool of academic writing that represents a distinct status group and credentials, in the form of academic qualifications. Bourdieu argues that 'titles of nobility, like educational credentials, represent true titles of symbolic property which give one a right to the share in the profits of recognition' (Bourdieu, 1989: 21) with educational credentials and recognition, comes power within the academy and beyond. Symbolic property and power (Bourdieu, 1989) afforded through academic qualifications and knowledge is an important consideration for all in or seeking to join the academy as academic qualifications are the gatekeeper.

Greenwood and Levin state that universities are, among other things, 'knowledge-producing systems' (2008: 65) through academic research and academic programmes of study. Interestingly, the Government Green Paper for Higher Education, *Fulfilling our Potential: Teaching Excellence, Social Mobility and Student Choice* (DfBIS, 2015), identified their core aims to 'raise teaching standards, provide greater focus on graduate employability, widen participation in higher education, and open up the sectors to new high quality entrants' (DfBIS, 2015: 7). The widening of the purposes of the university to beyond the knowledge-producing system that Greenwood and Levin (2008) indicate to include employability and widening participation are important in the notions of what knowledge is privileged: academic or vocational. These aspirational aims of government are problematic. In relation to raising teaching standards, Bourdieu, Passeron and De Saint Martin argue that the philosophical pedagogy within the academy reflects the 'superior level of the education system' (1994: 6) which academics occupy where there is a 'disdain' for reflexive and explicit teaching approaches:

> Their [academics] rejection of an explicit teaching practice follows from a perception of the student favoured by the professorial craft, one which is armed with all the certitudes and all the blindnesses of cultural ethnocentricism. (1994: 6)

If, as Bourdieu et al. (1994) suggest, the academy rejects or resists a transparent pedagogy, then the academy as a social space may struggle to change in light of these aims defined by the government (DfBIS, 2015). The notion of resistance is of relevance as where symbolic power is afforded to the academy and a need to protect this position, then it is unsurprising that those permitted to join it have done so through their aptitude in adhering to the conventions and demonstrating the characteristics that define it that equally reinforces the 'cultural ethnocentricism' (1994: 6) as Bourdieu et al. suggest.

Notions of struggle

Research conducted by Knight, Tennant, Dillon and Weddell (2006) with learners undertaking an early years FdA, which has resonance with this study, indicated that the learners felt greater job satisfaction and confidence, and that their work-based skills had improved by undertaking their programme. Knight et al. (2006) reported on six key factors that enabled the completion of the programme including high self-motivation; access to alternative sources of financial support; support and flexibility of tutors; strong peer support; workplace support; and support from family and friends. With the exclusion of the factor of financial support which this study did not investigate, the remaining five factors serve as important considerations for the participants and their experiences on the programme.

A critical component for learning is self-motivation and Illeris characterizes this in mature learners as 'a kind of ambition that implies a striving to realize more or less clear life aims relating to family, career, interest or something else' (2002: 216). Therefore, for many FdA learners, as work-based adult learners, the ambition that Illeris describes can be understood as wanting to learn something that is meaningful to them and a professional development course. As motivated learners there is some challenge for the academy to accommodate adults where theoretical knowledge is privileged over practice knowledge, and this is heightened when the academic tutor may seek to retain the power of knowledge through a lack of recognition of what the learner may bring to their learning. Equally the learner may be resistant 'in a more or less conscious way' to take responsibility for their own learning (Illeris, 2002: 221). It is only when the tutor insists on this, that the learner realizes the full responsibility that 'goal-directed, effective, transcendent and libidinal' learning occurs (Illeris, 2002: 221). In this way, the learner and the academic tutor are required to accept responsibility that each party has agency for learning to take place. This is a precarious state for learning, particularly where resistance can be present in both the academy and the learner. Resistance may be present due to multiple factors, and forms part of the 'struggle' that mature learners experience. Saccomanno (2017) refers to the notion of struggle as depicting the difficulties that the learner is facing and the strength of discomfort associated with these that requires deliberation or renegotiation of identities and sense of self.

During her studies Mariea, as a mature learner, had faced considerable opposition from her family about undertaking the FdA degree. Mariea was the first person in her family to attend university and applied to come on the programme without telling any of them. When she eventually did inform her family that she had secured and accepted a place on the FdA, there was initial resistance towards her decision by both parents and her sisters, which continued once the programme had commenced when they observed the amount of commitment and devotion of time to her studies that was required. Mariea's family suggested to her that she was going through a 'mid-life crisis' by deciding to undertake the degree. Over the course of the first year, her mother began to realize the determination that Mariea had to complete the course, despite being a single parent who was working full time. Mariea acknowledged this as an 'obstacle':

> ... [an] obstacle was probably parents, not very supportive with the whole further education, um at all. So ... mum's on board now, she sees how important it is and ... she is trying to be supportive, dad still doesn't get it but ... I'm sure he will in the future. (Mariea)

This support from her mother waivered when Mariea became pregnant during the first year of her studies. The baby was not planned and was her second child. Once Mariea's mother knew that she was pregnant, it was expected by the family that Mariea would give up her studies and 'throw in the towel' (Mariea). The baby was born in the first few weeks of the second year of her studies and following a difficult first semester and some low grades, she came to meet with me as her module tutor to discuss her progress. Mariea was distraught following a failed assignment. She acknowledged the demands of caring for a small baby along with her other daughter as a single mother and that it had proved to be challenging to complete assignments. She realized that something needed to change either in her management of her studies or that she would need to intercalate from the programme (normally up to a period of 12 months).

The struggle of managing the resistance from her family, her pregnancy and then her new baby re-established Mariea's fortitude and determination to complete her studies despite the personal challenges she faced. Her own alignment of her identity with the academy and her studies appeared important where there was a shift to apply for the programme, be accepted and then face considerable challenge to continue. The disequilibrium was resolved with her decision to continue studying on the course having found mechanisms to support her both emotionally and academically, exemplified through her perceived support from the relationship with a tutor. Postareff et al. (2017) argue that the interconnecting influences between emotions, learning, academic success and motivation are clear. The renegotiation (Saccomanno, 2017) of personal expectations triggered by changed personal commitments allowed for Mariea to realign to her long-established goal and ambition to complete and pass the degree programme.

Self-efficacy, agency and the capacity of mature learners for transformational learning

In undertaking a professional development programme, the FdA learners are given the opportunity to explore theories and evidence against their practice meaning schemes. In studying an academic programme, learners are able and expected to explore and write about knowledge that is not necessarily based solely on their experiences or beliefs. It is the exploration of new concepts, ideas and thinking that allows their professional understandings to be underpinned by a range of potentially contrasting theoretical frameworks. Mezirow (2009) suggests that these explorations are crucial to the making of new meaning schemes. The challenge for the work-based learner is that academic thinking and writing for assignments draws on the synthesizing of the two realities or sites of knowledge: their practice knowledge and academic knowledge. The member of the academy undertaking the marking of the work may also present a potential obstacle. The linking of what is known and understood in practice with theoretical knowledge makes for a difficult process as the close scrutiny, or reflections on practice in relation to theoretical frameworks may create a feeling of unease or dissatisfaction where these are unable to be easily aligned without a shift change in either domain. Mezirow (1990) outlines that in order to elicit a transformation of learning where the learner is changed, it is insufficient to just identify these habitual meaning schemes, there is a need to act, or engage with them in some way through critical reflection. Transformational learning can be inhibited as:

> A defining condition of being human is our urgent need to understand and order the meaning of our experience, to integrate it with what we know to avoid the threat of chaos. If we are unable to understand, we often turn to tradition, thoughtlessly seize explanations by authority figures, or resort to various psychological mechanisms, such as projection and rationalisation, to create imaginary meanings. (Mezirow, 2009: 3)

The cognitive demand of undertaking the linking of practice with theory to transform meaning schemes is challenging for many learners and in critically reflecting the learner may be unable to resolve the disequilibrium or feelings of unease where what they knew as a certainty (a prior meaning scheme) now becomes uncertain. The period of discomfort may last for some time and where a learner is unable to tolerate this or cannot make an alignment between the two sites of knowledge, resistance may occur (Taylor and Jarecke, 2009). A return to equilibrium can occur through the possible explanations of authority figures as Mezirow (2009) states. Alternatively, transformational learning is enacted where the learner is able to accommodate the new knowledge, theory, with the existing knowledge to re-establish a new and different state of equilibrium. The disequilibrium faced by the learner or what Mezirow describes as an 'intensely threatening emotional experiences' (2009: 7), or alternatively articulated as a struggle, surround the point of transformation and provide the possible template for how the academy may foster transformational learning.

Mezirow (2009) makes clear that transformational learning has been primarily researched in the field of adult education and as such was highly relevant to the participants in this study. 'Adulthood ... is the golden age in relation to both identity and transformational learning' (Illeris, 2014: 89) in that having established a reasonably stable identity from the age of mid- to late twenties that there is opportunity, perversely, to disturb this basis in relation to all parts of this identity. In addition to a more formed identity of the mature learner, a further condition for transformation is that the learner has a purpose for change. The decision to study on the FdA programme and having an identified purpose in relation to this is a key influence on their success which for the work-based learner may require the management of many demands on their time from family, work and their studies. The distinct purpose of undertaking the degree becomes a critically motivating aspect on their studies and propensity for change. The decision to study on a professional development course can be with the intention to improve their work with young children for the benefit of those they work with: children and colleagues. The intention may also be to gain the formal qualification in order to further the learner's career either within the sector, or to become a qualified teacher for example. These intrinsic and extrinsic motivators to achieving and completing the degree are importantly linked to a purpose for change. Motivation is a key aspect of transformational learning and, for adults, this motivation in learning is distinctly different to that of children (Illeris, 2002; Jones and Thomas, 2010: 72). Unlike children who attend statutory schooling, adults may have greater independence to choose and take responsibility for the choices they make.

Conclusion

To conclude, this qualitative, small-scale study was rooted in teaching students on an FdA programme and highlights the unique features of work-based, mature learners challenging the notion that students are a singular homogenous group. These findings contribute to other literature about non-traditional learners and more specifically to the more limited body of research that is concerned with the emotional and social aspects of learning, particularly of mature learners.

In summary, the academy needs to normalize and acknowledge the emotional struggles that adult learners experience in undertaking academic programmes such as an FdA. This will require greater transparency from the university and the future programme teams that represent formal learning differently from the outset to manage learners' expectations. The focus should now be on the *purpose* and *value* of the learning which is imperative to adult learning. This may be captured as individual purpose, programme and institutional purposes in order for a shared understanding that learning is indeed difficult, complex and is highly emotive. For many learners fear, doubt and anxiety surrounds academic endeavours as identified in this study. As Freire suggests:

> The fear itself is concrete. The issue is not allowing the fear to paralyse us, not allowing that fear to persuade us to quit, to face a challenging situation without effort, without a fight. (2005: 50)

The issue that Freire (2005) identifies is in using the struggle purposefully in an agentic way, whether the fear is real or imagined, as a catalyst for change. Learners need to be supported in accepting and expecting their struggles as part of the process of learning. As Mariea shared with me:

'I never ever thought I would get on the course, let alone complete the first year, so, it has been quite a whirlwind journey really. And it's funny, because when we first started, somebody said, 'you'll laugh, you'll cry, you'll get angry', and I said 'really?', but yeah you do don't you?'
(Mariea)

The fear that Freire (2005) suggests may also be evident in the academy through a resistance to reflexivity and transparency (Bourdieu et al., 1994) and would require institutionally wide reform, its own emergence, to acknowledge equity and notions of power between the university and learners and provides an opportunity to disrupt and interrupt dominant narratives present in the academy. Maclaren discusses pedagogy through Friere's concept of lovingness as characteristics of the progressive teacher, which include:

> ... those of humility, courage, tolerance, decisiveness, security, the tension between patience and impatience, joy of living. (2005: xxxi)

These are important characteristics for the transparent pedagogy needed by mature learners. The architype tutor is not a 'coddling parent' (Mclaren, 2005: xxxvi) rather one that challenges and assumes the role of critical friend in an adult, horizontal relationship (Rogers, 2003: 60) where trust and respect are reciprocal. The architype tutor represents a model for HE that can embody the complexity of transformational learning and champion the re-positioning of power within the academy of the FdA learner.

Critical reflective questions

1. Can the role of a critical friend present other challenges for mature learners?
2. How does the academic tutor become the architype tutor?
3. Does the critical friend to the student have to be the academic tutor?

References

Bourdieu, P. (1989), Social space and symbolic power. *Sociological Theory*, 7(1), 14–25.
Bourdieu, P., Passeron, J-C., and De Saint Martin, M. (1994). *Academic Discourse*. Cambridge: Polity Press.

Department for Business, Innovation and Skills (2015). *Fulfilling Our Potential: Teaching Excellence, Social Mobility and Student Choice*. London: HMSO. Fulfilling Our Potential: Teaching Excellence, Social Mobility and Student Choice. November (publishing.service.gov.uk).

Department for Education (2023). '*Studying Part-Time: Perspectives of Mature Students*' DfE Research report. Studying part-time: perspectives of mature students (publishing.service.gov.uk).

Friere, P. (2005). *Teachers as Cultural Workers: Letters to Those Who Dare Teach*. Cambridge, MA: Perseus Books Group.

Greenwood, D., and Levin, M. (2008). Reform of the social sciences and of universities through action research, in N. Denzin and Y. Lincoln (eds.), *The Landscape of Qualitative Research*, 57–86, London: Sage.

Hubble, S., and Bolton, P. (2021). '*Mature Higher Education Students in England*' House of Commons Library Briefing Paper No. 8809. 24 February. Mature higher education students in England (parliament.uk).

Illeris, K. (2002). *The Three Dimensions of Learning: Contemporary Learning Theory in the Tension Field between the Cognitive, the Emotional and the Social*. Denmark: Roskilde University Press. Mature higher education students in England (parliament.uk).

Illeris, K. (2014). *Transformative Learning and Identity*. Oxon: Routledge.

Jones, B., and Thomas, G. (2010). University continuing education: Changing concepts and perceptions, in B. Jones, R. Mosely and G. Thomas (eds.), *University Continuing Education 1981–2006: Twenty-Five Turbulent Years*, Leicester: National Institute of Adult Continuing Education.

Knight, T., Tennant, R., Dillon, L., and Weddell, E. (2006). *Evaluating the Early Years Sector Endorsed Foundation Degree – A Qualitative Study of Students' Views and Experiences*. Unassigned, 1. pp. 0–121. Retrieved from: http://heer.qaa.ac.uk/SearchForSummaries/Summaries/Pages/LTA257.aspx.

Lea, M., and Street, B. (1998). Student writing in higher education: An academic literacies approach. *Studies in Higher Education*, *23*(2), 157–72.

Maclaren, P. (2005). Preface: A pedagogy for life, in P. Friere (ed.), *Teachers as Cultural Workers: Letters to Those Who Dare Teach*, xxvii–xlix, Cambridge, MA: Perseus Books Group.

Mason, S., and Atkin, C. (2020). Capturing the struggle: Adult learners and academic writing. *Journal of Further and Higher Education*, *45*(8), 1–13. https://doi.org/10.1080/0309877X.2020.1851663.

Mezirow, J. (2009). Transformation learning theory, in J. Mezirow, E. Taylor and Associates (eds.), *Transformative Learning in Practice: Insights from Community, Workplace and Higher Education*, 18–33, San Francisco, CA: Jossey-Bass.

Mezirow, J. (1990). How critical Reflection triggers transformative learning. In J. Mezirow & Associates (eds.), *Fostering Critical Reflection in Adulthood*, 1–20. San Francisco, CA: Jossey-Bass.

Office for Students Insight 9 (2021). '*Improving Opportunity and Choice for Mature Student*' Insight 9 May 2021 Improving opportunity and choice for mature students (officeforstudents.org.uk).

Postareff, L., Mattsson, M., Lindblom-Ylänne, S., and Hailikari, T. (2017). The complex relationship between emotions, approaches to learning, study success and study progress during the transition to university. *Higher Education*, *73*, 441–57.

Rogers, A. (2003). *What Is the Difference?: A New Critique of Adult Learning and Teaching*. Leicester: National Institute of Adult Continuing Education.

Saccomanno, B. (2017). The aims of lifelong learning through the dynamic of ambition. *International Journal of Lifelong Education*, 36(5), 551–64. https://doi.org/10.1080/02601370.2017.1312579.

Taylor, E., and Jarecke, J. (2009). Looking forward by looking back, in J. Mezirow, E. Taylor and Associates (eds.), *Transformative Learning in Practice: Insights from Community, Workplace and Higher Education*, 275–89, San Francisco, CA: Jossey-Bass.

The Quality Assurance Agency for Higher Education (2015). *Characteristic Statement: Foundation Degrees*. Gloucester: QAA.

Is Ebenezer Scrooge Jewish? Countering Antisemitism and Considering Social Justice in the Teaching of *A Christmas Carol*

Ed Collyer

7

This chapter explores the implications of Ebenezer Scrooge's characterization within the context of nineteenth-century England. Traditionally, *A Christmas Carol* has been interpreted as a story of redemption. Closer analysis, however, suggests the novella is underpinned by the prejudices of Victorian England and draws on deeply embedded biases against the Jewish community. When *A Christmas Carol* remains a staple of England's GCSE curriculum, educators need to be empowered in approaching this text, and other similarly contentious classics, with an awareness of the biases that underpin them. This chapter advocates an approach that both accepts the literary merits of these books and challenges any contentious elements found within them. In exploring pedagogy, discussion and the use of contemporary resources, this chapter discusses ways in which educators can foster fairness, equality and social justice within their classrooms.

Introduction

Charles Dickens, one of the most celebrated and renowned authors of the nineteenth century, is known for blending characters and plot to satirize the social ills and inequality of Victorian England. *A Christmas Carol* (1843) applies a redemption narrative to its central character, Ebenezer Scrooge, to explore how anyone, no matter how selfish or miserly, can be redeemed and use their life to enact positive change on others. The novella's place as a staple within the General Certificate of Secondary Education curriculum (GCSE; AQA, 2015) means that teachers should be aware of this redemption arc as a literary method employed by Dickens in tandem with other, more implicit, aspects of Scrooge's characterization. English Literature's importance to all pupils within England is underscored by its recognition as a 'core subject', a status it has held since the Education Reform Act of 1988 (DfE, 2022). In comparison to other texts on the GCSE syllabus, *A Christmas Carol* is relatively short which, consequently, makes it a popular choice for GCSE study (AQA, 2015).

To equip teachers with the tools to approach the more implicit and, perhaps, more insidious elements of this work, this chapter explores an understudied aspect of Scrooge's characterization. Although there are some discussions of the religious aspects of the novella, Scrooge's portrayal as a member of the Jewish faith has not been sufficiently explored. The representation of Scrooge as Jewish and his supposed 'redemption' in embracing Christianity warrants closer scrutiny. As the novella retains a prominent place within the GCSE curriculum, it is important to tackle these characterizations to avoid unintentionally embedding bigoted or offensive stereotypes. This chapter explores Scrooge against a backdrop of the historical treatment of Jews within England and Europe. The purpose of this approach is manifold in unpacking both the portrayal of Scrooge as a member of the Jewish faith and to provide a foundation for teachers to employ pedagogy that allows students to approach the text in a socially just way. This chapter approaches the discussion with the understanding that antisemitism is still rampant. Allegations of antisemitism within the UK's Labour Party led to significant backlash from the public and internal evaluations within the party itself (EHRC, 2020). Additionally, Middle Eastern conflicts have led to spikes in antisemitic violence within the UK (CST, 2019) and the ongoing Israeli-Palestinian conflict has, similarly, led to a quadrupling of antisemitic hate crime in the UK (McGarvey, 2023). These examples demonstrate the persistence of antisemitic prejudice in societies that claim to cherish values of inclusivity and diversity. This chapter, then, emerges at an opportune time when educators will need further knowledge and skills to address and discuss antisemitism with their students.

How necessary is historical context?

It is accepted in literature studies that knowledge of a text's historical context or an author's biographical information can enhance how we view and how we engage with a text. When reading William Blake's poem 'The Garden of Love', for example, it is helpful to know that Blake was not anti-religious himself but was opposed to organized Christianity, seeing the institution of the church as an unnecessary mediator in humans' interaction with God. This then gives us valuable insights when, in the poem, he states that priests were 'binding with briars' (Blake, 1794) the speaker's 'joys and desires' (Blake, 1794). In reading these quotations without knowledge of Blake's personal ideologies, one could infer that the speaker's attitude is one of discontentment with the priests themselves. However, in viewing them through the knowledge of Blake's opposition to the church, there emerges an argument that Blake is not criticizing the priests specifically but using their image to make a wider criticism of the oppressive nature of organized Christianity.

Whilst historical context and biographical information *can* be helpful in reading texts, it is important to understand that the primary focus in literary studies should remain on the texts themselves. English teachers need to balance both understanding a writer's methods, without overemphasizing historical details at the expense of literary essence: teaching Literature should not be confused with teaching History. It has become a cliché within English teaching that any exploration of a Dickens' novel *must* begin with a discussion of how Dickens' father spent time in a debtor's prison which, subsequently, influenced his representation of the experience of the poor. Whilst this *may* have influenced his representation of the experience of certain issues within his work, there is more to be gleaned by looking at Dickens' work for a different perspective. Whilst Dickens' personal history may offer *some* contextual understanding, it is imperative not to let it overshadow other aspects of his work. A more holistic approach may also consider Dickens' narrative techniques, character development and symbolism. This is important in grounding the text within its history but equally important in ensuring that the literary merits of the text remain at the forefront of pedagogy.

Someone either studying or teaching Literature needs to carefully consider whether the context they are outlining adds to their analysis or pedagogy and their understanding of a text. This is a judgement I have had to make when writing this chapter. I accept that it may seem hypocritical to, on the one hand, state that context is not necessary for a thorough literary analysis whilst, on the other hand, appearing to unflinchingly segue into a section which outlines historical context before proceeding with literary analysis. The purpose of this chapter is, however, to provide a novel exploration of Scrooge's character within the context of Victorian England and the historical persecution of Jewish people. With this purpose in mind, the contextual factors I will outline are there to deepen literary analysis and strengthen my argument.

Throughout the nineteenth century, England underwent significant economic and social transformation. This shaped the narrative of *A Christmas Carol* as Dickens looked to criticize what he saw as perceived social ills and inequality. The era is renowned for encompassing a large part of the Industrial Revolution which had a significant impact on urban living, attitudes and, indeed, daily life (Morgan, 2004). The change from a pastoral way of life to rapid urbanization exemplified the inequality between the emerging, business owning, middle classes and the working classes (Cannadine, 1999). This influenced communication, global trade and transport which further confounded the socio-economic landscape (Johnson, 2005).

Workers' rights movements and intense debate on social reform added to the heightened awareness of social inequality (Smith, Dorling and Shaw, 2001). This was coupled with political turmoil. The Chartist movement, for example, advocated democratic rights in an attempt to reshape society (Chase, 2013). There was also fresh legislation, aimed at tackling issues such as workers' rights and the exploitation of child labour (UK Parliament, 2023).

The era is also recognized by its emphasis on morality, family and strict social hierarchies. The Church played a significant role in reinforcing these norms (Thompson, 1981). The clergy possessed significant power in spheres from education and arts to politics, holding substantial influence within both agrarian and metropolitan communities. Religion often was intertwined with social expectations, strengthening the eras social and moral values (Inglis, 2007).

Literature, particularly the works of Charles Dickens, was seen as a vehicle to explore social issues and political challenges of the time. Dickens often depicted the stark and brutal realities of the social divisions. The characterization within Dickens' work often was used as a device through which comment on and criticize social ills as readers were given insight into the lives of the poor against the backdrop of inequality encouraged by rapidly growing urban areas and industrialization.

The Jewish community in nineteenth-century England

Jewish people in England during the nineteenth century were initially faced with limitations on freedom and their roles within both the public sector and academia were subsequently limited. The century did, however, see the beginning of some more liberal attitudes and movements towards inclusivity. The Jewish Emancipation, which lasted between the late 1820s and the 1850s, aimed to remove some of these social and legal barriers (Henriques, 1968). Entry criteria for universities based on religion were removed, paving the way for some Jewish people to work and study at Oxford and Cambridge (Oxford University, 2021).

The tensions between Christianity and the Jewish community and the move towards inclusivity are illustrated by the 1858 case of Lionel de Rothschild. de Rothschild was unable to assume his position in the House of Commons for eleven years despite being elected consistently as an MP since 1847 (Henriques, 1907). The oath MPs were asked to swear contained Christian specific wording, which de Rothschild did not swear because of his Jewish faith. In 1858, the Christian wording was altered through the Jews Relief Act (1858). This then allowed de Rothschild to take his seat as an MP and paved the way for other, non-Christian MPs to take public office.

Jews were, stereotypically, viewed by nineteenth-century society as moneylenders and in other financial roles, a view that has medieval origins linked to both society and religion (Mell, 2017). The Christian faith prohibited Christians from lending money and charging interest, deeming it as 'usury' (Chazan, 1980). When there was a social and economic demand for moneylenders and Christians were unable to be fulfil them, Jews often assumed these positions.

In medieval Europe, Jewish people faced challenges which impacted their social roles and geographic locations. The 1290 Edict of Expulsion enacted by England's Edward I, prohibited Jews from living in England until the mid-seventeenth century, when it was repealed by Oliver Cromwell (Vital, 2001; Chazan, 2006). In France, Jews were periodically expelled, most notably in 1182 and 1306 (Schwarzfuchs, 1967; Jordan, 1989). Spain's King Ferdinand of Aragon and Queen Isabella of Castille mandated that Jews must either convert to Christianity or leave the country (Beinart, 2002). This view was similarly adopted by King Manuel I of Portugal in 1497 (Yerushalmi, 1976). Expulsions were not just held on a national level, but some were localized within nations, for example, Vienna's 1421 banishment (Widrich, 2013). Indeed, many areas implemented segregation, forcing Jews to occupy ghettos and wear attire such as the yellow badge (Cassen, 2017). Restrictions such as these, combined with bans on owning property or land, pushed Jew towards financial roles. Mell (2017) argues that the link between Jews and moneylending may be exaggerated but did, however, strengthen unjust stereotypes of Jewish people as greedy. These stereotypes remained even after the social epoch had changed.

In Charles Dickens' work, the character of Fagin from *Oliver Twist* (1838) is often remembered as his most problematic and prevailing example of a Jewish figure. Fagin is repeatedly referred to as 'the Jew' (p. 52). The casual and constant references to Fagin's faith alongside his criminality tie the two concepts together making Judaism and criminality inextricable within Dickens' representation. Dickens subsequence works, however, indicate that his personal stance towards Jews had altered. In *Our Mutual Friend* (1865) Dickens presents us with Mr Riah, a generous and respectable Jewish figure.

This forms a contrast to the representation of Fagin and, perhaps, could suggest an evolution of Dickens' views or an attempt to counterbalance earlier representations.

A Christmas Carol does not possess the same overt Jewish characterizations contained within *Oliver Twist*. It does at least imply that both Ebeneezer Scrooge and Jacob Marley are members of the Jewish faith and that Scrooge is not supposedly 'redeemed' until he embraces Christianity. The next section argues that Dickens establishes Scrooge as a Jewish character, as a basis for contesting that this representation warrants exploration with pupils in the English Literature classroom.

Exploring Jewish characterizations in *A Christmas Carol*

Ebeneezer Scrooge stands in stark contrast to the Victorian London setting that surrounds him. Goodwill and benevolence are openly cherished whilst Scrooge remains 'hard and sharp and flint' (p. 8). Scrooge's cold and miserly nature, when juxtaposed against this setting, signifies at the very outset of the novella that Scrooge is out of place and must transform if he is to endure. Scrooge's pariah status within this setting is confirmed in the image of him being 'solitary as an oyster' (p. 8). However, Scrooge does not seek to change; he is someone whom 'no warmth could warm, no wintry weather could chill' (p. 8). In constructing Scrooge in this way – as an unyielding and detached character in need of a transformation – Dickens offers a tale of redemption and suggests that this redemption cannot be complete without conversion from Judaism to Christianity. When viewed within the context of Dickens' wider work and the social milieu of the time, there emerges a convincing argument that Scrooge is depicted as a member of the Jewish faith.

Scrooge's description foregrounds his 'pointed' (p. 8) nose. Whilst this may be a physical representation of his sharp and miserly nature and, potentially, the cutting and derogatory comments he makes towards others, there remain connotations attached to this description which cannot be ignored. Historically, physical attributes have been linked to certain groups in derogatory and offensive ways. The 'hooked' nose has been a recurring stereotype of Jewish people, particularly within antisemitic cartoons of the nineteenth century (Stieg, 1975). Whilst the description of Scrooge's nose being 'pointed' (p. 8) does not contain the explicitly prejudiced connotations associated with the 'hooked' descriptor, its reference when taken alongside the social biases of the era makes it noteworthy. This argument is given further credence when, towards the end of the novel, during the final stave when Scrooge accepts Christmas and, by extension, Christianity, Dickens describes Scrooge shaving. He writes:

> Shaving was not an easy task, for his hand continued to shake very much; and shaving requires attention, even when you don't dance while you are at it. But if he had cut the end of his nose off, he would have put a piece of sticking-plaster over it, and been quite satisfied. (p. 88)

Here, Dickens introduces a hypothetical situation in the final chapter, or 'stave', of the novella in which Scrooge realizes that his excitement has caused him to behave irresponsibly and dance with excitement whilst shaving. However, he continues to dance nevertheless, indifferent to any personal harm he may inflict. The idea that Scrooge would be perfectly happy, having caused himself significant personal injury, with simply applying a plaster to his nose could signify an abandonment of his Jewish faith. Whilst the association with Jewish people and hooked noses remains unfortunate, it is difficult to overlook how Dickens would have been unaware of this stereotype when it was prevalent in publications of the period and such an act may well have resonated with the prevailing prejudices of the time.

Throughout the narrative, Dickens has Scrooge develop from a figure steeped in avarice to a character underscored by benevolence and charity. At the start of the novel Scrooge, quite blatantly, rejects Christmas and its associations with goodwill. In interactions with his nephew, Fred, and two men collecting for a charity, Scrooge is firmly established as an outsider and directly opposed to their warm and kind representations and, by proxy, their Christian sentiments. This rejection of charity and goodwill when tied in with Scrooge's greed echoes the stereotypes of Jewish moneylenders. Dickens' characterization of Scrooge alienates him from the Christian celebration of Christmas. Yet, as Scrooge encounters the three spirits, he very quickly is placed on an obvious trajectory towards accepting Christianity. Each spirit could be seen as a representation of core Christian beliefs. The Ghost of Christmas Past, both bright and revelatory, could embody Christian enlightenment. The Ghost of Christmas Present, with its emphasis on compassion and altruism, personifies the Christian emphasis on charity. Finally, the Ghost of Christmas Yet to Come, with its eschatological appearance and actions, reminds us of the Last Judgement and cements Scrooge's next course of action: to seek salvation. Scrooge's character only fully endears himself to the audience after his Christian epiphany. This transition from miserable outsider to endearing figure may suggest that endorsing Christian values is a commendable endeavour. It is worth noting, however, that the third spirit places Scrooge into emotional distress. Visions of Scrooge's impending death serve as instruments of psychological torture and intimidation forcing him to accept Christmas and Christianity.

Dickens' nomenclature within *A Christmas Carol* further reinforces Scrooge's, and his equally avaricious business partner Jacob Marley's, Jewish identities. 'Ebeneezer' and 'Jacob' are names engrained within Hebraic backgrounds. Samuel 7:12 of the Old Testament documents how Samuel created a memorial of a stone and named the stone 'Ebeneezer', meaning 'stone of help'. Similarly, 'Jacob' is drawn from the book of Genesis and is the name of the patriarch who wrestled an angel and was renamed 'Israel'. As a writer, Dickens is renowned for his characterization and the names he gives his characters. With this inclination in mind, the naming of both Scrooge and Marley with names entrenched in foundational Jewish texts seems intentional. In naming his characters in this way, Dickens reinforces Scrooge and Marley's separation and hostility towards the Christian values held by much of Victorian England.

Pause for thought: Vignette – Becoming an Ally

Emma is a high school English Literature teacher. During a discussion on *A Christmas Carol,* Jack, one of Emma's students, appeared subdued. Jack was usually very eager to share his ideas with the class. However, today, Jack was more withdrawn and did not want to actively partake in the lesson.

After the lesson, Emma spoke with Jack to see what was wrong. He said that he 'felt uncomfortable when Jenna said how Scrooge has some stereotypically Jewish characteristics. My grandparents told me about how they faced antisemitism growing up and the discussion made me a bit upset'.

Reflection

This vignette demonstrates the power literature has on individuals and how so many of students' personal histories could potentially render them emotionally vulnerable. *A Christmas Carol,* like much of Dickens' work, has been celebrated for its literary merits. However, for Jack, the prejudicial implications of Scrooge's representation resonated with his personal history and the history of his family.

Educators need to approach classic literature in a balanced way that appreciates the artistic merits of a literary text, whilst sensitively exploring any contention that may be associated with it. Teachers need to find space for students to voice any discomfort and turn the classroom into an inclusive space that fosters collective growth and understanding.

Education is not about simply transferring knowledge from teacher to student. It is about helping students to learn to empathize and understand others and to think critically. Literature can be a powerful way to approach this as it often offers a space for open dialogue and the sharing of personal experience. However, students should only be encouraged to share any personal experiences if they are comfortable to do so and, as a teacher, you feel the classroom is a safe space to encourage this.

Evaluating Dickens' Representation of scrooge and crafting inclusive and socially just classrooms

As teachers take the role of promoting social justice within their classroom, they must be equipped to recognize problematic representations in literary classics like *A Christmas Carol*. Such issues are not solely in the realm of nineteenth-century literature but span centuries; many of the works of Shakespeare, for example, contain problematic elements. *The Taming of the Shrew* (1590) portrays hugely problematic depictions of the treatment of women as one of the play's central characters, Katherine, goes from being strong willed and independent to subservient to her abusive husband, Petruchio. On the surface, this appears to be a misogynistic and offensive plot. On the other hand, you could argue that the play is so hyperbolically offensive that it is lampooning the idea that women must be subservient to their husbands, rather than promoting it, by escalating a stereotype of women to ridiculous proportions. Whether Shakespeare intended the play to be offensive was just unintentionally reflecting the values of the time or was crafting a witty send up of Elizabethan attitudes towards women, we will never know. What we can do, however, is teach students that Shakespeare was one of, if not, the greatest playwrights and poets of all time but that he also wrote some problematic things that need unpacking within classrooms to ensure teachers promote social justice. The same can be said of Charles Dickens. Teachers can teach that Dickens was one of the greatest writers of the nineteenth century but that he also wrote some problematic things which they can then address through dialogue with classes.

To craft socially just classrooms, teachers must acknowledge prejudice within texts so that they are able to facilitate discussion with their classes around these issues. Stating that Dickens was a talented and important writer is not a blanket endorsement of everything he wrote. Equally, in stating that I find his portrayal of Scrooge antisemitic, I am not saying that everything he wrote was unacceptable or lacking merit. Recognizing prejudice, especially when it can be overlooked, is often the first step to tackling it. Once it has been recognized, the duty then falls to the teacher to deal with it sensitively, inviting their students to question the portrayals.

One of the most powerful tools teachers have for developing pedagogy is their colleagues. This chapter was inspired by conversations over lunch with my own colleagues. English departments are often the largest departments in schools and can contain teachers with varying years of experience. It is important for teachers, irrespective of their time in the profession, to spend time sharing ideas and exploring classroom interactions. In taking this collaborative approach, teachers can harness each other's wisdom to develop strategies for tackling issues within literary texts sensitively. In a mutually supportive environment such as this, teachers of all career stages can be empowered to undertake the challenge of teaching classic literature that balances the literary merits of the text with tackling its contentious aspects.

It is helpful to view literary texts as part of a web, where they are in dialogue with other texts of the era and the wider social norms of the time. If a teacher was to address the antisemitic elements of Scrooge's portrayal without referring to other texts of the period, students could possibly come away thinking that Dickens was the only writer who published antisemitic sentiments. Utilizing these texts to help students form a more holistic understanding of antisemitism in the period could help broaden the potentially myopic view of the period that could unintentionally be fostered by exploring a single text. A valuable resource contemporary to the nineteenth century is *Punch Magazine*. Rosenblum argues that the magazine is 'spattered with acid allusions to the Jews' (p. 203). However, Rosenblum also contends that, despite derogatory portrayals of Jewish people, the magazine itself wasn't inherently antisemitic. He suggests that *Punch's* purpose was to critique society indiscriminately. However, even if a wider, indiscriminate critique of society was *Punch's* aim, the persistent portrayal of Jewish people in a negative way cannot be explained away as social commentary. Thus, comparisons could be drawn between *Punch* and Dickens' work, with the texts forming a web that interlink with one another.

Open dialogue is fundamental in shaping socially just classrooms and a teacher holds the power to facilitate this dialogue and create a space in which everyone feels able to be heard and to ask questions, without fear of getting something wrong or using a term incorrectly. Facilitating effective dialogue can take students from being readers to analysts capable of recognizing and, importantly, articulating and explaining the biases they encounter. A practical approach here could be the 'Socratic seminar', a technique whereby students discuss a text by posing open-ended questions and responding by pointing to moments within the text to support their view. Within this paradigm, the teacher adopts the role of a moderator, steering the discussion and pushing pupils for deeper reflection. To enhance this, pupils could be given perspectives to adopt that are not, perhaps their own. This could help them develop their own point of view by considering other perspectives in a way they may not have considered fully before.

Recognizing prejudice within historical texts could also be used a springboard for pupils to start critically assessing the representations in the twenty-first century, leading them to become more aware of issues surrounding social justice today. For example, after reading *A Christmas Carol* or after addressing the antisemitism within it, students could be tasked with finding similar themes or biases within a modern-day news article, book or film. Certainly, books by David Walliams have been singled out recently for containing racist portrayals of characters (Flood, 2021) and may be a starting point for teachers to begin comparing and contrasting nineteenth-century values with twenty-first-century values.

Ultimately, by utilizing some of these strategies to help pupils explore the contentious issues within classic literature educators can – regardless of their level of experience – develop learning environments that cultivate a deeper understanding of classic literature and a deeper understanding of twenty-first-century society. This could be key in nurturing students into informed, critical individuals with a keen social consciousness and an awareness for spotting injustice.

Conclusion

The aim of this chapter was to explore the representation of Scrooge as a member of the Jewish faith and the implications of his Christian epiphany. Whilst Dickens' portrayal of Jewish characters has often courted controversy, most notably the character of Fagin in *Oliver Twist,* exploration of Scrooge as Jewish character has been limited.

Unpacking Scrooge's character arc as he develops from a miserable, miserly pariah to a happy, reformed pillar of the community presents an opportunity for dialogue around cultural representation. Scrooge's salvation, when viewed from the perspective outlined in this chapter, sends a problematic message that salvation can only be found within Christianity; a version of Christianity that Scrooge is abused and bullied into accepting.

This chapter suggests that awareness is the key to forming socially just classrooms. That awareness, first of all, has to start with the teacher. A teacher must feel empowered to break out of and challenge traditional readings of texts. Whilst these readings may be tried and tested in getting pupils to pass exams, the question emerges of whether it is ethical for a teacher to ignore the antisemitic elements of *A Christmas Carol* once they are aware of them in favour of dedicating class time to teaching more conventional readings of texts. Educators bear the responsibility of allowing pupils the time and space to acknowledge biases within texts and to give them a safe and supportive platform on which to discuss it. This, then, means that the teacher's role is to help pupils understand the world in which they live through the literature they teach.

Most critically, this chapter reinforces the need for educators to revisit and revise the curriculum they teach. Whilst teachers may they are limited by exam specifications, which dictate the texts that need to teach, they can always alter the way they are taught and the elements that are discussed. This will help develop students into discerning readers and thinkers who are equipped with the ability to leave school and go into the world with an understanding of fairness, equality and social justice.

Critical reflective questions

1. How does Dickens' representation of Scrooge reinforce stereotypes of Jewish people?
2. How can educators balance lesser discussed elements of texts, with more traditional readings that will enable pupils to perform in an exam?
3. In what ways can teachers balance the celebration of a work's literary merits with its more contentious elements?
4. How can teachers utilize resources, both modern and contemporary to a text's time period, to demonstrate how the text forms part of a textual web, as opposed to being isolated.
5. What strategies can teachers use in their teaching of classic literature to impart knowledge and promote fairness, quality and social justice for all?

References

AQA (2015). *English Literature*. Retrieved from https://filestore.aqa.org.uk/resources/english/specifications/AQA-8702-SP-2015.PDF.

Beinart, H. (2002). *The Expulsion of the Jews from Spain*. Liverpool: University of Liverpool Press.

Blake, W. (1794). The garden of love, in *Songs of Innocence and of Experience*, Gutenberg: Online https://www.gutenberg.org/cache/epub/1934/pg1934-images.html.

Cannadine, D. (1999). *The Rise and Fall of Class in Britain*. New York: Columbia University Press.

Cassen, F. (2017). *Marking the Jews in Renaissance Italy*. New York: Cambridge University Press.

Chase, M. (2013). *Chartism: A New History.* Manchester: Manchester University Press.

Chazan, R. (1980). *Church State and Jew in the Middle Ages.* West Orange, NJ: Behrman House.

Chazan, R. (2006). *The Jews of Medieval Western Christendom 1000–1500*. New York: Cambridge University Press.

CST (2019). *Antisemetic Incidents Report.* London: CST.

DfE (July 15 2022). *Research Review Series: English*. Retrieved from DfE Web Site: https://www.gov.uk/government/publications/curriculum-research-review-series-english/curriculum-research-review-series-english.

Dickens, C. (1838). *Oliver Twist.* London: web-books.com.

Dickens, C. (1865). *Our Mutual Friend.* London: Gutenberg.

Dickens, C. (1943). *A Christmas Carol.* London: Lbiblio.

EHRC (2020). *Investigation into Antisemitism in the Labour Party*. London: EHRC.

Flood, A. (2021). HarperCollins removes story from David Walliams' book the world's worst children, *The Guardian*.

Henriques, H. (1907). The political rights of English Jews II. *The Jewish Quarterly Review*, *19*(4), 751–99.

Henriques, U. (1968). The Jewish emancipation controversy in nineteenth-century Britain. *Past & Present*, *40*, 126–46.

Inglis, K. (2007). *Churches and the Working Classes in Victorian England*. London: Routledge.

Jews Relief Act 1858, c. 49. (1858). Retrieved from https://www.legislation.gov.uk/ukpga/Vict/21-22/49/enacted

Johnson, P. (2005). *Market Disciplines in Victorian Britain*. London: London School of Economics.

Jordan, W. C. (1989). The Jews of the royal domain, in *The French Monarchy and the Jews: From Philip Augustus to the Last Capetians,* 3–22, Philadelphia, PA: University of Pennsylvania Press.

McGarvey, E. (2023). Antisemitic incidents 'quadruple in UK' since Hamas attack in Israel, *BBC News*. https://www.bbc.co.uk/news/uk-67095846

Mell, J. L. (2017). *The Myth of the Medieval Jewish Moneylender*. Cham: Palgrave Macmillan.

Morgan, K. (2004). *The Birth of Industrial Britain.* London: Pearson Longman.

Oxford University (2021). *Opening Oxford: 1871–2021.* 16 June. Retrieved from Oxford University Web Site: https://www.ox.ac.uk/news/2021-06-16-opening-oxford-1871-2021.

Schwarzfuchs, S. R. (1967). The expulsion of the Jews from France (1306). *The Jewish Quarterly Review*, *57*, 482–9.

Smith, G., Dorling, D., and Shaw, M. (2001). *Poverty, Inequality and Health in Britain: 1800–2000*. Bristol: The Policy Press.

Steig, M. (1975). A chapter of noses: George Cruikshank's psychonography of the nose. *Criticism*, *17*(4), 308–25.
The Holy Bible (n.d.) holybooks.com.
Thompson, F. (1981). Social control in Victorian Britain. *The Economic History Review*, *34*(2), 189–208.
UK Parliament (2023). *The 1833 Factory Act*. Retrieved from UK Parliament Web Site: https://www.parliament.uk/about/living-heritage/transformingsociety/livinglearning/19thcentury/overview/factoryact/.
Vital, D. (2001). *A Political History of Jews in Europe*. Oxford: Open University Press.
Wagner, K. (2018). Savage warfare: violence and the rule of colonial difference in the early British Counterinsurgency. *History Workshop Journal*, *85*, 217–37.
Widrich, M. (2013). The willed and unwilled monument. *Journal of the Society of Architectural Historian*, *72*(3), 382–98.
Yerushalmi, Y. H. (1976). *The Lisbon Massacre of 1506 and the Royal Image in the Shebet Yehudah*. Cincinnati, OH: Hebrew Union College Press.

Drama and Mathematics Educators Working Together: Working at Social Justice with Teachers

Tony Cotton and Helen Toft

Introduction

This book takes it as given that teachers have agency. It also acknowledges that education is a contested terrain, and that within this terrain it can be challenging for educators to take action (particularly in the area of social justice). We began writing this chapter in August 2023, during the Edinburgh Fringe Festival where we saw *After the Act*, a play by the Breach Theatre company,[1] which explored the implementation of section 28 of the Local Government Act 1988. This Act stated that no local authority could, 'intentionally promote the teaching in any maintained school the acceptability of homosexuality as a pretended family relationship' (National Archives). This production included, as a song, Margaret Thatcher's speech to the 1987 Conservative Party conference (available at the British Political Speech archive), when she announced:

> And in the inner cities – where youngsters must have a decent education if they are to have a better future – that opportunity is all too often snatched from them by hard left education authorities and extremist teachers. And children who need to be able to count and multiply are learning anti-racist mathematics – whatever that may be.

For us, this speech shows Thatcher acknowledging the centrality of mathematics education as offering improved life chances for young people while concurrently suggesting that 'hard left' activists were acting against social justice by imposing 'anti-racism' views on the education system. Further there is some sense that mathematics is value-free, and the concept that mathematics and issues of social justice might be connected is ridiculed. The Conservative Government of 2023 appears to be rehashing these arguments under an 'anti-woke' agenda with Oliver Dowden (who was Conservative Party chairman from 2021 to 2022) stating a West 'confident in its values' would not be 'obsessing over pronouns or indeed seeking to decolonise mathematics' (Guardian, 2022).

Success in high-stakes examinations in mathematics gives access to higher earnings, promotes greater equality and enables us to have greater control over our lives. The recent Covid-19 pandemic provided a useful example of such control where much of the information regarding the infection was presented as mathematical data; the more confident people were in making sense of this data, the more able they were to make choices on how they could live life more safely. Here, mathematical literacy had a direct impact on the way we make life-changing decisions. Consequently, one of the activities shared later in the chapter directly addresses the Covid-19 pandemic.

The Breach Theatre company explained that they had created the play *After the act* from interviews with a large number of teachers and students during the implementation of section 28. They made connections between this historical event and the current debates which have been termed 'culture wars', noting how issues of trans rights and transphobia seem to have become foregrounded, with trans people replacing minority ethnic groups as scapegoats and symbols of 'woke' culture. They were surprised when we told them that we had announced to the students we taught in the 1980s that we had made a conscious decision to ignore the requirements of section 28. This action had been particularly relevant to some of the students we taught as these young people were living in secure same-sex parent families. However, we also acknowledged how difficult it was to make such a stand and that not all teachers would feel able to take such action; similarly, we wonder, how many teachers feel embattled by current Government edicts.

Gillborn (2008) reminds us that, 'in the education system racism is figured in the distribution of material and educational resources and even in teachers' notions of ability and motivation'. Hence the very fabric of the education system works against some groups of learners. A 2017 study on pupils found that, where learners were sorted in this way, lower sets were mostly populated by Black pupils (Francis et al., 2017). It also noted the impact of teacher assumptions that Black and some brown pupils were not good at maths where this assumption led to the placing of those children in lower sets (Francis et al., 2017). Mathematical literacy is a social justice issue and can either be supported or stifled. In this chapter we demonstrate how, through employing techniques 'borrowed' from drama education, mathematical literacy can be developed for all learners and how these opportunities may be welcomed by learners who have previously experienced discrimination.

The aim of this chapter is to show how the two disciplines of drama and mathematics can be connected under the common banner of social justice, and how, through working in a collaborative and committed manner, educators with a shared understanding of the importance of social justice can face the challenges present in the settings in which we work.

Making connections: Mathematics and drama

> The ability to operate mathematically is an aspect of human functioning which is as universal as language itself. Attention needs constantly to be drawn to this fact. Any possibility of intimidating with mathematical expertise is to be avoided (from the guiding principles of the *Association of Teachers of Mathematics (ATM)*).

> We are committed to developing a child-centred, humanising curriculum with an internationalist perspective. We are constantly asking ourselves 'what does the child need to know?' in order to be 'at home' in the world (from the guiding principles of the *National Association for the Teaching of Drama (NATD)*).

As we began our work together exploring how drama and mathematics can support each other in enabling learners to develop skills in both areas through working in a cross-curricular way, we were struck by the similarities, and subtle differences between the guiding principles of our two professional organizations. We were particularly struck by the underlying commitment to issues of social justice in the two sets of guiding principles.

We the writers of this chapter are partners, both in terms of being married and in terms of working together – we have taught and worked in teacher education together for over thirty years. We do not, however, share subject backgrounds. Tony is a teacher of mathematics with a nervousness about learning and teaching though drama; Helen is a teacher of drama with a nervousness (verging on fear!) of all things mathematical. We would argue that this makes us an ideal partnership to explore how we can intertwine mathematics and drama to explore elements of social justice.

Over the years, we have explored this subject in many different contexts. We realized that although many people might see the subject disciplines of mathematic and drama as different, the aims and guiding principles of the associations suggest that we share common beliefs about the purpose of education. One of the challenges faced by all educators is the focus in many schools on curriculum 'delivery' and on coverage of subject-specific objectives rather than on exploration of ways in which subject areas can collaborate. Our alternative hypothesis is that, in such an objective-led curriculum, cross-curricular work can support us in ensuring that objectives from different disciplines are experienced in the same lesson by learners, which could be argued to be a highly economical way of teaching. This alternative approach to the curriculum is offered by many International Schools who follow the International Baccalaureate programme (IB). The IB curriculum has an expectation that all students should become:

Inquirers: Students should develop their natural curiosity.
Knowledgeable: Students should explore concepts, ideas and issues that have both a local and global significance.
Thinkers: Students should think critically to engage themselves in figuring out complex problems.
Communicators: Students should express themselves and information through a variety of modes of communication.
Principled: Students should act honestly and with a strong sense of fairness, justice and respect for the dignity of the individual, groups and communities.
Open-minded: Students should appreciate their own cultures and personal histories and are open to the perspectives, values and traditions of other individuals and communities.
Caring: Students should show respect and compassion towards the needs of others.
Risk-takers: Students should approach unfamiliar situations with courage, as well as defend their beliefs.
Balanced: Students should understand the importance of intellectual, physical and emotional balance to achieve personal well-being.
Reflective: Students should give thoughtful consideration to their own learning and experience.
https://ibo.org/benefits/learner-profile/

For Helen this list of attributes is something that she feels would quite naturally be expected in a classroom focused on developing skills in drama. For readers who teach in the Early Years, or perhaps who teach social studies in secondary schools, this may also seem quite natural.

However, when we have asked teachers of mathematics to reflect on how they develop this learner profile through their teaching of mathematics, they often see these concepts as more challenging. It may be helpful for you as the reader at this point to reflect on a recent 'lesson' you taught; use this profile to analyse the dispositions you paid most attention to, and those you may not have developed. In our experience we have found that working together, drawing on and combining the disciplines of mathematics and drama, allows us to focus on these dispositions rather than solely on particular skills contained within the mathematics or drama curricular.

In the following two section, we share exemplar lessons, designed through example to develop this argument further. The first of these draws on a workshop we developed for the 2016 ATM Easter Conference, and the second on mathematical modelling to explore a history of pandemics.

Exemplar 1: A refugee journey

What follows describes a workshop we devised to explore debate around the refugee 'crisis'. Two guiding principles from the associations for drama and mathematics give context here:

> Learning becomes deeply social (and sometimes personal) through play because learners know that they are contracting into fiction and they understand the power they have within that fiction to direct, decide and function (from the NATD guiding principles).

> Teaching and learning are cooperative activities. Encouraging a questioning approach and giving due attention to the ideas of others are attitudes to be encouraged (from the ATM guiding principles).

Our initial activity was to invite participants, in groups of five, to engage in three activities that would traditionally be more directly linked to drama. Our intention was to explore whether engagement in these activities would bring people together, both literally and metaphorically, and introduce ideas of boundaries and enclosures, danger, safety and protection. We believe that such activities have a place in all mathematics teaching, as the development of a community of learners supports the exploration and discussion of complex ideas. The three activities were:

> **Bomb and shield:** This game was developed by Augustus Boal as a part of his *Theatre of the oppressed* project (Boal, 1985). Theatre of the oppressed has the explicit aim of using education to help people understand their social reality, in order to change it. In this game, participants spread out around the room. Without revealing their choices, each person chooses one person in the room to be a 'bomb' and another to be their 'shield'. The aim of the game is to keep your shield between you and your bomb as people move around the room. The activity saw plenty of frantic movement as we counted down from 10 to 1, when the bomb 'explodes'.
>
> [N.B. It is worth noting that, since the time when this game was devised by Boal, the context has become very close to real life. We now

choose to introduce it as *Aliens and defenders* when we work with young learners. In Boal's time, there were few suicide bombers who would, literally, blow themselves up.]

Touching the floor: Whilst *Bomb and shield* introduced ideas of safety, danger and protection, the next game brought us closer together. We shouted out a number and each group, whilst remaining in contact with each other the whole time, had to keep this number of body parts on the floor. Ten was easy as the group simply held hands with ten feet touching the floor. For numbers greater than ten, some of the group were required to add hands, or noses, or foreheads to the floor. For numbers less than ten, individuals would have to balance and for numbers less than five, one of the group would need to be entirely supported.

Smallest area: Our final activity in this section invited each group to find the smallest area that they could all balance within. We asked them to mark out this area with masking tape and to calculate the area. Again, we were subtly introducing the idea of confinement and support. This activity also involved the groups in some estimating, measuring and calculation, marking the transition to mathematics.

The journey from Syria

The next section of the workshop required each group of five to make twenty miniature people using modelling clay. We asked that these should be a twentieth of the average size of the individual members of each group. We left the definition of 'average' to each group, and they interpreted this in a variety of ways, although there was some evidence of measurement and division. We were fascinated by the care that people took in making these models, even though we had not yet told the groups what we would be using the models for.

> While the participants were working on this task, they were set another
>   problem:
> How long would it take you to walk 4,320 km?

Again, we did not offer a context for this problem. As groups finished the modelling, we drew together to create a map on the floor of the space using masking tape. At this point, we explained why we had chosen 4,320 km; it is the distance from Aleppo, Syria to Calais, France. Google map suggests this journey would take 831 hours to walk. We agreed through discussion that this would take a minimum of three months if we included sleeping breaks and difficulties in crossing borders. The participants then used the information given below to create a 'map' from masking tape, marking out the various points along a line.

> Syria to Turkish border nearest Greece: 1,500 km
> Syria to Macedonian border: 2,000 km
> Syria to Austria/Germany border: 3,100 km
> Syria to Germany/France border: 3,700 km
> Syria to Calais: 4,320 km

The next task was to place the 100 'people' along the route from Syria to Calais. Each model represented one per cent of the people displaced in and from Syria as a result of the war. Another set of information was needed for this task. [Figures given were accurate in April 2016, for current data see UNICEF, Syrian refugee response.]

The population of Syria is 22.8 million. It is estimated that 6.6 million have been displaced within the country and 4.8 million displaced to other countries. Therefore, approximately 50 per cent of the population have been displaced, 29 per cent internally and 21 per cent to other countries.

As the models were placed onto the 'map' line, the atmosphere changed. A sense emerged from the group of not wanting to put the models in danger. We realized the extent to which the participants had contracted 'into fiction and understood the power they have within that fiction to direct, decide and function' (from the guiding principles of the NATD quoted above). We had clearly found ways to meet the requirements of another guiding principle of which states:

> The power to learn rests with the learner. Teaching has a subordinate role. The teacher has a duty to seek out ways to engage the power of the learner.
> *https://www.atm.org.uk/ATM-aims-principles*

The final act for the group was to place the English Channel on the 'map'. The group calculated that this was approximately the width of one of the

Table 1 Refugees Recorded in Different Countries

The following numbers of refugees were in these countries:	
Turkey	2.8 million
Lebanon	1.5 million
Jordan	1.5 million
Germany	500,000
Macedonia	400,000
France	10,000
UK	8,000
Refugees in Dunkirk and Calais camps	6,000

tape measures we had been using, according to the scale used. One participant looked back at the image of the journey, with our models spread out along the line of the 'map' and said, 'If you had come all that way, of course you are going to try and get over the channel.' The activity had successfully modelled the tiny proportion of Syrian refugees that have reached the channel; the 6,000 people in the camps at Dunkirk and Calais were represented by 0.1 per cent of a person (represented by an arm), with a finger representing the refugees who had successfully and safely reached the UK.

We will save reflections on this session for the end of the chapter when we have described the second activities, when we will draw together the two exemplars.

Pause for thought: Vignette

As we returned from a break during the workshop, we noticed one of the participants had stayed in the room, sitting with his thoughts. We noticed he had tears in his eyes. He smiled and said, 'Isn't it strange how attached you can become to little clay figures.'

For this participant, the stories of refugee journeys were being rewritten by engaging with mathematics through drama activities. Here mathematics had allowed us to share data which offered a big picture view of a specific situation and which challenged misconceptions often spread by mainstream media.

Exemplar 2: Modelling the spread of a pandemic

We opened this chapter by sharing the commitment of the NATD and the ATM to developing a 'humanizing' curriculum. Humanizing a curriculum is, in itself, a move towards a more socially just curriculum. The second workshop we describe used mathematical modelling and the experience of the Covid-19 pandemic and was influenced by another ATM guiding principle:

> The power to learn rests with the learner. Teaching has a subordinate role. The teacher has a duty to seek out ways to engage the power of the learner.

We began the workshop with the activity below.

Activity

You need about twenty people. Give each person a small piece of paper. Nineteen pieces are blank. One piece has a cross on it. Tell everyone to keep their piece of paper secret and invite the group to move around and then pair up. Everyone looks at their pieces of paper, the person who has paired up with the person with a cross adds a cross to their paper. Repeat this twice more. Invite the group to estimate how many people will now have crosses, in effect who has 'caught' the virus.

Then repeat the activity. This time if someone meets up with a 'cross' rather than immediately writing a cross they toss a coin. If it comes down 'heads' they write a cross, if 'tails' the paper remains blank. Again, invite an estimate of how many of the group now have the 'virus'.

This activity can be seen as a way of modelling the spread of the Covid-19 virus. In particular, research was reported by The Guardian that shows that the spread of the virus 'was linked to a 53 per cent fall in the incidence of the disease'. Tony was fortunate enough to be working in Belize recently and used this activity in all five areas of the country in which he ran workshops to illustrate how mathematics can be intimately tied to our lived experiences and to emphasize how an understanding of mathematics can impact on important life choices that we might make. These are the results from those workshops:

Punta Gorda	12	9
Dangriga	14	9
San Ignacio	9	7
Belize City	12	7
Corozal	14	3
Totals	61	35

Looking at the final totals across the five workshops, you can see that thirty-five people 'caught the virus' in the second version of the simulation compared to sixty-one in the first version. This works out as a reduction of 57 per cent. Interestingly, this shows that adding in the coin tossing element (which gives a 50 per cent chance of catching the virus) almost exactly replicated the scientific research in terms of 'reducing the incidence'.

We first came across a version of this activity at a conference in South Africa in the 1990s. It was introduced by a team of educators who had been working in rural South Africa where the incidence of HIV was very high. In this example not only was mathematics seen as an integral part of health education, but mathematics education was seen as important even for young learners who were unlikely to live to complete their schooling. This was the first time an important question was raised for me: what form of mathematics education could we offer learners as useful, exciting, interesting, and empowering in its own right rather than as a means to any other end such as examinations, progression through education or usefulness to a country's economic development?

Participants, whether students or teachers (and we have used this activity with participants from seven-years-old to seventy), can explore the statistics illustrating the differential impact of a virus on different groups of people. Through this practical activity, participants can explore how they might develop a mathematical model to illustrate differential impact. We then explored this subject further through use of an historical example: the events in the village of Eyam.

The roses of Eyam and the creation of a visual timeline

One of the key skills of an historian is having a well-developed understanding of chronology. We believe that 'feeling at home in the world' requires an understanding of how personal and community chronologies fit into the broader picture, and that we can draw on the idea of scaling from mathematics to do this. In this activity we ask participants to construct a timeline, usually from 0 to 2023, or whatever the current year is, by marking out the perimeter of the room in masking tape divided into 100-year sections. There is always interesting mathematical discussion as we calculate an appropriate scale so that the timeline will fit the space we are working in.

The next stage of the activity is to ask participants for historical events that they know of, or that are important to their families or communities. It does not matter whether or not participants know the dates of these events – after all, history is much more than simply remembering dates and the web is a great resource for finding such information if necessary. Participants place these events on the timeline on sticky notes and we invite them to comment, particularly on the parts of the timeline which appear 'empty' (and ask why this may be). This is also an opportunity to think about any historical events which are missing. Do the events that are recorded show the richness of the shared histories of all communities? Is there an unintended euro-centric bias evident?

From general to specific: Eyam

At this point we begin to explore the example of a specific event in history. The story of the plague village of Eyam offers a great opportunity to 'help pupils to understand the complexity of people's lives, the process of change, the diversity of societies and relationships between different groups, as well as their own identity and the challenges of their time', as identified as an objective in the English National Curriculum for History.

The first step in this activity is to invite participants to construct a scale plan of the village on the hall floor, using masking tape and pictures of some of the key places in the village. We explain that they will need to be able to move around the village, so the plan needs to be big enough to allow this to be possible.

The participants are then allocated a character from the village. For example, one might be the Reverend William Mompesson, who was the newly appointed Rector of Eyam when the plague broke out. He was a young academic, and his previous experience had not prepared him for the horror and responsibility he faced. He lived in the village with his wife, Catherine, another character who might be 'played' by a participant. Although the Mompessons sent their children away in the summer of 1666, Catherine refused to leave the village and died from plague herself in August 1666.

Another participant might be invited to play Thomas Stanley who had been the Rector of Eyam until 1660. He returned to Eyam when William Mompesson took over and, since he had the trust of most of the villagers, was fundamental in convincing the villagers to quarantine themselves to prevent the plague spreading elsewhere. Final examples include Marshall Howe, who was the village sexton responsible for burying the victims, Emmot Sydall and Rowland Torre, who were engaged when the plague broke out, and Rowland, a farmer in a nearby village who used to walk up the Delph to meet with a villager, Emmot, and who, when she stopped coming, could only fear the worst.

The participants work as a group, standing on an appropriate site on the map, and discuss how they feel at this moment in history and discuss their possible responses to the crisis. This leads to a whole group discussion about the responses of the village to the arrival of the plague, 'Should I stay, or should I go?'

Finally, we use the speech from the play *The Roses of Eyam* delivered by Thomas Stanley, read by a participant. The participants then reflect again on their feelings and responsibilities, and on what decisions they might make.

Conclusion

It seems a little strange to write a section entitled 'conclusions,' when a chapter such as this rather intends to elucidate a starting point. We hope that what we have shared provides a 'stopping off point' in our shared journey as we all work for social justice, and we hope the next stopping off point might be the classrooms in which you work as you try out the activities we have shared. As a way of drawing this section of the journey to a close we would like to share the work of Munir Fasheh, a Palestinian academic and teacher. In 'Mathematics Teaching 251', he challenges readers to think of learning and assessment through new eyes. He defines *mujaawarah* as a personal and communal freedom to learn and act in harmony with well-being and wisdom. We invite you to spend a moment thinking of how often such a freedom exists in our mathematics classrooms and whether or not the activities described above offer participants personal and communal freedom to learn and to act in harmony, with well-being and with wisdom. In the same article, Munir redefines assessment in terms of an Arabic term *yuhsen*. *Yuhsen* is a combination of one's performance in action and one's relationship to who and what is around, and so offers an alternative view of assessment. For Munir Fasheh, a person's worth is judged by looking at the interconnectivity of:

- How well they use a skill.
- The beauty of the outcomes.
- How useful the outcomes are to the community.
- How respectfully the process is engaged in.
- The humility of the act.

Again, we invite you to use these statements to reflect on and evaluate the activities outlined above. Our final thought takes us back to both the value of cross-curricular work and to the importance of collaboration across disciplines. We offer the words with which Munir Fasheh closed his piece in MT251:

'Beyond right and wrong there is a field; I will meet you there.'

Critical reflective questions

Think back to an activity which you have used in a classroom in which you work, whether as a teacher, a teacher educator or a community teacher. Use the list below, which draws on Munir Fasheh's description of *Yuhsen* to reflect on the 'worth' of the activity:

1. To what extent did you notice learners developing new skills and using skills they already had fluency in?
2. Was there a shared excitement in the 'beauty' of the outcomes?

3   Will participants be able to use the skills they have developed and the outcomes of the activity to develop the communities in which they live?
4   Was a mutual respect between learners and between learners and teachers evident throughout the process?
5   Was humility evident in both learners and teachers?

Note

1   For more details on Breach Theatre, go to https://www.breachtheatre.com/.

References

ATM guiding principles (2023). These can be found at https://www.atm.org.uk/ATM-aims-principles (accessed 5 October 2023).
Boal, A. (1985). *Theatre of the Oppressed*. London: Theatre Communications Group.
British Political Speech archive (2023). http://www.britishpoliticalspeech.org/speech-archive.htm?speech=133 (accessed September 2023).
Cotton, T., and Toft, H. (2018). Teaching mathematics through drama, in *Mathematics Teaching 263*, 15–19. Derby: Association of Teachers of Mathematics.
Cotton, T., and Toft, H. (2019). Mathematics and drama: The case of history, in *Mathematics Teaching 269*, 41–2. Derby: Association of Teachers of Mathematics.
Fasheh, M. (2016). Over 68 years with mathematics, in *Mathematics Teaching 251*, 6–10. Derby: Association of Teachers of Mathematics.
Francis, B., Connolly, P., Archer, L., Hodgen, J., Mazenod, A., Pepper, D., Sloan, S., Taylor, B., Tereshchenko, A, and Travers, M. (2017). Attainment grouping as self-fulfilling prophecy? A mixed methods exploration of self-confidence and set level among Year 7 students. *International Journal of Educational Research, 86*, 96–108. Elsevier.
Gillborn, D. (2008). *Racism and Education: Coincidence or Conspiracy*. London: Routledge.
Heathcote, D., and Bolton, G. (1995) *Drama for Learning: Dorothy Heathcote's Mantle of the Expert Approach to Education*. Portsmouth, NH: Heinemann USA.
House of Commons (2020). *Unequal Impact? Coronavirus and BAME People: Third Report of Session 2019–21*. https://committees.parliament.uk/publications/3965/documents/39887/default/ (accessed 12 October 2022).
IB Learner Profile (2023). Available at http://www.ibo.org/globalassets/publications/recognition/learnerprofile-en.pdf (accessed 11 December 2023).
National Archives (2023). Local Government Act 1988 can be found at https://www.legislation.gov.uk/ukpga/1988/9/contents (accessed September 2023).
The Guardian (2022). *Tory Party Chairman Says 'Painful Woke Psychodrama' Weakening the West*. https://www.theguardian.com/politics/2022/feb/14/oliver-

dowden-says-painful-woke-psychodrama-weakening-the-west (accessed 12 October 2022).

The National Association for the Teaching of Drama guiding principles can be found at (2025). http://www.natd.eu/ (accessed on 15 March 2025).

UNICEF (2023). Data on the Syrian refugee response can be found at https://data.unhcr.org/en/situations/syria (accessed September 2023).

Meeting Our Responsibilities to All: Re-Cripping Classroom Texts

Clare Lawrence and Clare Mahon

9

Introduction

There is increased awareness as we approach the second quarter of the twenty-first century that literature studied in schools carries within it important messages about our society's identity. Happily, many schools are working to 'decolonise' their curricula (Elliott and Courtney, 2023) and examination boards are widening text options for GCSE. Recognition of the contribution of writers of colour, and critical awareness regarding representations of race and ethnicity within texts are beginning to redress the historical dominance of white euro-centricity. Gradually, books read in schools are starting to more accurately reflect the diversity of the world, and of those who read and teach them.

This cannot yet, though, be said for the minority members of our communities who are disabled. The emergence of Disability Studies and of critical phenomenological approaches to the understanding of lived experience of disability (Dickel, 2022) are yet to have much impact in our classrooms. The texts taught and read still overwhelmingly feature nondisabled protagonists and are overwhelmingly authored by nondisabled writers. If we aspire that the texts we share with pupils should be both mirrors and windows (Bishop, 1990), then we must acknowledge that they are currently ones with disappointingly foggy glass.

Further, on the occasions where disability is portrayed in texts, the way that this occurs needs conscious and careful scrutiny. This chapter explores the teaching of two widely found and highly respected classroom texts – *Of Mice and Men* by John Steinbeck (1937) and *Wonder* by R. J. Palacio (2012).

It identifies and critiques the potentially ableist narratives within the texts and questions how as teachers we might foreground these, and so support pupils to use the texts to consider ideas of ableism and inclusivity.

Of course, we need to tread a careful path here, between mediating the pupils' readings of the texts and protecting those readers' rights to authentic engagement with them (Mason and Giovanelli, 2017). In order to develop as readers and as critical thinkers, children need freedom to make their own personal responses to texts (Collyer et al., 2022). However, they also need access to alternative views of the world if they are to develop a critical understanding of the portrayals made by writers (Dressel, 2005). They may lack the lived experience to be able to create schemas and the maturity of reading needed to challenge certain narratives they encounter (Gray and Rogers, 1956; Manzo and Manzo, 1993) and may be more likely to internalize ideas presented to them by the authoritative figure of the writer (Powell and Snow, 2007). How teachers might navigate this tricky terrain is explored here, using the theoretical lens of Crip theory and the proposed strategy of 're-cripping'.

The concept of re-cripping

Crip theory emerged from within Disability Studies, with the term 'crip' being both consciously reclaimed (McRuer, 2006) and widened to no longer refer solely to those with physical impairments but also to those with intellectual and sensory impairments (Sandahl, 2003). 'Cripping' is a radical act in the disability world, bringing disability to the forefront of society's attention, and refusing to allow it to be elided or overlooked. The concept of re-cripping literature, therefore, refers to the treatment of disabled characters *as* disabled, thereby bringing disability back into the discussion (Loftis, 2021). This means treating disability as integral to disabled characters and acknowledging that it plays a role within the text. Loftis – a disabled Professor of English – uses the example of *Richard III* (Loftis, 2021), arguing that debate over whether or not the real King Richard was disabled is unhelpful and irrelevant to study of Shakespeare's play. This play consciously portrays King Richard as 'deformed, unfinished' (*Richard III,* I:i). Loftis calls for the character Richard in the play to be treated as a disabled character in his own right, separate from the historical Richard III, and for him to be studied, performed and discussed as such.

Re-cripping is a strategy which teachers may apply when discussing both Lennie in *Of Mice and Men* and August in *Wonder*. Rather than simplifying August to someone who 'looks different', highlighting that he has an impairment and is therefore disabled in discussions with the class could be a powerful way to re-crip this text. Similarly, discussing Lennie as intellectually disabled rather than simply 'childlike' (for example, Yorknotes, n.d.) will re-crip *Of Mice and Men* and help to move discussions to less ableist positions.

In the classroom, pupils and teachers have the opportunity to unpick representations, enabling them to challenge ideas they see both in the text and in their contemporary society. Although authorial context is addressed as part of the National Curriculum and is important in appreciating how the world has changed over time, pupils do not always have the tools to distance themselves from the implications which are conveyed to them in writing (Powell and Snow, 2007). Encountering these texts in the classroom may lend validity to the author's perceived positionality if this is not challenged by the teacher (Casalme, 2016). These representations studied in school hold within them powerful narratives about disability and these narratives merit scrutiny in a modern classroom context.

Unpacking representation in the sample texts

The ableism in *Of Mice and Men* (Steinbeck, 1937) is overt and 'of its time' and is present in the text from the outset. Lennie is not described to the reader as being his own character, but rather as being everything that George is not, or as lacking everything that George has. This difference works to separate the disabled character from the nondisabled character, to ask the reader to see Lennie as different from George and from themself. There is no concept that the reader may identify with Lennie; Steinbeck works to 'other' Lennie from the outset.

Lennie is not positioned as being merely different from George, but as inferior to him, closer to an animal than another human. This begins with describing the way he drags his feet as similar to 'the way a bear drags its paws' (Steinbeck, 1937: 2) and re-emerges when he arrives at the water pool and drinks with 'long gulps, snorting into the water like a horse' (Steinbeck, 1937: 3). Both of these animals are physically very powerful, dangerous in their own ways. Lennie is not depicted as an easily controlled, reserved animal, fully managed by his handler, but as something which must be contained to prevent risk to himself and others, a lot which falls to George (Steinbeck, 1937: 3). There is an unease in this relationship, either in the potential retribution that Lennie as a beast might face if he does not obey his handler, or in the backlash that George might receive if he pushes this well-trained animal too far. Steinbeck continues this uneasy metaphor when he has George state that he 'wisht [he] could put [Lennie] in a cage' (Steinbeck, 1937: 13).

In many ways, *Wonder* (Palacio, 2012) is a product of a more accepting society, containing more inclusive views of disability than those portrayed in *Of Mice and Men*. However, there are narratives within it which nonetheless require scrutiny, despite the book's celebrated tone of acceptance.

Wonder's first-person narrative is intriguing because of its comparative rareness; it is much less common to see stories told by disabled people than stories featuring or about them (Tarvainen, 2019). The novel, right from the beginning, positions the disabled character, August, as having his own voice, and so *Wonder* seems to offer August more agency than *Of Mice and Men* does to Lennie. August states in the first line that he 'know[s he's] not an ordinary ten-year-old-kid' (Palacio, 2012: 3). August explains that he 'feels ordinary' (Palacio, 2012: 3), but that it is the way in which other people react to him that tells him that he is not (Palacio, 2012: 3). The narrative suggests that August's disability is something which is imposed upon him by other people, not something which he sees as an integral part of himself. *Wonder* therefore seems to support the Social Model view of disability (Oliver, 1986) which argues that it is not individual impairments which are the disabling factor in people's lives, but society's refusal to accommodate these differences.

However, there are challenges to accepting this positionality in the text. Rather than wishing for societal acceptance, August states that 'If [he] found a magic lamp' his one wish would be to have a 'normal face' (Palacio, 2012: 3). He chooses to change his outward appearance rather than hoping that people might come to appreciate him for who he is. August's vocalization of this position may imply to young readers that the answer to disability is that it is removed, that people would be better off if they did not have impairments. Palacio presents this idea on the very first page but then works through the narrative of the novel to challenge it, encouraging the reader to consider their reactions towards an acceptance of disability.

Both texts also contain additional ableist narratives. These can be sorted into three categories: narratives of death, of the unborn and cure narratives.

The death narrative in *Of Mice and Men* is plain to see: George shoots Lennie in the back of the head at the end of the book. This plot-point is made more problematic when we acknowledge that this act is presented as the most reasonable way to deal with Lennie's disability. George's other options as presented in the text are to have Lennie tied up 'like a dog' (Steinbeck, 1937: 71), to allow him to be lynched by the angry mob or to let him starve to death as he wanders in the wilderness. Lennie's murder is presented as the kindest and the most reasonable option. It is compounded by having the authoritative character of the narrative, Slim, destroy four runts of his dog's litter (Steinbeck, 1937: 39), as well as endorsing the shooting of Candy's elderly dog (Steinbeck, 1937: 51). Slim also justifies George's action in killing Lennie, resting his hand on George's shoulder and telling him that George 'hadda' do it (Steinbeck, 1937: 121).

The death narrative in *Wonder* is better hidden, although one way in which it appears is a direct mirroring of *Of Mice and Men* through the euthanasia of the family's dog, Daisy. Palacio highlights Daisy's old age and provides an obvious reminder of her deteriorating state when she is sick in the hall after a family dinner (Palacio, 2012: 191). August's mother says that they 'don't want her to suffer' (Palacio, 2012: 221), telling August that it is kinder for Daisy to be euthanized than to live in pain. Although Palacio positions the decision in *Wonder* to be made genuinely out of concern for the suffering of the animal, death is, as in *Of Mice and Men,* presented as a viable option when faced with suffering. This is compounded by a comment made by one of August's classmates, a boy who is meant to be his friend. This boy claims that, if he looked like August, he would kill himself (Palacio, 2012: 77). It is a harsh reality that individuals with a physical disability are three times more likely to have attempted suicide than nondisabled individuals (Khazem et al., 2021). The idea of a disabled life being a kind of torture is a concept prevalent around discussions regarding disabled children as found in 'Worth living or worth dying? The views of the general public about allowing disabled children to die' (Brick et al., 2020). This paper uses Wilkinson's (2011) definition of a 'Life Not Worth Living' (LNWL) as 'A life in which future burdens for the individual outweigh benefits. There is negative net future well-being' (Wilkinson, 2011: 21).

Unborn narratives, rather than eradicating disabled lives, are those which indicate that it would be better that those lives had never started in the first place. In *Of Mice and Men*, Lennie's sexuality is treated as troublesome and dangerous. Multiple times, Lennie acts in a way which could be understood to have sexual undertones – first in Weed before the start of the novella, then at the end right before the murder of Curley's wife. Steinbeck may be responding to the fact that, rather than euthanasia, forced sterilization was a widespread form of eugenics at the time he was writing (Amy and Rowlands, 2018; Ciancio, 2020). In California, where the novella is set, over 20,000 people were sterilized before 1964, a third of whom were considered 'mentally insufficient' (Ciancio, 2020). Sterilization in California continued until 2013 (Ciancio, 2020).

In *Wonder*, although the topic of sterilization is once again not made explicit, August does make it very clear that his condition was a complete surprise to his parents at his birth (Palacio, 2012: 6–7). This may reflect that over half of parents choose to abort their child where impairments are found on pre-natal tests (97 per cent in Australia (Maxwell et al., 2015) and 67 per cent in the USA (Natoli et al. Yes,012)). Furthermore, the reader is told that August's sister, Via, aims to become a genetic scientist (Palacio, 2012: 190).

Palacio seems to be positioning Via as interested in the implications of August's genetics on her future children. This would likely come in the form of the pre-natal testing which results in such high abortion rates. Saxton (2016) goes as far as to call pre-natal testing a form of eugenics.

Finally, the cure narrative in *Of Mice and Men* is presented in the form of the dream which Lennie and George have of the farm where Lennie can have his own role and social standing, no longer disabled by his condition. This dream emerges in Chapter One (Steinbeck, 1937: 17) and re-emerges frequently throughout the text (for example, Steinbeck, 1937: 17, 63, 86). Although the dream seems to offer comfort to both characters throughout the novella, it disappears following the death of Curley's wife, when George admits, 'I think I knowed from the very first. I think I knowed we'd never do her' (Steinbeck, 1937: 107). The dream is therefore presented as fundamentally impractical, something which offers comfort but no actual likely fulfilment. Death is presented as the only 'cure' for Lennie's disability.

In *Wonder*, there are many medical interventions which August goes through, with varying levels of consent on his part. He tells the reader that he has had twenty-seven surgeries so far (Palacio, 2012: 4), some for medical reasons – for example, to modify his jaw (Palacio, 2012: 50) – and others for cosmetic reasons (Palacio, 2012: 88). As August says to Jack when asked why he does not just get plastic surgery to change the way he looks, 'Hello? This *is* after plastic surgery' (Palacio, 2012: 64, emphasis in original). Although Palacio has August make light of the situation here, this does raise the question of how far medical intervention is beneficial for him.

Pause for thought: Research

In their 2022 paper, Heineke, Papola-Ellis and Elliott suggest a four-step framework to support text-choice for classroom use that will allow all children – including those from minority groups, such as those with disabilities – to see themselves in the texts they read. They draw on the theoretical frameworks of Culturally Sustaining Pedagogy, which aims to emphasize the 'strengths, languages, and cultural practices of learners who have been historically situated as deficient' (Heineke et al., 2022: 277) and Critical Literacy, which 'seeks to disrupt the status quo in traditional schooling and promote social action' (Heineke et al., 2022: 277). Their framework incorporates four steps:

1. Teachers are encouraged to get to know the identities of the children they teach, to explore their 'multifaceted identities' (Heineke et al., 2022: 278) and their experiences, and to move beyond superficial labelling.

2 Teachers should ensure that texts are given a central role in the learning and in developing literacy of their pupils.

3 Teachers are urged to select texts that prioritize 'relevant and authentic portrayals that capture multifaceted identities and experiences' (Heineke et al., 2022: 278).

4 Teachers should integrate texts into the classroom thoughtfully and purposefully, supporting children to connect with what they read.

Giving central place to quality texts that provide genuine, thoughtful and authentic portrayal of diverse identities and lived experiences resonates as being at the heart of good practice. Yet, as discussed in this chapter, texts may be flawed and may include elements of both overt and hidden ableism. Much of what constitutes the 'canon' of literature includes elements of discrimination, and teachers may have little choice in the selection of these older texts in response to the demands of examination boards.

Of the steps outlined in the framework, the first may be perhaps both the most important and the most difficult. We seem to have moved away from a child-centred learning approach in many of our schools, and properly 'getting to know' the pupils we teach can feel almost intrusive. Yet without awareness of the diversity in the pupils before us, how can we support the fourth suggestion of this framework? It is a challenge to support pupils to make personal connections if we are unaware what connections there are to be made.

Additionally, teachers may feel inadequate to the task of supporting those connections. They may, for example, have had no training regarding teaching a child with visible differences and may therefore shy away from introducing a text such as *Wonder* if a pupil in that class has a physical disability such as a craniofacial abnormality. The UK charity *Changing Faces* Advocates in its resources for teachers for an 'understanding of the basic psychological and social issues that arise' for these pupils. For teachers who do not have basic psychological training, it is perhaps even more important that the texts they choose are robust and that they feel robustly able to critique them regarding the issues they present.

Re-cripping in the classroom

The concept of re-cripping requires above all that disability is acknowledged. Lennie is not 'childlike', and August is not merely 'different looking'. If the portrayals are to be discussed in the classroom with any degree of seriousness, the characters' impairments and what causes them to be disabled (whether that is those impairments themselves or society's view of them) need to be acknowledged. Within her text Palacio states that August is 'neither disabled, handicapped, nor developmentally delayed in any way' (Palacio, 2012: 163). Acknowledging that August *is*, in fact, disabled does not challenge Palacio's narrative that August is the same, deep down, as everyone else, but it does begin to allow for honest discussion of the discrimination he faces. Consideration of Via's view of him, her decision not to have children and of the implications of her wish to study genetics need to be brought into the open, as does the implication of Jack's assertion that he would kill himself if he shared August's disability. Steinbeck's framing of Lennie as animalistic and George's murder of him require that Lennie's disability be acknowledged and squarely faced if discussion is to have any depth.

One of the most powerful methods of re-cripping a text that features a disabled character is through performance (Loftis, 2021). One of the problems with nondisabled actors taking on disabled roles is the perception of disability as performative, something which can easily be separated from the individual. Loftis discusses performances of *Richard III*, which she describes as a role typically played by handsome, appealing actors as a way to test their ability to act 'ugly' or 'crippled' (Loftis, 2021). There is an understanding that, once the performance has finished, these actors can return to their position in society as attractive, untainted. Research has shown that simulating disability does not improve attitudes towards disability and does not increase willingness to interact with disabled people (Nario-Redmond et al., 2017).

In film adaptations of *Of Mice and Men* (Milestone, 1939; Badiyi, 1981; Sinise, 1992) Lennie is played by nondisabled actors, who undertake the challenge of being disabled for only as long as they are on screen. This 'uncripping' is also seen in the film adaptation of *Wonder* (Chbosky, 2017). In this film August is played by a nondisabled child actor who dons prosthetic makeup in order to undertake the role. These prosthetics earned BAFTA, Oscar and Critic's Choice nominations. However, the make-up artists could not move the actor's eyes down his face nor change the shape of his jaw, as Palacio describes in the text (Palacio, 2012: 88). Tollefson (2018), a professor of facial plastic and reconstructive surgery, states that the prosthetics in *Wonder* are substantially different to the faces of those with Treacher Collins Syndrome, and that *Wonder*'s prosthetics will not prepare those watching the film to meet people with this syndrome. With nondisabled actors assuming disabled roles, the focus can therefore slide from portrayal of a fully rounded character to prescription of how the actor might portray the impairment. Disabled characteristics and behaviours become scrutiny to what is 'realistic' and what is 'too much' and may be watered down to become palatable. August being played by a boy with real craniofacial abnormalities could change the audience's response when he first appears on screen to reflect the reactions of other characters in the book. The audience response to Lennie's murder may be similarly altered if a disabled actor is shown being killed. We are past the point as a society where a white actor would wear blackface to show how difficult it is to live with racism. Why is this not the case with disability?

However, although it may be powerful if teachers had the opportunity to show pupils performances of the texts featuring disabled actors, this is not something over which they have direct control. Therefore, if re-cripping is to be used by teachers as a means to introduce discussion of disability in the classroom, it may need to happen in other ways. Re-cripping the participants of the conversation and therefore directly addressing disability within the classroom is a method worth considering, albeit with perception and sensitivity (Collins et al., 2018). This might start with opening the door for disabled pupils to speak and to contribute their lived experiences to the conversation. Open discussion by all pupils, including those who may have disabled friends, family or are themselves disabled, should support positive prefiguring and re-cripping of the texts. Lennie being shot in the back of the head seems a lot less acceptable when Lennie reminds you of your own brother.

Widening access to disabled voices might also take the form of more diverse curricula. Reading other texts which prioritize disabled voices alongside each other and comparing narratives may be a way in which to do this. One of the central issues with both *Of Mice and Men* and *Wonder* is that they are not written by disabled writers. The nondisabled writer uses their imagination to invite a supposed nondisabled reader to imagine what the lived experience of the characters might be. Of course, this is an accepted element of art: Shakespeare was not a Danish Prince nor was Dickens a house-breaker. However, including authentic voices from writers with lived experience has the potential to enrich the reader's engagement, and awareness that some readers will share this lived experience enriches it further. Texts for children and young people which feature disability are gradually becoming more available (Nikolajeva, 2016) and giving pupils access to diverse voices, indeed including disabled queer characters, or disabled people of colour, will allow them to consider disability through a number of different lenses. As well as fiction, introducing non-fiction materials about disability may be a way to ensure disabled voices are heard, including seizing opportunities to discuss disability with disabled people invited into the classroom.

One of the most overlooked and yet most potentially powerful methods of re-cripping within the classroom is the increased visibility of disabled teachers. The high status of the teacher within the classroom challenges the very concept of 'dis'-ability (Ware et al., 2020). The presence of teachers who are visibly disabled or feel confident to disclose hidden disabilities automatically prefigures texts involving disability in a particular way. The individual with the most authority in the classroom acknowledging their status as disabled means that the pupils in the class have access to a conceptualization of disability which is successful, capable of leadership and able to live a full and fulfilling life into adulthood. There is a power in acknowledging the influence of disabled teachers who may 'offer a unique knowledge standpoint, challenge the animosity of dominant cultural beliefs around disability ... and provide a source of resistance, solace and resolution for students they teach' (Pritchard, 2010: 43). Greater visibility of disabled teachers would enable pupils to see someone whose disability has not been erased, someone who has not been 'cured', yet someone who is living proof that impairment is not something which has to weigh them down nor define them. George's actions at the end of *Of Mice and Men*, Jack's assertion that he would kill himself if he looked like August or Via's apparent determination not to have children like her brother are then filtered through the understanding that they question the value of the teacher's very existence. The teacher themself becomes a form of prefiguring.

Conclusion

There is considerable research evidence that having a 'teacher like them' enables pupils to become more successful in life (see, for example, Egalite and Kisida, 2018; Gershenson et al., 2018; Pritchard, 2010). However, as disabled activist Stella Young asserts in her 2014 TED Talk, 'For lots of us, disabled people are not our teachers or our doctors or our manicurists.' Many people do not see disabled people outside texts or other media and, although the ideal answer to the challenges of the texts discussed in this chapter may be to see more disabled teachers in the classroom, this is clearly not an imminent solution while statistics suggest that only 0.5 per cent of teachers identify as disabled (Gov.co.uk, 2017).

Instead, taking opportunities to re-crip our classrooms enables us, even when we find ourselves in a space with very few disabled voices, to remain aware of a disabled perspective. We can encourage disabled activists or speakers to come into these spaces. We can choose to include materials produced by disabled people, and bring disabled voices into our classroom through texts, films and other materials.

Most importantly, perhaps, we can re-crip ourselves. We can consciously seek interaction with diverse people in our lives, can be critically alert to portrayals of disability in our teaching, and ensure that our own schemas are robust, well rounded and suitable. Whether or not we identify as disabled ourselves, we need to make careful decisions about the form and content of what we say and to encourage pupils to follow suit, engaging with potentially ableist narratives as we encounter them, both in texts and in society.

Critical reflective questions

1. What measures do you take to explore the multifaceted identities and experiences of those you teach? Does your awareness of these influence your choice of texts?

2. When exploring texts that include subject matter with which you are not familiar through experience, how can you ensure that portrayals are relevant and authentic, and how do you support thoughtful and purposeful connections between text and readers?

3. To what extent does the language of 're-cripping' challenge you and those you teach? Are you confident with language that is deliberately provocative?

4. Research (for example, Chatzitheochari et al., 2016) suggests disabled pupils are at greater risk of bullying than nondisabled peers; Government statistics (2023) suggest that 24 per cent of the UK population – yet just 0.5 per cent of teachers – are disabled. Disability awareness does not appear at any point in the National Curriculum and schools have no requirement to address it. How can we as teachers – both disabled and nondisabled – address this inequity of experience?

Texts

Palacio, R. J. (2012). *Wonder*. London: Penguin Random House.
Steinbeck, J. (1937). *Of Mice and Men*. New York: Covici, Friede, Inc.

References

Amy, J. J., and Rowlands, S. (2018). Legalised non-consensual sterilisation–eugenics put into practice before 1945, and the aftermath. Part 2: Europe. *The European Journal of Contraception & Reproductive Health Care*, *23*(3), 194–200.
Badiyi, R. (Producer and Director) (1981). *Of Mice and Men*. [Motion Picture].

Bishop, R. S. (1990). Windows and mirrors: Children's books and parallel cultures. In *California State University Reading Conference: 14th Annual Conference Proceedings*, March, 3–12.

Brick, C., Kahane, G., Wilkinson, D., Caviola, L., and Savulescu, J. (2020). Worth living or worth dying? The views of the general public about allowing disabled children to die. *Journal of Medical Ethics*, 46(1), 7–15.

Casalme, A. G. (2016). Engaging children in discussions of disfigurement and disability: The wonder of palacio's wonder. *The Cutting Edge: The Stanford Undergraduate Journal of Education Research*, 1(1), 26–44.

Chatzitheochari, S., Parsons, S., and Platt, L. (2016). Doubly disadvantaged? Bullying experiences among disabled children and young people in England. *Sociology*, 50(4), 695–713.

Chbosky, S. (Director). (2017). *Wonder* [Motion Picture]. United States: Lionsgate.

Ciancio, S. (2020). *Eugenic Sterilization Laws in the U.S. Human Life International*. Retrieved from https://www.hli.org/resources/eugenic-sterilization/#:~:text=By%201930%2C%2030%20states%20had%20passed%20laws%20that,parents%20of%20children%20likely%20to%20experience%20various%20disorders.

Collins, K. M., Wagner, M. O. C., and Meadows, J. (2018). Every story matters: Disability studies in the literacy classroom. *Language Arts*, 96(2), 114–18.

Collyer, E., Norton, G., Lawrence, C., Reeve, S., Siddiquee, R., Meacham, A., and Harrison, K. (2022). Responding to pupil led tangential thinking: A case study of teaching romantic poetry in a post-16 setting. *English in Education*, 56(1), 47–58.

Dickel, S. (2022). *Embodying Difference: Critical Phenomenology and Narratives of Disability, Race, and Sexuality*. Berlin, New York, London: Springer Nature.

Dressel, J. H. (2005). Personal response and social responsibility: Responses of middle school students to multicultural literature. *The Reading Teacher*, 58(8), 750–64.

Egalite, A. J., and Kisida, B. (2018). The effects of teacher match on students' academic perceptions and attitudes. *Educational Evaluation and Policy Analysis*, 40(1), 59–81.

Elliott, V., and Courtney, M. (2023). Teaching poems by authors of colour at key stage 3: Categorising what is taught. *English in Education*, 57(2), 91–101.

Gershenson, S., Hart, C. M., Hyman, J., Lindsay, C., and Papageorge, N. W. (2018). *The Long-Run Impacts of Same-Race Teachers* (No. w25254). National Bureau of Economic Research.

Gov.co.uk (2017). *National Statistics: School Workforce in England: November 2016*. Department for Education. Published Thursday, 22 June 2017 (online).

Gov.co.uk (2023). *UK Disability Statistics: Prevalence and Life Experiences* Research Briefing. Published Wednesday, 23 August 2023 (online).

Gray, W. S., and Rogers, B. (1956). *Maturity in Reading: Its Nature and Appraisal*. Chicago, IL: University of Chicago Press.

Heineke, A. J., Papola-Ellis, A., and Elliott, J. (2022). Using texts as mirrors: The power of readers seeing themselves. *The Reading Teacher*, 76(3), 277–84.

Khazem, L. R., Anestis, M. D., Gratz, K. L., Tull, M. T., and Bryan, C. J. (2021). Examining the role of stigma and disability-related factors in suicide risk through the lens of the Interpersonal Theory of Suicide. *Journal of Psychiatric Research*, 137, 652–6.

Loftis, S. F. (2021). *Shakespeare and Disability Studies*. Oxford: Oxford University Press.

Manzo, U. C., and Manzo, A. V. (1993). *Literacy Disorders: Holistic Diagnosis and Remediation*. New York: Harcourt Brace Jovanovich College Publishers.

Mason, J., and Giovanelli, M. (2017). 'What do you think?' Let me tell you: Discourse about texts and the literature classroom. *Changing English*, *24*(3), 318–29.

Maxwell, S., C. Bower, and O'Leary, P. (2015). Impact of prenatal screening and diagnostic testing on trends in Down syndrome births and terminations in Western Australia 1980 to 2013. *Prenatal Diagnosis*, *35*(13), 1324–30.

McRuer, R. (2006). *Crip Theory: Cultural Signs of Queerness and Disability (Vol. 9)*. New York: New York University Press.

Milestone, L. (Producer and Director) (1939). *Of Mice and Men* [Motion Picture]. United States: United Artists.

Nario-Redmond, M. R., Gospodinov, D., and Cobb, A. (2017). Crip for a day: The unintended negative consequences of disability simulations. *Rehabilitation Psychology*, *62*(3), 324.

Nikolajeva, M. (2016). Recent trends in children's literature research: Return to the body. *International Research in Children's Literature*, *9*(2), 132–45.

Oliver, M. (1986). Social policy and disability: Some theoretical issues. *Disability, Handicap & Society*, *1*(1), 5–17.

Powell, M. B., and Snow, P. C. (2007). Guide to questioning children during the free-narrative phase of an investigative interview. *Australian Psychologist*, *42*(1), 57–65.

Pritchard, G. (2010). Disabled people as culturally relevant teachers. *Journal of Social Inclusion*, *1*(1), 43.

Sandahl, C. (2003). Queering the crip or cripping the queer?: Intersections of queer and crip identities in solo autobiographical performance. *GLQ: A journal of lesbian and gay studies*, *9*(1), 25–56.

Saxton, M. (2016). Disability rights and selective abortion. In L. J. Davis (ed.), *The Disability Studies Reader*, 73–86. 4th edn, London: Routledge.

Sinise, G. (Producer and Director) (1992). *Of Mice and Men* [Motion Picture]. United States: Metro-Goldwyn-Mayer.

Tarvainen, M. (2019). Ableism and the life stories of people with disabilities. *Scandinavian Journal of Disability Research*, *21*(1), 291–9.

Tollefson, T. T. (2018). Apprehending otherness through wonder: A facial plastic surgeon's review of the book and movie. *Jama*, *319*(7), 640–2.

Ware, H., Singal, N., and Groce, N. (2020). The work lives of disabled teachers: Revisiting inclusive education in English schools. *Disability and Society*, 1–23. www.aqa.org.uk/news/new-texts-and-poetry-bring-greater-diversity-to-aqas-english-literature-gcse-qualification.

Wilkinson, D. J. (2011). A life worth giving? The threshold for permissible withdrawal of life support from disabled newborn infants. *The American Journal of Bioethics*, *11*(2), 20–32.

Yorknotes (n.d.). Lennie. Retrieved from https://www.yorknotes.com/gcse/english-literature/of-mice-and-men/study/characters/02020200_lennie.

'Rethinking Childhood Development: Critiquing Norm-Referenced Approaches in Early Years Education'

Nyree Nicholson

Introduction

The EYFS curriculum in England assesses children aged birth to five (DfE, 2024). The curriculum centres around an outcomes approach, with an emphasis on measuring and documenting children's stages of development. This chapter, based on primary research, examines how early childhood practitioners use statutory criteria to assess and support children's development. The current English education system divides children into several educational stages based on their chronological age, ranging from birth to sixteen. This system, which dates back to roughly 1860, has been criticized for its factory-like approach, emphasizing standardized development and progression (Leland and Kasten, 2002: 5). Children in early childhood settings are evaluated against Early Learning Goals (ELG) under the EYFS with the goal of detecting developmental gaps, particularly the attainment gap between children from different socioeconomic origins. This norm-referenced approach implies a linear, chronological development paradigm, labelling deviations from the norm as 'abnormal'.

Child development, which includes physical, emotional and cognitive growth, is recognized as a complex and nonlinear process. Despite this, educational and health services frequently use normative criteria to assess cognitive and physical growth. This chapter explores the concept of 'normal' development, asserting that it excludes children who develop at varying rates or under various conditions. The chapter emphasizes the problematic aspect of normalizing child development, including the risk of neglecting individual differences and the diversity of varied developmental pathways, it examines the difficulties of early childhood education in England, namely the norm-referenced approach to child development and questions the validity and ethical consequences of existing assessment processes, emphasizing the importance of a more inclusive and flexible approach that recognizes and celebrates each child's unique developmental path.

Defining early development: A norm referenced approach

Child development is the term used to describe a child's progress in physical, emotional and cognitive growth and theorists consistently agree that children develop skills at different rates (Bukatko and Daehler, 2012). According to Palaiologou (2019), development is a social term that organizes and categorizes development. Development, from the standpoint of developmental psychology, is lifelong and may be characterized as 'patterns of change' that occur throughout an individual's life (Palaiologou, 2019: 94). This perspective highlights that development is not linear, with a beginning and an end point, but rather continuous, temporal and changing.

Armstrong (1995) highlighted the increased contemporary scrutiny of children's development. Educational surveillance assesses cognitive and physical development, while health services measure health-related variables like weight (Ware and Harvey, 2013). Honig (1983) noted how research has established developmental standards to gauge a child's cognitive and physical growth, emphasizing the importance of documenting and standardizing developmental stages for confirming normative development. However, Armstrong (1995) criticized the attempt to define 'normality' or 'average development', arguing that it labels anything outside these limits as 'abnormal', which he termed the 'problematisation of the normal' (Armstrong, 1995: 396).

Armstrong (1995) maintained that development is an individual experience that occurs at varying rates. As a result, attempting to normalize development is risky since it implies that some children will never achieve the same level as their peers in spite of endeavours to ensure that all children develop in the same ways at the same time as in the factory model of education (Robinson, 2011). Hauerwas (2005: 37) termed the widespread acceptance of socially defined normality as the 'tyranny of normality'. Hauerwas (2005: 40) explained 'the most stringent power we have over another is not physical coercion but the ability to have the other accept our definition of them'. Emphasizing this point is Tayler et al.'s (2015) study that investigated the variability of developmental trajectories by tracking the development rates of 2,498 three- to four-year-old children across three years. Tayler et al. (2015) discovered that the development trajectory differed depending on the child's background, showing that defining 'normal' development is difficult and depends on a multitude of circumstances.

Overview of the early years curriculum

The EYFS, comprising seven areas of learning and seventeen ELGs, undergoes assessment at the foundation stage's end to form the Early Years Foundation Stage Profile (DfE, 2023). Children are categorized into emerging, expected, or exceeding levels based on these ELGs (Glazzard, 2014). Exceeding children outperform their age's expected development, while expected children meet the normative standard, leaving emerging children falling behind. Children not meeting these norms might be identified as having a SEND, signifying an educational performance gap (DfE, 2015).

Edgington et al. (2012) argue that EYFS's prescriptive nature aims to normalize and standardize development, potentially harming children. Robinson (2010b) suggests global governments view learning as a linear process, structuring education like fast-food chains for uniform outcomes. This approach was described by Pen Green (2018: 10) as a 'norm-referenced measure that only succeeds in recognising delay'. Neaum (2016) highlights a tension between an ideology setting preset competencies and a deficit-based approach filling perceived skill gaps.

Child assessment in education serves multifaceted purposes, evaluating development, identifying strengths and targeting support areas. Tracking progress through ELGs and creating individual profiles for children below or emerging levels enables early intervention (Roberts-Holmes and Bradbury, 2016). However, Palaiologou and Male (2019) argue this approach turns children into performers with observable and measurable outcomes, increasing pressure to fulfil government agendas promoting normative development. According to Palaiologou and Male (2019: 26), this approach does not allow scope 'for the child to be a child, instead creating the performer child, where outcomes, goals and outputs are observable and measurable'. The image of a performer child suggests increasing pressure on the child and providers to fulfil government agendas that support the idea of normal child development.

Defining normalization

The tension between assessment-driven education, highlighted by Palaiologou and Male (2019), and normalizing child development, as studied by Deleuze (1992), raises questions about the impact of assessments on children and society. Assessments, while meant to monitor progress and maintain standards, also affect children's experiences and pressures, reflecting contemporary governance and control. This correlation warrants a deeper examination of the interplay between individuality, societal norms and education.

Normative development is typically established by calculating averages from a group of children (Armstrong, 1995). Studies like Bates et al. (1994), Rescorla and Alley (2001) and MacRoy-Higgins et al. (2016) have computed normative language measures from their study cohorts, but the challenge lies in the methods and criteria used for these calculations. Nicholson's (2020) research on normative language development found inconsistencies among studies, indicating significant variability in how averages are calculated and defined.

The problem with normative approaches

The issue of normativity in developmental assessments, as discussed earlier, is complicated by the challenges in calculating averages and the lack of study consistency, as highlighted by Nicholson (2020). This 'massive variability' in averages, noted by Bates et al. (1994: 94), underscores the complexity of defining and applying normative parameters, echoing Armstrong's (1995) concern about labelling deviations as abnormal causing feelings of failure and highlighting the subjectivity and ethical aspect of defining 'normative' growth levels is evident. Moreover, in a quest to define and achieve normativity, there is a subtle yet significant risk of diminishing the richness of individual differences. The homogenization that often accompanies standardization efforts can lead to a loss of diversity, a key driver of innovation and societal progress. This perspective echoes Deleuze's (1992) insights on societal control mechanisms. In the realm of education, the emphasis on uniformity and standardization risks yielding a generation that, while uniform in its capabilities, may lack the diversity and creative spark essential for societal advancement.

This reflection brings the discussion back to the ethical and moral considerations of such a norm-referenced approach. The pursuit of standardization, intended to chart progress and development, must be balanced against the risk of eroding the unique qualities that each child brings to the learning environment. Deleuze's (1992) notion of individuals being perceived as 'dividuals' in control societies is particularly relevant here, as it stresses the potential loss of individuality in the face of widespread standardization.

In culture, behaviour and values shape social acceptability (Foucault, 2005). Foucault suggested society dictates normativity, specifying not only what to be and do but how to do it, thereby limiting acceptable conduct. Normalization, (Taylor, 2009), embeds accepted norms, leading to unquestioned acceptance within a group, potentially excluding non-conformists. This process is referred to as 'normalising the norm'.

Done et al. (2018) argued that education aims to help all children meet specific criteria. Educators, according to Ofsted (2017), are responsible for ensuring children maintain pace with their peers. Children who deviate from the expected learning development (ELD) standards require extra resources to either achieve success or fulfil potential. The ELD represents the educational goal, and additional resources are allocated to support children falling short of it, however no additional resource is provided to children who may exceed ELD. In neoliberal systems practitioners bear the responsibility for children's progress (Brill et al., 2018). Hutchings (2015) highlights how the pressure to achieve ELD places strain on both struggling children and the practitioners who support them. Roberts-Holmes et al. (2019) also noted that children were conscious of testing and experienced feelings of failure. Hutchings (2015) further emphasizes that highlighting gaps in understanding can result in feelings of failure for both practitioners and children.

Brookes et al. (2013) claim the English education system resembles a conveyor belt, progressing children by age. It aligns with the 'factory model of education' (Leland and Kasten, 2002: 5) focused on cost-effectiveness (Robinson, 2010a). This system emphasizes conformity, and labels pushes non-conformists labelling them having SEND while failing to provide for talented young people. This language dates back to the industrialization era, when the major goal was to provide education in the most cost-effective way possible to meet the needs of a market driven economy, as discussed by Robinson (2011).

Robinson (2010a) suggests that an efficient approach involves grouping subjects based on children's chronological age, emphasizing social conformity and standardization, often resulting in the labelling of non-conforming children. Society uses labels to organize individuals (Algraigray and Boyle, 2017), indirectly shaping them by imposing specific standards, attitudes and beliefs (Costas, 2012). Labels reinforce accepted norms, excluding behaviours that deviate from established criteria. Those outside society's 'normal' boundaries may be seen as needing 'correction' for acceptance, similar to the principles of the medical model of disability, which aims to address, treat or adapt perceived disabilities (Andrews et al., 2000: 259).

In early childhood education, labelling is evident. The term SEND, according to Ekins (2015: 93), is a 'social construct' applied to individuals meeting specific criteria, while Hausstatter and Thuen (2014: 192) see it as identifying a 'deviant group' who don't meet expected standards. Robinson (2010b) suggests that divergent children think creatively and critically, challenging educational conditioning. This governmental push for uniformity may hinder creativity and individuality. Jones (1972) highlighted how labels can create self-fulfilling prophecies, leading parents and children to accept limitations, potentially discouraging teachers from offering encouragement.

Pause for thought: Vignette

While being interviewed a highly dedicated early childhood practitioner recounted her experiences of working with young children from many cultural backgrounds, many of whom speak English as an additional language (EAL). She shed insight into the difficulties encountered while implementing a normative curriculum to children with varying cultural norms and traditions.

The practitioner observed that the traditional curriculum frequently ignored the unique developmental norms of children who speak EAL. When these children were examined using a curriculum that rigorously followed normative standards, they may appear to be delayed in specific areas such as self-care skills and language proficiency, impacted by their home nations' cultural customs and expectations. However, it is critical to understand that while these variations in performance do not always imply developmental delays, they are frequently misinterpreted as such due to the structure of the curriculum.

This interview emphasized the importance of recognizing and integrating cultural difference in developmental norms, especially when implementing a standardized curriculum for children who speak English as an additional language. This culturally sensitive approach would ensure that their development and progress were accurately assessed and effectively supported, while also honouring and valuing the distinct skills and abilities that each child brings to the learning environment.

Reflection

The assumption that a rigid curriculum, lacking in flexibility to accommodate diverse learning abilities, may amount to neglect. In the academic year 2022/2023, 20.2 per cent of all students in schools were identified as EAL speakers. For some, especially newcomers to the country who may not comprehend English beyond basic communication, isolation can be a challenge. While translators can address immediate communication needs like expressing basic necessities, it may take years for children to attain the language proficiency necessary to fully engage with the curriculum.

Within your own educational settings, how do you provide support to children and young individuals who might struggle to grasp the curriculum's concepts? Is your approach more than merely superficial, ensuring that these young learners can adapt and comprehend what is expected of them within the school environment?

Methodology: Exploring practitioners experience of working in early years education

This study explored the identification, assessment and support of speech, language and communication needs in two-year-old children. The research involved fifteen practitioners from two different geographical locations. All participants were working in early years and were females with ages ranging from twenty to six years. Their employment duration in the sector varied from three to thirty-seven years.

The research methodology employed conversational interviews with each participant. These interviews were designed to foster open dialogue, with questions generated based on the participant's responses and experiences. Using a semi-structured, overarching themes guided the conversation, and facilitated unstructured exploration of topics, permitting the discussion to evolve naturally. This flexibility enabled in-depth consideration of topics introduced by either party, ensuring a comprehensive exploration of the subject matter. Each participant was assigned a pseudonym to protect anonymity.

Findings: The standardization strain: Exploring inequalities in early years assessment

One of the main themes from this research was participants who focussed on the unfairness and inequity of assessment procedures within the early years' curriculum. When seen in conjunction with personal surveillance experiences and external expectations, the participants' perspective on evaluation and their role in monitoring the development of children became clearer. They characterized assessment as primarily a means of measuring children's progress against the EYFS Development Matters Framework (DfE, 2023) and highlighted it as an important component of their responsibilities, relying on observations to collect data. Tracking individual children's progress within their settings was thought critical, particularly in identifying those who were falling behind or emerging in their achievement of ELGs. Less attention was given to children who exceeded expectations and the focus remained on meeting developmental milestones and closing gaps in children's profiles. This emphasis on normative development was encouraged by external authorities such as the Local Authority (LA) and Ofsted, which monitored and rated settings based on children's ELD achievement. This persistent surveillance appeared to impact practitioners daily activities, developing a sense of responsibility for upholding normativity in child evaluation and meeting external expectations.

Assessment as a driver for normalization

The participants primarily viewed assessment as a means to determine children's development against the EYFS Development Matters Framework (DfE, 2012). They recognized assessment as an essential aspect of their role, relying on observations to gather data. Tracking individual child progress within their settings was deemed vital, particularly to ensure age-appropriate development. Nine of the fifteen participants explained how data was compiled based on child observations, which served as a process to detect children who were at the 'below' or 'emerging' stage of achieving the ELGs (Glazzard, 2014). Keyleigh, a setting manager, highlighted how the application is used in practice:

> *I can look at the whole nursery ... [as] red, green and blue, red they're below, green their on target, blue they're above so I can at a glimpse ... look at all the observations and see exactly where all the children are*

Keyleigh's practice involved addressing gaps in children's profiles compared to ELGs by communicating with their key workers and devising plans to support children in achieving ELD. This practice highlighted the setting's focus on using assessment to identify children's developmental stages and those who may not meet expected levels. In contrast, the responses from all fifteen participants revealed a lack of consistent methods for assessing a child's development within an ELG or determining their status as 'emerging', 'expected', or 'exceeding' in line with Glazzard's (2014) model. Instead, participants relied on 'best-fit decisions' based on the child's performance across various activities, demonstrating the subjectivity of the assessment process.

Using normative benchmarks to label children

Participants discussed the suitability of the EYFS (DfE, 2012) as an assessment tool, highlighting its adequacy for typically developing children and identified its limitations for children with SEND or EAL backgrounds. Ayla's (a practitioner) frustration with the system was evident when assessing a child with English as a second language, as the assessment labelled the child as underperforming despite Ayla's professional opinion to the contrary. Ayla expressed frustration when assessing a child whom she worked with, whose first language was Polish and stated that according to the assessment, *'the child is underperforming, but he's not'*. Ayla's comments seemed to suggest that the system did not accurately represent the abilities of some of the children she worked with. According to Ayla, the current system labeled any child failing to meet the ELD for their age and stage as an *'underperformer'*. This observation aligns with Palaiologou and Male's (2019) assertion that the system tends to promote the idea of a performer child, emphasizing measurable and observable outcomes. Pascale et al. (2019: 51) also suggest that the EYFS fails to adequately support the development of 'less advantaged children', potentially leading them to 'underachieve'.

Participants acknowledged their role in identifying development gaps and assisting children in reaching ELD, emphasizing tailored interventions to maintain the normalization process. They also discussed interventions for children not meeting ELD in various areas of learning, reflecting their awareness of government policies and expectations. In this context the EYFS (DfE, 2012) can be seen as a system that promotes normativity by recognizing deficiencies, and through maintaining normativity in children's development and suggesting the practitioners' acknowledgment and acceptance of responsibility for maintaining the normalization process. These insights highlight potential ethical and social concerns within the system.

The challenge of measuring normative development and seeking external support for children below the normative standard was a recurring theme. Armstrong (1995) raised concerns about normalizing children's development based on fixed assessments, potentially leading to feelings of failure for those falling outside normative parameters. Consequently, the EYFS (DfE, 2012) can be seen as promoting normativity by identifying deficiencies. Keyleigh emphasized this notion by stating that tailored interventions were created to: *'help them and bring them up to where they need to be*'. Keyleigh's emphasis on tailored interventions to bring children up to expected levels demonstrated her commitment to addressing developmental gaps, even if appearing to ignore that children often need to revisit areas of learning multiple times before they have fully mastered specific skills or understood concepts. It was evident that Keyleigh acknowledged and accepted her role in maintaining the normalization process; a position supported by the SENDCoP that children who do not attain ELD require 'assistance' (DfE, 2015: 67).

Participants mainly focused on aiding children in achieving development levels, reflecting participants' awareness of government policies and expectations. Interventions to support children in reaching ELD were a major topic discussed by all but one participant, with a consensus that interventions were provided for children not meeting ELD in one or more areas of learning.

Participants emphasized the challenges in measuring normative development and securing external support for children falling below this perceived standard. In her role as a manager, Aleigha stressed that external organizations demanded data-based evidence of children's below-expected development levels to justify the need for additional assistance in reaching ELD.

> ... it is literally 'this is where they should be that's not where they are' so it gets highlighted as a concern

Aleigha's belief in children reaching a specific level aligned with the concept of normalization or standardization. Armstrong (1995) expressed concerns regarding efforts to normalize children's development, considering the diverse rates at which children progress. Armstrong (1995) argued that determining normative development through fixed assessments and averages presupposes that any child deviating from these norms is considered abnormal, evidencing again that a deficit mentality.

The use of surveillance to promote a normative agenda

The pressure to ensure children met the ELG was evident through participants' experiences with the Local Authority (LA) contacting them about children at the below or emerging stage of ELGs. Corrie mentioned sending data to the LA and how they would inquire about children who were behind. She stated,

> We send all our data to early years, three times a year, and they'll come back to us and tell us where the gaps are .....they will then ring me, or someone will come in, and they'll say, this child, this child and this child they're red they're behind ... ... what you doing, why are they behind, blah, blah.

Participants felt compelled to conform to the EYFS Development Matters (DfE, 2012) despite its non-statutory nature due to the panoptical perception of government surveillance. Similarly, Kailah expressed the pressure to provide evidence for Ofsted inspections, saying,

Ofsted come in and say 'which one's your key children tell me where that child's sat at.' But like I say it's having, I hate the word evidence to say that that child can do it.

The fear of government influence on funding and functioning, as well as the government's agenda for standardization, as discussed by Robinson (2010b), may help to explain why participants complied with the normalizing process of child assessment despite reservations about its accuracy in reflecting children's abilities.

The sense of monitoring was evident when Poppy and Corrie discussed sending children's profiles to the LA, which questioned gaps when children did not meet ELD according to ELG. The LA resembled Deleuze's (1992) control system where he explains that power can be asserted through processes made by one organization and imposed on another, and could therefore be seen as crossing a boundary. The LA's data request could be viewed as boundary-crossing to guide practitioners towards normativity, even though there was no legal obligation to provide it (Costas, 2012: 378). The goal of normative maintenance could be seen in the earlier comment made by Corrie:

they're red they're behind ... ... what you doing, why are they behind?

Corrie's remark implies that the LA controls normativity through data monitoring and follow-ups, aiming to keep practitioners focused on ELD. The LA could cease funding for settings rated 'satisfactory or requires improvement' or below by Ofsted (DfE, 2023:19). While official paperwork lacked a clear responsibility for data submission, participants in one LA routinely sent child development data against ELGs. This reflects what Taylor (2009: 47) calls 'normalising the norm', where participants no longer question or oppose data submission, routine behaviours and local policies.

Participants discussed using development trackers to collate, monitor and evidence children's development, aiding managers in identifying gaps in profiles. Keyleigh mentioned using a digital system, where 'red' signifies children below ELD, prompting discussions with keyworkers. This role transformed Keyleigh into an audit monitor, surveilling key workers whose children didn't achieve ELD. Other participants also emphasized internal monitoring as a method for managing normalization. Chloe, a deputy manager and SENDCo, mentioned questioning staff to justify their entries, illustrating how managers contributed to the control system for achieving normativity.

Conclusion

The impact of a normative culture within the context of early childhood education and development has significant implications for both children and society in the long term. The statutory requirement to assess and measure children against ELGs in the EYFS has led to a system that emphasizes uniformity and standardization in children's development. The goal is for all children to achieve at least the expected level of development (ELD) in specific areas, with the intention of closing the attainment gap, particularly for children from low-income households, who have SEND or use EAL.

This norm-referenced approach assumes that child development is linear and progresses chronologically, which overlooks the reality that children develop skills at different rates. Development is a complex and continuous process that cannot be neatly categorized into normative parameters. This approach to defining 'normal' development can lead to feelings of failure for children who fall outside these limits. Furthermore, the use of normative benchmarks and labels, such as SEND and EAL, can have long-term consequences for children. The pressure to conform to normative standards can stifle creativity and individuality, as children are expected to fit into a predefined mould of development. This can result in self-fulfilling prophecies where children and parents accept limitations, and potentially discouraging teachers from providing encouragement.

The normative culture in early childhood education also extends to the surveillance and monitoring of children's development by external authorities, such as the Local Authority and Ofsted. This constant surveillance creates a sense of pressure among practitioners to adhere to normative expectations, even if they have reservations about the accuracy of assessments. The fear of government influence on funding and the drive for standardization further perpetuate the normative culture within the education system.

In conclusion, the normative culture in early childhood education has far-reaching implications for children's development and society as a whole. It can lead to a one-size-fits-all approach that does not account for the diverse rates at which children develop. It can also limit creativity and individuality and perpetuate feelings of failure for children who do not conform to normative standards. The constant surveillance and monitoring by external authorities further reinforce the pressure to conform to these standards. To promote social justice and the well-being of children, it is crucial to critically examine and challenge the normative culture within early childhood education and consider alternative approaches that value and celebrate individual differences. Practitioners must critically consider their role within these frameworks to prioritize children's best interests and be willing to challenge elements that conflict with their values (Taylor, 2009).

Critical reflective questions

1 How does the current emphasis on normative developmental assessment in education impact the recognition and support of individual differences among children in your setting?

2 In what ways do external pressures from educational standards and governing bodies influence educators' approaches to assessment?

3 Considering the potential ethical implications, is it justifiable to use normative benchmarks for assessing children's development, especially when considering children with special educational needs or from diverse linguistic and cultural backgrounds?

4 What are the consequences of increased surveillance and accountability measures (like those from Ofsted) on the quality of education and the well-being of both educators and children?

References

Algraigray, H., and Boyle, C. (2017). The SEN label and its effect on special education, (*Labelling and Diagnosis*) *Educational and Child Psychologist, 34*(4), 70–9.

Andrews, J. E., Carnine, D. W., Coutinho, M. J., Edgar, E. B., Forness, S. R., Fuchs, L. S., Jordan, D., Kauffman, J. M., Patton, J. M., and Paul, J. (2000). Bridging the special education divide. *Remedial and Special Education, 21*(5), 258–67.

Armstrong, D. (1995). The rise of surveillance medicine. *Sociology of Health and Illness, 17*(3), 393–404.

Bates, E., Marchman, V., Thal, D., Fenson, L., Dale, P., Reznick, J. S., Reilly, J., and Hartung, J. (1994). Developmental and stylistic variation in the composition of early vocabulary. *Journal of Child Language, 21*(1), 85–123.

Brill, F., Grayson, H., Kuhn, L., and O'Donnell, S. (2018). *What Impact Does Accountability Have on Curriculum, Standards and Engagement in Education? A Literature Review*. Berkshire: National Foundation for Educational Research.

Brooks, R., McCormack, M., and Bhopal, K. (2013). Contemporary debates in the sociology of education: An introduction, in R. Brooks, M. McCormack, and K. Bhopal (eds.), *Contemporary Debates in the Sociology of Education*, 1–19, Basingstoke: Palgrave Macmillan.

Bukatko, D., and Daehler, M. W. (2012). *Child Development: A Thematic Approach*. 6th edition. Basingstoke: Wadsworth Cengage Learning.

Costas, J. (2012). 'We are all friends here' reinforcing paradoxes of normative control in a culture of friendship. *Journal of Management Inquiry, 21*(4), 377–95.

Deleuze, G. (1992). Postscript on the societies of control. *October, 59*, 3–7.

Department for Education (2012). *Development Matters in the Early Years Foundation Stage*. Runcorn: DfE.

Department for Education (2015). *SEND Code of Practice: 0 to 25 Years*. https://www.gov.uk/government/publications/send-code-of-practice-0-to-25.

Department for Education (2023). *Early Education and Childcare: Statutory Guidance for Local Authorities*. London: DfE.

Department for Education (2024). *Early Years Foundation Stage: Development Matters*. London: DfE.

Done, E. J., Andrews, M. J., and Evenden, C. (2018). (C) old beginnings and technologies of rectification in early years education: The implications for teachers and children with special educational needs. *International Journal of Early Years Education*, 1–14. DOI: 10.1080/09669760.2018.1547633.

Edgington, M., Hooper Hansen, G., and Simpson, K. (2012). *The Revised EYFS: Too Little, Too Late | Nursery World*. http://www.nurseryworld.co.uk/nursery-world/opinion/1106010/revised-eyfs-little-late.

Ekins, A. (2015). *The Changing Face of Special Educational Needs: Impact and Implications for SENCOs, Teachers and Their Schools*. London: Routledge.

Foucault, M. (2005). *The Order of Things*. London: Routledge.

Glazzard, J. (2014). Observation and assessment, in P. Mukherji and L. Dryen (eds.), *Foundations of Early Childhood: Principles and Practice*, London: SAGE Publications.

Hauerwas, S. (2005). Chapter 1. timeful friends: Living with the handicapped. *Journal of Religion, Disability and Health*, 8(3–4), 11–25.

Hausstatter, R. S., and Thuen, H. (2014). Special education today in Norway. *Special Education International Perspectives: Practices across the Globe Advances in Special Education*, 28, 181–207.

Honig, A. S. (1983). Programming for preschoolers with special needs: How child development knowledge can help. *Early Child Development and Care*, 11(2), 165–96.

Hutchings, M. (2015). Exam factories, in *The Impact of Accountability Measures on Children and Young People*, 1–14, London: NUT.

Jones, R. L. (1972). Labels and stigma in special education. *Exceptional Children*, 38(7), 553–64.

Leland, C. H., and Kasten, W. C. (2002). Literacy education for the 21st Century: It's time to close the factory. *Reading and Writing Quarterly*, 18(1), 5.

MacRoy-Higgins, M., Shafer, V. L., Fahey, K. J., and Kaden, E. R. (2016). Vocabulary of toddlers who are late talkers. *Journal of Early Intervention*, 38(2), 118–29.

Neaum, S. (2016). School readiness and pedagogies of competence and performance: Theorising the troubled relationship between early years and early years policy. *International Journal of Early Years Education*, 24(3), 239–53.

Nicholson, N. (2020). *Supporting Children with Identified Speech, Language and Communication Needs at Two-Years-Old: Voices of Early Years Practitioners* [Postdoctoral, University of Lincoln]. https://bgro.repository.guildhe.ac.uk/id/eprint/813/.

Ofsted (2017). *Bold Beginnings: The Reception Curriculum in a Sample of Good and Outstanding Primary Schools*. Ofsted. https://schoolsweek.co.uk/wp-content/uploads/2017/11/28933-Ofsted-Early-Years-Curriculum-Report.pdf.

Palaiologou, I. (2019). What do student teachers need to know about child development, in C. Carden (ed.), *Primary Teaching: Learning and Teaching in Primary Schools Today*, 93–110, London: Learning Matters.

Palaiologou, I., and Male, T. (2019). Leadership in early childhood education: The case for pedagogical praxis. *Contemporary Issues in Early Childhood*, 20(1), 23–34.

Pascal, C., Bertram, T., and Rouse, L. (2019). *Getting It Right in the Early Years Foundation Stage: A Review of the Evidence*. London: The British Association for Early Childhood Education.

Rescorla, L., and Alley, A. (2001). Validation of the Language Development Survey (LDS): A parent report tool for identifying language delay in toddlers. *Journal of Speech, Language, and Hearing Research*, *44*(2), 434–45.

Roberts-Holmes, G., and Bradbury, A. (2016). Governance, accountability and the datafication of early years education in England. *British Educational Research Journal*, *42*(4), 600–13.

Roberts-Holmes, G., Lee, S. F., Sousa, D., and Jones, E. (2019). *Research into the 2019 Pilot of Reception Baseline Assessment (RBA)*. London: UCL Institute of Education. https://neu.org.uk/media/9116/view.

Robinson, S. K. (2010a). *Bring on the Learning Revolution!* https://www.ted.com/talks/sir_ken_robinson_bring_on_the_learning_revolution.

Robinson, S. K. (2010b). *Changing Education Paradigms*. https://www.ted.com/talks/sir_ken_robinson_changing_education_paradigms.

Robinson, K. (2011). *Out of Our Minds: Learning to Be Creative*. Chichester: John Wiley and Sons.

Tayler, C., Cloney, D., and Niklas, F. (2015). A bird in the hand: Understanding the trajectories of development of young children and the need for action to improve outcomes. *Australasian Journal of Early Childhood*, *40*(3), 51–60.

Taylor, D. (2009). Normativity and normalization. *Foucault Studies*, 45–63. https://rauli.cbs.dk/index.php/foucault-studies/article/download/2636/2653/.

The Pen Green Center (2018). *A Celebratory Approach to SEND Assessment in the Early Years*. Corby, Northamptonshire: Pen Green Centre for Children and Families. https://www.pengreen.org/wp-content/uploads/2018/05/A-Celebratory-Approach-to-SEND-Assessment-in-the-Early-Years.pdf.

Ware, R., and Harvey, J. (2013). Health Surveillance, in J. Harvey and V. Taylor (eds.), *Measuring Health and Wellbeing*, 68–89, London: Learning Matters.

Lived Experiences of Black, Asian and Minority Ethnic Students on White Majority Higher Education Campuses in the UK: Can You See Me?

Sheine Peart and
Hadiza Kere Abdulrahman

Terminology

The authors are aware of and acknowledge the challenges and limitations of the acronym BAME. However, as a broadly understood term in education we have, reluctantly, opted to use the term as an interim measure for this study.

Introduction

The population of the UK has been diverse for many years. As the populations of Black, Asian and Minority Ethnic (BAME) groups have increased so have the legal protections and other securities afforded to these groups. However, students from diverse backgrounds remain under-represented in HE and UK higher education and academia remains overwhelmingly White (Tate and Page, 2018; Bhopal and Pitkin, 2020). This White-centric perspective informs and determines the structures, policies and organization of HE, that can produce outcomes including, for example, the 'whitewashing' and exclusion of minority students in predominantly White spaces or some groups being disadvantaged by the education system. Both Peart (2013) and Gilborn (2008) have argued that some inequalities are so structurally ingrained that failure and marginalization of certain groups are almost inevitable – Black students appear to be one such group. While all universities openly state their support for diversity on campus, contrary to such claims some students from BAME backgrounds do not always feel included in university life and, significantly, believe they experience a range of adverse outcomes in comparison to their White peers. This chapter provides an exploration into the lived experiences of BAME students in a majority White university campus in the United Kingdom.

Informed by the Critical Race Theory (CRT) method of counter-narrative, this chapter centralizes the voices of the student participants and positions their words alongside existing literature to highlight the salience of race while simultaneously scrutinizing the culture of Whiteness. Through listening to participants in a research project entitled 'Tell It Like It Is', the lived realities of these students were captured; this explored their sense of belonging and presents their honest reflections of what it means to learn, live and exist in such a space.

In exploring Black, Asian and Minority Ethnic students, the term BAME is often used as a descriptor. BAME is used to refer to groups of people who are visibly different in terms of skin colour, cultures, traditions and/or religions, and in so doing, it inevitably centres Whiteness. It has even been adopted by the UK government for statistical purposes (Wilkins and Lall, 2011) and is used on grounds of convenience, obfuscating the true workings of race and racism in British society. Accepting its contestations and limitations (Abdulrahman, 2020), the term BAME is used here acknowledging that ethnic labels have complex meanings in British society. Its sparse use in this chapter is as a space-holder (for lack of any better alternative) and specifically in terms of the experiences of minoritized and non-white students in predominantly white spaces including UK HEIs.

UK higher education institutions as 'white spaces'

Higher education institutions have a present and a past that is deeply rooted in Whiteness, this being the foundation upon which they have been built. Cabrera (2016) states HEIs were not created to be racially inclusive and have been struggling with the legacy of White privilege ever since. Through varying guises and reinventions, HE particularly within the west has been designed to facilitate and entrench the power and privilege of the dominant White majority often at the expense of minoritized ethnic groups who remain on the periphery of the academy (Heleta, 2016). Academia has long been a vehicle for the symptomatic ways in which Whiteness is constructed as normative and illustrates how differing discursive techniques of White privilege operate together to racialize, marginalize and exclude ethnic minorities from academic spaces.

Within this context, space is configured as the physical environment as well as the policies, climate and organization culture of an institution. According to Cabrera et al. (2016), the intersection of Whiteness and space is designed to produce comfort for White individuals creating an embedded White Cultural ideology. This same ideology places Whiteness at the centre of all being and uses Whiteness as a lens to privilege certain cultural practices, traditions and perceptions of knowledge which in turn are positioned and taken for granted as a norms at HEIs. White Cultural ideology provides the basis for White Institutional Presence which has four key attributes: White ascendancy; Mono-culturalism; White estrangement; and White blindness. Whiteness is used as an instrument of power and privilege, and particular types of knowledge, notably the contributions and achievements of BAME communities, continue to be omitted from the curricula (Arday et al., 2021) which impacts engagement, inclusivity and belonging. These White-centric exclusionary messages are reinforced by the physical infrastructure of universities (such as statues and framed pictures) which send messages about who is welcomed and who is excluded.

In describing and attempting to define Whiteness and its wider impact, it is important not to conflate this concept with 'White People' or with the global influence of majority White nations. It is not solely about individuals or nation states but the Whiteness of institutions and the way in which those institutions are constructed and operate. Leonardo (2002) makes an important distinction, arguing that 'Whiteness' is a racial discourse whereas the category 'White people' represents a socially constructed identity. Whiteness also refers to a deeply ingrained way of being in the world that includes behaviours, habits and dispositions. Collins et al. (2020) also describe Whiteness as a discourse, ideology and social habit used to understand historical and contemporary HEI practices and policies. Through acknowledging the centrality of Whiteness and the different ways it functions in the academy, this chapter uses BAME students' voices to examine the very concept, and to clear a space for counter-narratives and by presenting different equally valuable ways of being and existing.

Experiences of BAME students within UK higher education

Transitioning to HE represents a challenge for all students as they move from a familiar to a new environment. In this regard, all students can expect to face some challenges. However, 'in the process of adapting to the college milieu Black students face distinctive challenges' (Cole and Arriola, 2007: 380) which are above and beyond those experienced by their White counterparts. As such BAME students living this experience represent a valid data source because of their intimate knowledge of campus situations. Consequently, to develop a more informed understanding of the experiences and lived realities of these students in majority White university spaces, it is necessary to explore how Whiteness impacts on Black, Asian and Minority Ethnic students, their engagement and sense/feelings of belonging in HEIs. By placing their experiences at the centre of the argument, the impact of Whiteness on the learning experience can be better appreciated.

For Black, Asian and Minority Ethnic students studying in UK HEIs, the literature presents a dominant theme of unbelonging, experiencing 'otherness' and of being made to feel an outsider (Bunce et al., 2019; Universities UK and National Union of Students, 2019). In this respect the UK mirrors findings in the US where 'many African American students attending PWIs (Predominantly White Institutions) experience feelings of incongruence' (Bonner and Evans, 2004: 10) indicating the global nature of racial inequality.

In the UK there are persistent, inadequately explained HE attainment gaps between UK-domiciled students from BAME groups and White students (Advance HE, 2018; Bunce et al., 2019). These gaps emerge in on-course assessments, year-to-year progression and summative assessment outcomes. Further, Wong et al. (2020) observed that across UK higher education, there are still concerns about differential final degrees outcomes which refers to the difference in the proportion of White and BAME students awarded a 'good degree' (a first or upper-second class degree classification). In 2017/2018 this attainment gap was 13 per cent and more research was needed to understand the experiences of BAME students in higher education. Further 'in 2018–19, there was a difference of 22.1 percentage points between the proportion of White and Black students getting a 1st or a 2:1' (Guild HE: nd).

Racial inequality in HE is often implicit with reported experiences such as microaggressions. In his work, Allen (1997: 182) found that racism was 'subtle, it is the glance and the unsaid. It is these kinds of experiences that many black students often have to endure on their passage through higher education and beyond'.

The dominance of Whiteness as the normative position affects the culture of HE, informs the prevailing climate and influences all provision so that BAME students are ignored, held at a distance or provided with an ill-matched learning experience (Cabrera et al., 2017) and subjected to 'a pathologizing gaze on racialized bodies that have historically been constructed as a problem for education' (Burke, 2018: 367). Moreover, the taught curriculum where

BAME communities receive negative, no or token recognition and where anti-racist strategies have 'failed to permeate ... courses in a more rigorous way' (Allen, 1997: 182) have further contributed to creating a hostile learning environment for BAME students. In addition, colour-blind attitudes where the significance of race has been ignored or the distinctive needs of BAME students were assumed to be identical in all regards to those of their White counterparts have produced a situation which confirms the outsider status of BAME students and questions HEIs 'real commitment to racial equality' (Allen, 97: 184). This differential treatment has produced profound and lasting impacts on BAME students and significantly influenced their sense of belonging in HE as 'authentic university students' (Burke, 2018: 366).

Pause for thought: Research

In 2020, in recognition of the widespread and pervasive nature of racism in the Higher Education sector which included name-calling and being excluded by peers, Universities UK published guidance to help universities tackle racism within the sector. The guidance was a call to action and identified twelve key recommendations where Universities could take specific steps in their organizations to eradicate racism. In 2023, Universities UK revisited this work to consider what progress had been achieved. While 68 per cent of organizations had developed an institution wide response for addressing racial inequalities and 76 per cent of staff and students stated they knew how to report incidences of racial harassment, at the same time more than half of students who responded (55 per cent) had experienced some form of racial harassment, indicating the need for further work in the sector.

Reflection

The co-ordinated action taken by Universities UK confirms a seriousness of intent to directly address and challenge racism in HE. And, although progress has been made, it appears over 30 per cent of organizations do not yet have a defined plan to tackle racism. Further, the levels of student harassment remain high across the sector. In your own institution are you aware of your organizations policy regarding racial harassment? Is this policy readily available to all staff? Has your organization provided training to staff and students to help them both identify and tackle racism and are relevant systems in place to support those who have been the victims of racism? Though policies are an important step in the journey to make organizations more equitable and safe for all users, unless they are supported by clear implementation strategies and identified lines of accountability, real progress is likely to remain frustratingly elusive.

Methodology: Researching Black students' lives in HE

This research was motivated by the University's existing organizational agenda to better understand the academic and social experiences of minoritized students studying at the university and recognizing the unique situation of this group who (as well as being a minority in terms of national demographics) formed an even smaller population of the student body, being approximately only two per cent of the overall student group, and thus are accurately described as a hyper-marginalized population. Recognizing the significance of such hyper-marginalization and its potential impacts, in the words of one of the research participants, attending the university required applicants to be '*extremely brave and courageous and not care what other people think because [they would] have to take some hits*'.

The research was centred on three key questions, and specifically sought to explore:

- What were Black Asian and Minority Ethnic students' experiences of engaging with Higher Education?
- What were their daily interactions with people, structures and systems? and
- What, if any, were their perceptions of discrimination within HE?

In order to research these questions, the project placed the student voice at the centre of the study, recognizing students were experts of their individual situated realities and were best placed to represent their experiences. As the potential target population was comparatively small, research participants were drawn from across the university from degrees with a foundation year through to Masters level courses. Using existing student project recruitment systems, Black Asian and Minority Ethnic students were invited to engage with a small-scale research project. Online recruitment messages and strategically placed posters were displayed for approximately one month. From a potential population of approximately fifty students, nine students (including two males) expressed an interest in engaging with the project. The final sample comprised five female students: two younger students studying a UG course together with one mature student also studying a UG course; and two mature students studying a Masters course. The two male students who initially expressed an interest in the project declined to take part in the final study. Being adults, all research participants provided informed consent prior to engaging with the project.

Data was collected through one semi-structured interview with each research participant. Prior to this data collection exercise, and to ensure participants were fully aware of their commitment, a group orientation meeting was held to 'establish a climate of trust' (Denscombe, 2010: 182) between participant and researcher. All interview data was collected by a single researcher who, like the research participants, was a Black woman, and who remained constant throughout the data collection process to promote consistency. A framework of twenty common core questions were used for all interviews and areas of note were 'enhanced by probes' (Schensul et al., 1999: 149). Interviews were used for 'discovery rather than checking' (Denscombe, 2010: 182) and each took place at the university and lasted approximately one hour. All data was audio-recorded and later transcribed. Interview data was then analysed for 'recurring words, phrases and topics' (Maykut and Morehouse, 1999: 133) which were used to create research themes. Culturally consistent pseudonyms have been used to present student quotes to help retain a sense of authenticity.

Findings: Revealing the terrain of HE

The 2010 Equality Act, and the Public Sector Equality Duty (PSED) created by the Act, obliges organizations to positively promote equality for and between races. Within the normative discourse of Whiteness and particularly for HEIs with small numbers of students from BAME groups, PSED assumes heightened protective significance as organizations may not, through a combination of normative practices, a dominant monocultural Whiteness perspective, and as a result of lacking effective or appropriate communication channels, be aware of the ways in which minoritized populations experience the environment and services provided. Thus, BAME service users can potentially be in even greater jeopardy through invisibility, minimization or denial of circumstances which can work against minority populations. Consequently, this research was significant for both BAME students and the organization itself.

Student support mechanisms

The findings relating to student support were not consistent across the research participants. Jennifer (PG student) stated there was '*a divide between postgrads and undergrads'* and it appeared the university was *'organized with undergrads in mind'*. She further claimed this was *'a real issue if you want people to be included'*. While this comment was not specifically related to a racialized experience, within the context of the educational journeys of BAME students attending HEIs, as many students of colour return to education later in life due to earlier educational challenges this observation was pertinent. In addition, because some BAME students find *'education really overwhelming'* (Coral, mature UG student), it added a further layer to potentially exclusionary mechanisms worthy of organizational consideration.

Although all research participants were positive about the individualized personal support they received from their university course tutors, a point attributed to the personal approach of academic staff, with Amber (UG student) commenting *'everyone's so chilled out ... the staff are really nice'* and Courtney (PG student) stating the lecturers *'were very approachable'* it was apparent culturally congruent support which recognized the importance of being a racialized minority, was not routinely made available to BAME students. Instead generic counselling, accommodation, careers and financial guidance were provided. While such services may have met some student needs, they were not necessarily best placed to accommodate the specific needs of BAME students. This cultural homogenization which assumed Whiteness as the norm became apparent to Courtney (PG student) who noted when she moved into university halls of residence she was *'different to everyone else'* and the only *'person of colour ... among 70 people'*. The lack of overt organizational acknowledgement prompted Ashley (UG student) to state *'it would be better to speak from someone who is from a similar background ... because a White British person would not always understand the hardship'*, an assertion which supports Fordham's (1996) concept of fictive kinship between populations who accept a shared common heritage and highlighting the need to provide culturally relevant support *'by someone who we can recognise'* (Courtney, PG student) to assist BAME students navigate new or challenging situations (Wright, Standen and Patel, 2010).

Taught and hidden curricula

All participants recognized the White-centric nature of the taught and hidden curricula at the university and even when relevant opportunities were presented, for example in exploring the over-representation of Black males in the UK prison population in a sociology module, there was *'no specific focus on race issues'* (Amber UG student). This position was confirmed by Ashley who stated *'we talk about Europe and slightly outside of Europe, but I've never heard anything other than that. We don't really visit the topics of Africa'*.

Amber also felt there was a lack of *'representation or acknowledgment of BAME students'*. Further when issues of race emerged in different topics this sometimes provoked negative comments from other White students and not all lecturing staff appeared adequately capable of managing such challenges, or recognized they had strayed onto a *'touchy subject'* (Courtney, PG student) which might make BAME students feel more vulnerable or uncomfortable. Courtney added that some staff *'could do with training'* to help them appreciate *'what it is like for people of colour to be in that environment'*. However, when or if BAME students tried to address these issues with some academic staff, rather than being listened to their contributions were *'kind of shooed away'* (Amber, UG student) adding this left students feeling as though they were being constructed as *'the angry Black girl who's using the race card.. because she can'*. In a similar exclusionary manner, when searching for source material Amber also reported that she hadn't *'really seen much'* in terms of race in the university library. This presented another area of concern as the university had purposely developed and curated a number of collections focussing on race, equality and inclusion yet these collections did not seem to be obvious to students.

Because of their broader life experiences and being in a minority in many different situations in the UK, some students had become almost immune to being excluded. When discussing imagery and representation at the university, Amanda stated *'I've got used to a lot of things being overlooked and things like that'* (mature student on UG course) and appeared to have little expectation her specific cultural needs would be considered or actively taken into account. This cultural colour-blindness was exemplified by Courtney's experience, when early in her university career a White person was selected to *'represent Black people'* with the rationale provided there was *'not a big population'* of Black people to approach to complete this task, the implication being that cultural congruence was not a requirement to effectively fulfil this role.

The student union

The Student Union appeared to hold greater significance for the two undergraduate participants, with Jennifer stating post graduate students were *'not here to hang about in the SU'* or to *'mess about'*. However, Jennifer also recognized her invisibility as a woman of colour and that she was *'unrepresented'* in the university's *'democratic processes'*. Consequently, having previously *'been involved in local government'* and being aware of the importance of the SU's organizational influence, Jennifer *'became involved with the Student Council'* as a conscious choice to be more engaged with the structures of the university.

The undergraduate students appeared particularly frustrated the SU did not appear to actively include BAME students in its thinking or provision. Amber was clear on this point stating

> *just knowing that you've got BAME students in your uni, you should make an effort to include them in something or just to reach out ... I've not seen any effort made by any higher up representatives to include minorities. All that is being chucked at you from the SU is about sports and gender equality. It's the same two things every term ... other groups might want some inclusion in our community*

Ashley, the other undergraduate student who took part in the research was similarly clear commenting *'I didn't feel like the SU was a very welcoming place to go ... I felt like an outsider. I didn't feel very comfortable a few times going in there so I decided I wasn't going back.'* Even though Amber considered putting herself forward to *'be the one to kick start a society for BAME students [she did not] feel confident enough to stick [her] neck out'*. Ultimately she acknowledged the lack of *'a sense of belonging'* and resigned herself to there being *'something missing'* in terms of inclusive practice. Ashley, who started her studies after Amber, also thought there needed to be

> *some sort of BAME student ambassador to represent the people of colour at the university and it was absolutely disgusting that in the whole time that they've had a students' union they haven't had one ... different races out there should be represented*

However, Ashley chose to address the situation differently and at the next round of student elections stood for and was elected to the SU as the Equality Officer.

Conclusion

The findings of this small-scale qualitative research help to provide a picture of the daily lives of minoritized students in one small UK university and demonstrate that these students continue to have a less inclusive and more challenging experience of HE than their White peers. These findings are significant within the context of changing national demographics. Census data from 2021 compared to 2011 for the UK shows that the populations of BAME residents have risen, from 1.8 per cent to 2.5 per cent of the population for Black residents and from 7.5 per cent to 9.3 per cent for Asian residents. At the same time the population of White residents has fallen from

86.0 per cent to 81.7 per cent (Office for National Statistics). In line with this national picture, increasing numbers of BAME students are making the decision to attend university, taking the first step into what is usually a long, and often challenging journey. While this statement may be accurate for most student groups, it is particularly significant for BAME populations, who, in addition to academic demands, can expect racism and its various expressions, to be 'central to their experiences of higher education' (Allen, 1997: 182). However, despite this changing national picture, 'like other professions in Britain, the academic establishment has been slow to respond to the multiracial nature of British society' (Allen, 1997: 184). As a result, many HEIs appear to have made few provisions for increasing numbers of BAME students who may, on entering university, encounter a curriculum which does 'not reflect minority groups' experiences' (Universities UK and National Union of Students, 2019: 2).

While it might be possible for organizations to use a critical mass/cost argument to explain why some culturally specific services, such as ethnically congruent counselling, are not provided for Black, Asian and Minority Ethnic students, the same argument cannot be used to justify lack of awareness of academic staff who, as a result of the 2010 Equality Act and as public sector workers, are meant to promote equality between various groups. The data from this research indicated that not all staff had developed this critical understanding (or the requisite skill set) and even though on a personal level most students had positive academic relationships with teaching staff they experienced 'academic environments that, although not outwardly hostile provided little or no support to Black students' (Alford, 2000: 3). As a result, many students were put in a position where they had to 'devise coping skills that allow them to function in the college academic environment' (Alford, 2000) to enable them to complete their studies.

All HEIs setting higher level tuition fees are required by The Office for Students (OfS) to publish 'Access and participation plans [which] set out how higher education providers will improve equality of opportunity for underrepresented groups to access, succeed in and progress from higher education' (OfS: nd). For most organizations to achieve this goal some staff training has been provided to help staff can more effectively support BAME populations. However, in some organizations this training has been reduced to 'a 10-minute online training course with a multiple-choice assessment' (Tate and Page, 2018: 142). While such training may achieve non-specified minimum compliance standards, it does not adequately recognize the all-pervasive nature of racism and the damming impacts of the many different presentations of racism on BAME students; and unless and until HEIs work to counter the 'structural and systemic racism' (Tate and Page, 2018) common in many universities, it is likely that BAME students will continue to be routinely disadvantaged and encounter many forms of racist practices.

For BAME students to 'have a good sense of belonging at their university' (Universities UK and National Union of Students, 2019: 2), HEIs must acknowledge the ways in which BAME students have been othered and marginalized by HE. Universities need to engage with challenging and difficult 'conversations about race and changing the culture' (Universities UK and National Union of Students, 2019) if they are to unravel the complex and intersectional ways in which BAME students are disadvantaged. Furthermore, 'close attention must thus be paid to the different practices and contexts in which the inequalities of race, ethnicity and difference are formed and reformed' (Burke, 2018: 365). Universities must move beyond 'limited short-term strategies' (Rollock, 2018: 314) and start to develop with BAME communities different situated strategies which robustly engage with the challenges of racism and work to actively dismantle structures of oppression.

Critical reflective questions

1 Within your own organization, how is data on racial harassment collected and used? How does this data feed into institutional decision-making and policy development?

2 In what ways has your organization worked to capture the voices of minoritized populations? What culturally specific support systems have been developed to meet the needs of diverse student populations?

3 Adopting the 'nothing about us without us' principle and accepting that communities need to be included in the development of any responses which directly affect them, how has your organization sought to engage with minority communities and seek their views on moving forward?

References

Abdulrahman, H. K. (2020). Am I different? Social identity, difference, exclusion, and the (un)happiness of the 'black and minority ethnic' child in *Bring My Smile Back: Working with Unhappy Children in Education*, 1–16, New York: Nova Science Publishers.

Advance, H. E. (2018). Equality in higher education, Staff statistical report 2018. *Advance HE*, 6.

Alford, S. M. (2000). A qualitative study of the college social adjustment of black students from lower socioeconomic communities. *Journal of Multicultural Counselling and Development*, 28, 2–15.

Allen, P. (1997). Black students in Ivory Towers. *Studies in the Education of Adults*, 29(2), 179–90.

Arday, J., Belluigi, D. Z., and Thomas, D. (2021). Attempting to break the chain: Reimaging inclusive pedagogy and decolonising the curriculum within the academy. *Educational Philosophy and Theory*, 53(3), 298–313. https://doi.org/10.1080/00131857.2020.1773257.

Bhopal, K. and Pitkin, C. (2020). 'Same old story, just a different policy': Race and policy making in higher education in the UK. *Race Ethnicity and Education*, 23(4), 530–47.

Bonner, F. A. and Evans, M. (2004). Can you hear me? voices and experiences of African American students in higher education, in D. Cleveland (ed.), *A Long Way To Go*, 3–18, Switzerland: Peter Laing

Bunce, L., King, N., Saran, S., and Talib, N. (2019). Experiences of black and minority ethnic (BME) students in higher education: Applying self-determination theory to understand the BME attainment gap, *Studies in Higher Education*, 46(3), 534–47.

Burke, P. J. (2018). Trans/forming pedagogical spaces: Race, belonging and recognition in higher education, in J. Arday and H. S. Mirza (eds.), *Dismantling Race in Higher Education: Racism, Whiteness and Decolonising the Academy*, 365–82, Cham: Palgrave Macmillan

Cabrera, N. L., Franklin, J. D., and Watson J. S. (2016). Whiteness in higher education: The invisible missing link in diversity and racial analyses. *ASHE Higher Education Report*, 42(6), 7–125.

Cole, E. R. and Arriola, K. R. J. (2007). Black students on white campuses: Toward a two-dimensional model of black acculturation. *Journal of Black Psychology*, 3(4), 379–403.

Denscombe, M. (2010). *The Good Research Guide for Small Scale Social Research Projects*. 2nd edition. Maidenhead: Open University Press.

Fordham, S. (1996). *Blacked Out, Dilemmas of Race, Identity and Success at Capital High*. Chicago, IL: University of Chicago Press.

Gillborn, D. (2008). Education policy as an act of white supremacy: Whiteness, critical race theory and education reform. *Journal of Education Policy*, 20(4), 485–505,

Guild, H. E (nd). *Anti-Racism Programme: Briefing 3: Learning Teaching and Student Achievement*. London: Guild HE.

Heleta, S. (2016). Decolonisation of higher education: Dismantling epistemic violence and Eurocentrism in South Africa. *Transformation in Higher Education*, 1(1), 1–8.

Leonardo, Z. (2002). The souls of white folk: Critical pedagogy, whiteness studies, and globalization discourse. *Race Ethnicity and Education*, 5(1), 29–50,

Maykut, P. and Morehouse, R. (1999). *Beginning Qualitative Research: A Philosophic and Practical Guide*. London: Falmer Press.

Office for National Statistics (2021). *Census 2021: Ethnic Group England and Wales*. Available at: https://www.ons.gov.uk/peoplepopulationandcommunity/culturalidentity/ethnicity/bulletins/ethnicgroupenglandandwales/census2021#:~:text=the%20%22Asian%2C%20or%20Asian%20British,was%2081.0%25%20(45.8%20million) (accessed 31 December 2022).

Office for Students (nd). *Access and Participation Plans*. Available at: https://www.officeforstudents.org.uk/advice-and-guidance/promoting-equal-opportunities/access-and-participation-plans/ (accessed 1 January 2023).

Peart, S. (2013). *Making Education Work – How Black Men Navigate the Further Education Sector*. Stoke on Trent: Trentham Books.

Rollock, N. (2018). The heart of whiteness: Racial gesture politics, equity and higher education, in J. Arday and H. S. Mirza (eds.), *Dismantling Race in Higher Education: Racism, Whiteness and Decolonising the Academy*, Cham: Palgrave Macmillan.

Schensul, S. L., Schensul, J., and LeCompte, M. D. (1999). *Essential Ethnographic Methods*. California: Altamira Press.

Tate, S. A., and Page, D. (2018). Whiteliness and institutional racism: Hiding behind (Un) conscious bias. *Ethics and Education*, 3(1), 141–55.

Universities UK (2020). *Tacking Racial Harassment in Higher Education- Executive Summary*. Available at https://www.universitiesuk.ac.uk/sites/default/files/uploads/Reports/tackling-racial-harassment-in-higher-education-exec.pdf Universities UK accessed 3 November 2023.

Universities UK (2023). Tacking racial harassment in higher education – progress since 2020. Available at https://www.universitiesuk.ac.uk/sites/default/files/uploads/Reports/tacking-racial-harassment-progress-since-2020.pdf Universities UK 3 November 2023.

Universities UK and National Union of Students (2019). *Black, Asian and Minority Ethnic Attainment in UK Universities: #Closing the Gap Universities UK and National Union of Students*.

Wilkins, C. and Lall, R. (2011). 'You've got to be tough and I'm trying': Black and Minority Ethnic student teachers' experiences of initial teacher education. *Race, Ethnicity and Education*, 14(3), 123–34.

Wong, B., Elmorally, R., Copsey-Blake, M., Highwood, E., and Singarayer, J. (2020). Is race still relevant? Student perceptions and experiences of racism in higher education. *Cambridge Journal of Education*, 53(3), 359–75.

Wright, C., Standen, P. J., and Patel, T. (2010). *Black Youth Matters: Transitions from School to Success (Critical Youth Studies)*. Abingdon: Routledge.

Is This Going to Hurt? Engaging in Structural Cultural Change through Implementing Black History Month (BHM) as an Institutional Endeavour in a Small UK University

Sheine Peart and Rachael Fell-Chambers

Introduction

Embracing diversity and celebrating difference remains an elusive aspiration for some universities with history, tradition and normalized culture acting collectively to position minority groups at the fringes of the organization. As a consequence of the Macpherson Report (1999), universities must provide an appropriate and professional service to people which should not be adversely influenced by their colour, culture or ethnic origin. Universities must also uphold strengthened legal protections provided to minoritized ethnic populations. Specifically, the Equality Act 2010 requires publicly funded organizations to meet the distinctive cultural needs of minority groups and the Public Sector Equality Duty (PSED) obliges organizations to 'improve society and promote equality in every aspect of their day-to-day business' (Equality and Human Rights Commission, 2022). All Universities are required to meet this obligation irrespective of the numbers of ethnic minority students who attend any given institution. The geographical location of the organization and racial demographic of leadership teams may create a monolithic approach to diversity, supporting colour-blindness and further exasperating inequality. Ray (2019: 12) suggests that organizations should assume they are 'contributing to racial inequality unless the data shows otherwise' and Rollock (2018: 315) states that in some learning environments 'course content dismisses or subjugates their identity or history' therefore, minority students are immediately and automatically disadvantaged through casual alienation processes.

Even though all universities state their desire to be inclusive organizations, research has repeatedly demonstrated that Black minority students feel marginalized and less well catered for than their white peers. To counter such persistent inequalities, the Office for Students (OfS, 2022) has committed to ensuring that all groups should be able to access, succeed and thrive in higher education and be able to be recognized as a full member of the Academy. Not satisfied with progress across the higher education (HE) sector in 2023 the OfS published reforms to its approach to regulating equality of opportunity across English HE providers; this included the implementation of an externally validated Access and Participation Plan (APP). Under statute, organizations are required to set-out their commitment to promote equality of opportunity for underrepresented groups identifying key risks that students are facing. Plans are expected to be 'highly impactful', contain 'ambitious targets' and detail robust evaluation of effectiveness (OfS, 2023).

To tackle racial equalities within higher education, Advance HE refreshed the Race Equality Charter in 2023. Recognizing the strengths of embracing intersectionality, the Charter encourages organizations to reflect on their cross-institution practices to support the HE sector in reaching its full potential benefiting from the talents of the whole staff and student population. Correspondingly, the centre for Transforming Access and Student Outcomes in Higher Education (TASO) (2023) developed resources to support organizations with planning interventions and evaluation activities aimed at tackling the persistent unequal educational attainment between Black minorities and White students in HE. The Theory of Change toolkit facilitates disrupting monolithic practices and actively promotes change (TASO, 2023). However, unlike the OfS Access and Participation Plan, both initiatives from TASO and Advance HE rely on voluntary participation which could lead to uneven activity across the sector and low levels of engagement, thus maintaining the status quo. The invisible culture of Whiteness, which has silently evolved to dominate many large mainstream institutions including education, often fails to even recognize inequality and through either active aggression or indifference normalizes discrimination leaving it unchallenged.

Census data from 2022 for England and Wales, compared to 2011, recorded that the overall population of the Black minorities had increased from 1.9 million to 2.4 million, while the population of mixed groups (i.e. identifying as having one parent from a minority ethnic group) was 1.7 million compared to 1.2 million in 2011 (Diversity UK, 2023). This population change has been reflected in the numbers of Black minorities who have chosen to enter HE with number increasing overtime so that in 2021, 48.6 per cent of Black state school-aged pupils over eighteen chose to progress to HE and 40.8 per cent of Mixed pupils also chose this route (Gov.UK, 2022). This changing demographic obliges Universities to examine their provision and revisit taken for granted positions and convenient assumptions and work towards achieving equity between and across communities and counter existing or emerging inequalities.

This research explored how a group of White staff experienced engaging in active cultural change designed to disrupt assumed narratives about race by scrutinizing their responses to this development. Using Black History Month as a mechanism to open conversations and to revisit current provision, this project investigated what it means to occupy a shared space which values diversity and celebrates difference.

This small-scale research completed by two researchers working at one University, one who identified as Black the other as White, explored staff responses to introducing and embedding Black History Month (BHM) into the fabric of the organization as a way of questioning current provision and exploring future options. This paper investigates the perceived and actual impact of adopting an institution wide strategy, details the methodology used in this study, discusses study findings and considers implications for organizations. Although umbrella terms are problematic for the way that they exclude groups and concurrently homogenize or erase differences between populations and individuals, drawing together the four categories in the 2021 UK census of Black, Black British, Caribbean or African, the term Black minorities has been used in this research as a unifying descriptor of all four groups and to identify targeted populations.

Race relations in the UK

The UK has a long history of race relations where many 'have been taught to believe that there are distinct biological and genetic differences between races' (DiAngelo, 2019: 15). While 'race is an invalid scientific concept' (Cole, 2012: 49) differences between racial groups, which are often solely based on visible features, have been used to create an order where some groups are identified as superior and others necessarily inferior. The belief of a hierarchy of races is a cornerstone of racism and has used and continues to use, pseudoscience to legitimate the adverse treatment of one group while favouring another. Beliefs on the ordering of races also helped to justify Britain's colonization of nations throughout the globe and produced a set of persistent attitudes, practices and procedures which continue to structurally disadvantage some groups. In this self-proclaimed hierarchy, White British people identified themselves as natural rulers, genetically endowed with superior wisdom and capabilities, to whom other groups should defer. Such racist attitudes have contributed to many negative outcomes for Black minorities in the UK including a persistent education achievement gap, poorer employment opportunities and over-representation in prison populations. This antagonistic space made it easy to discriminate against Black minorities and provided little room to acknowledge or celebrate the positive contributions of Black peoples.

In the UK 'racially related issues have been addressed via a range of formal and informal dictates' (Quraishi and Philburn, 2015: 38) and the first Race Relations Act was introduced in 1965. This Act was designed 'to prohibit discrimination on racial grounds in places of public resort; to prevent the enforcement or imposition on racial grounds of restrictions on the transfer of tenancies; to penalize incitement to racial hatred' (Gov.UK, 1965). Further Acts and Amendments focused on race were passed in 1965, 1968, 1976, 1977, 1992, 1998, 2000 and 2002 before the introduction of the 2010 Equality Act which brought together all pieces of equality legislation under a single umbrella Act. Since 1965 the narrow scope of legal protections provided to different racial groups has been extended and the Equality Act directs organizations to adopt a pro-active response and put measures into place which would prevent discrimination from occurring and to develop co-operative ways of working and being together. However, none of these pieces of legislation have provided guidance on how organizations may achieve such positive collaboration, instead each public body has been left to develop its own situated response. While this has led to the development of good practice in some areas, it has also enabled other organizations to continue to accept poor or damaging practices, or worse still to 'recreate white supremacy on a daily basis' (Leonardo, 2009: 264).

Although legislation may have been helpful in curbing some of the worst excesses of racism and 'such measures have undoubtedly moved us forward and improved society no end' (Quraishi and Philburn, 2015: 38) laws alone will not eradicate racism because 'the ways in which racism is embedded has not been confronted' (Bhavnini, Mirza and Meetoo, 2005: 29) and if 'the purpose of education is to challenge and undermine that racism' (Cole, 2012: 89) other mechanisms which require educators to engage at a deeper, more critical level are needed to eliminate racism from all education structures and systems. Further recent landmark events such as Black Lives Matter (BLM) may signal the Equality Act requires urgent review.

Using Black history month as a catalyst for change

'If we assume that racism exists in our societies, then we need to "step in" to ensure that it is reduced or eliminated altogether' (Bhavnini, Mirza and Meetoo, 2005: 25) and because 'the hidden curriculum of Whiteness saturates everyday ... life' (Leonardo, 2009: 267) educators need to deconstruct the racist structures they occupy and rebuild positive, educationally inclusive practices to meet legislative obligations and to better serve the needs of all students, staff and other university users. It is only through such action that the UK's 'racist society' (Cole, 2012: 53) can be dismantled. The development of positive relationships between different groups, coupled with a willingness to work with others, is often predicated on a greater understanding which requires 'continued, on-going dialogue about race-related issues' (Tatum, 2009: 281). Therefore, developing a space where White people can start to examine 'how much of their lives and the lives of people of color have been affected by racism in our society' (Tatum, 2009: 279) and where Black minorities can share their experiences from the 'point of the oppressed' (Leonardo, 2009: 265) creates opportunities for collaborative action and forming new futures.

Within education, the development of more positive relationships necessarily requires the examination of persistent behaviours and structures which privilege one group over others, either intentionally or unwittingly, and the rejection of overt or subtle forms of discrimination. BHM, recognized in the UK since 1987, provides an opportunity to conduct such an examination and to reconfigure working practices. BHM is a vehicle which facilitates an annual 'public opportunity to celebrate Black cultures' (Spencer, 2020: 265) and to 'disrupt systemic racism [and] combat negative constructions of racialization' (King and Brown, 2014: 25); it is an anti-racist structure which is 'grounded in the egalitarian principle that social and institutional arrangements should be designed to give equal consideration to all' (Terzi, 2008: 143) and may be a useful tool in helping Black minorities feel more welcome and part of the university community.

The research site, in common with a growing number of UK organizations, used BHM to refocus service users' minds recognizing the contributions and achievements of peoples from the African diaspora. This endeavour assumes a heightened significance in some parts of the UK where there are smaller populations of Black minorities and where these contributions have been denied, ignored, marginalized, subject to 'hostile political discourse' (Bernard, 2018: 389) or 'expertly ignored' (Van De Mieroop, 2016: 3). Even though BHM has been criticized for failing to 'fulfil the goal of critically reshaping inequitable curriculum, BHM is a rare time that many … teachers recognise the histories of Black people in classrooms' (King and Brown, 2014: 24). While it appears that 'the UK has retreated from multiculturalism' (Mathieu, 2018: 44), BHM can be used as a platform to challenge colonial attitudes which position 'western capitalism and culture' (Tikly, 2004: 175) as a superior form of civilization and to counter the view that Black minorities occupy 'a state of natural inferiority to Whites' (King and Brown, 2014: 23). Further, BHM is uniquely positioned to facilitate 'an opportunity for communal learning, pride, and the literal prizing of knowledge concerning the Black diaspora' (Spencer, 2020: 272). In doing so, BHM can be a tool to challenge 'institutionally racist' (Doharty, 2019: 111) embedded curricula of many education organizations.

Lack of curricula diversity combined with a mainly White demography within some localities results in opportunities to develop awareness of Black history being limited and western-centric ideology being maintained. For these students and staff, amplification of Black history throughout an organization may stimulate a consideration of how 'their worldviews might be implicitly racialised, and to challenge ingrained habits of thought' (Singh et al., 2023: 241). Events provided through BHM can be 'transformative influences on students' learning' (King and Brown, 2014: 26).

Pause for thought: Research

Institutional culture describes the ethos of an organization and its accepted norms. It is an invisible code which pervades all aspects of the institution, creating the lived reality of attending that institution; more simply it can be described as 'the way we do things around here' (Universities UK, 2020: 5). The culture of an institution is critical in determining how welcome members of that organization feel. Having a positive institutional culture can help to promote feelings of security and belonging. Universities UK, which represents over 140 higher education institutions, has published guidance stating 'creating a safe space for conversations about racial inequality and committing to becoming allies in dismantling racism, at their institution and more widely, can also improve experiences of inclusion and help to deliver a change in university culture' (Universities UK, 2020: 5).

To accompany the guidance Universities UK published a set of case studies provided by different universities showing what action had been taken to tackle racial harassment on campus including senior leadership training, setting up anti-racist groups, and developing racist incident reporting tools. Each of these projects was customized to the organization and tailored to the specific institutional circumstances.

Reflection

HE has recognized that removing racism from education is a process which requires dedication from the whole organization with staff at all levels and in all departments working to make the university a place where people can live, work and learn together. Achieving this outcome requires commitment from the whole institution and support from outside including families, communities, local and national government agencies, and other networks. Racism cannot be countered by adopting a simplistic 'one-size-fits-all' approach. Each university must first of all determine what specific action needs to be completed so that the organization can respond appropriately. The OfS regulatory requirement to produce a localized equality of opportunity risk register through the APP goes some way towards this. Equally, such action cannot solely be imposed by a top-down model as a policy which is not supported, is a policy which will fail. In the same way any grass roots action which does not receive the support of the management team will also not succeed. In your own organization, are you aware of the action your organization has chosen to support and progress? What support is given to staff to raise issues so that matters can be discussed and an agreed co-created response can be developed? Systems which are developed by and invested in by the community have both a greater chance of success and are more likely to persist into the future.

Methodology: Living the change, staff experience of engaging in BHM

This research explored how university staff perceived, received and responded to the introduction of BHM. Although some staff had previously independently supported BHM, this was the first time the organization had adopted an institutional wide approach which actively sought to engage participation from all parts of the University. The research intended to ask staff to engage in a deeper level of critical reflection and to explore if, or how implementing BHM, could support an organizational ambition of creating a community built on mutual trust and respect. Prior to any data collection ethical approval was obtained via standard university procedure.

Specifically, the research focused on three main areas of interest, namely:

- What were the possible demographic challenges of introducing BHM in a predominantly White area of the UK?
- What were the institutional issues of trying to raise the profile of BHM?
- What were the perceived impacts of hosting BHM for staff and students?

Using a phenomenological approach, E-questionnaires were distributed to twenty-seven potential participants who took part in the planning, organization and implementation of BHM at the end of a month-long programme of events which were facilitated or provided by internal staff and students and included poetry, lectures, film and storytelling. In addition, where a relevant curriculum link could be achieved, teaching staff revisited their schemes of work to foreground the contributions from the African diaspora. Acknowledging the possibility of inherent bias, as those who had chosen to help organize BHM were the same members of the university being asked to evaluate the project, as insiders they were also well-placed to comment on the implementation and effectiveness of the BHM initiative.

To protect participant anonymity, questionnaire data was distributed and mediated by an external IT organization. All members of the planning and delivery group which included students, members of the University leadership team, teaching staff, and university support services were invited to take part. The participant pool incorporated representation from different racial groups and different genders with the youngest participant being in their early twenties and the oldest in their mid-sixties. The questionnaire comprised seventeen free response questions and achieved a 22 per cent response rate with six questionnaires returned. Although this could be considered a low response rate, it is consistent with the typical response rate for surveys (Opie, 2019). All participants were informed at the outset of the research that their responses may be used to produce research outputs.

Survey data was analysed by reading and re-reading multiple times and scrutinizing the written responses to determine meanings and patterns across the participants' replies. Conscious of the subjectivity of the interpretation process, both researchers ensured reflexivity was practised in order to maintain the integrity of the data analysis process (von Unger, 2021). Rivas (2012: 368) suggests that by reading and re-reading data several times before coding, 'sensitivity to meaning is enhanced'. Data was then coded and this information was used to generate research themes. As participant numbers were small, data was not analysed according to the participants' particular features such as age, gender or other characteristics, rather an overview approach was adopted which drew together all data to produce a final set of findings.

Findings – Outcomes of changing practice

Questionnaire data was analysed thematically (Braun and Clarke, 2006) and produced three principal themes: 'Levels of Participant Awareness and Motivation to Engage', 'Organizational Support' and 'Ownership of the Initiative'. Although there was a degree of overlap between each of these themes, there were also distinct features.

Theme One: 'Levels of Participant Awareness and Motivation to Engage'

There was some awareness of BHM in the planning group and all members demonstrated an active willingness to organize events. Despite BHM arriving in the UK in 1987, two members of the group stated they had no awareness of this national event and did not, at the start of the planning process, realize the university had committed to being part of these celebrations stating, *'I don't think I was aware'* and *'I didn't know the university was taking part'*. There was also a general perception of a *'lack of interest'* across the university. While the first comment signals a lack of knowledge regarding BHM, the second is more ambiguous. As an organization-wide approach had not previously occurred, the staff member may have thought the established pattern of institutional disengagement was being repeated and had accepted the university did not celebrate BHM; this disconnection was echoed bluntly in the third comment. These low levels of awareness and lack of connection may have been linked to the demography of the region where there were few Black minorities and traditionally the local council and regional services appeared to have paid little attention to BHM. For these staff members, BHM also served as an education tool, for as a result of taking part in planning and attending events, staff members had a greater awareness of the contributions of Black minorities; the significance of BHM for the whole organization and how BHM events could benefit staff, students and the wider public.

While the planning team were positively motivated to promote BHM many faced challenges in overcoming staff and student inertia and securing attendance at events, noting *'the lack of support at events from students/staff/ wider community'*. Again, this perceived level of lower engagement may have been a reflection of organizational history and a university population not used to this provision being offered who consequently neither expected nor looked forward to the annual arrival of BHM. Although lack of support may not have impacted on staff on a personal level, as they had invested effort to organize or resource events, low audience engagement may have influenced staff commitment to supporting future events and was therefore a matter of concern; indeed it could be part of the pain of organizing and delivering BHM in a university setting.

Theme Two: 'Organizational Support'

The planning team solely comprised willing volunteers and while the team had some administrative standing in that it reported to the university's Access and Participation Committee (APC), it lacked organizational authority and lacked dedicated funding to progress work. This led to several participants to comment on the need for a *'central budget'*, for once the BHM programme had been agreed by the planning team, they had to return to the APC to request funds to support events. In this way, funding for BHM was *'provided by a number of departments'* who each contributed different sums. While this support was sufficient to ensure that BHM *'actually happened'* there was a feeling across the group that greater support needed to be shown by the university leadership team with participants commenting *'senior management need to be visibly involved'* and *'a firm commitment from SLT is required'*.

This is supported through the work of Singh et al. (2023: 241) who state that 'Decision-makers within higher education, have an important function when getting to grips with the negative consequences of minoritisation within Western universities.' Furthermore, greater support from the senior management team is consistent with Kotter's (2012) assertion that for lasting organizational change to occur, in addition to building ground-level community endorsement, there must also be support at management level and succession planning to ensure the continuation of provision.

Theme Three: 'Ownership of the Initiative'

There was general agreement that in addition to a stand-alone central programme of events, there needed to be integrated curriculum provision that would secure greater engagement by students who appeared indifferent to the programme of events. This could be supported by academic teams through embedding activities within the curriculum planning. Findings also highlight the importance of building environments to share and build on each other's ideas freely, generating space to hold courageous conversations to open 'the vision of what is possible and ... how to take steps to turn that vision into a reality' (Munby, 2019: 54). There were mixed messages regarding ownership of the project with some believing events should be led by management while others favoured a more distributed leadership approach (DeFlaminis, Abdul-Jabbar and Yoak, 2016). Though staff support for BHM existed in pockets throughout the University, it was felt there needed to be more robust institutional support. While not offering a template for action, the findings of this study provide a useful reference point for organizations with small populations of Black minorities who are seeking to enhance the educational experience of all users, promote BHM and challenge 'systematic and incidental racism' (Peart, 2018: 545) by working across groups to secure action and to challenge attitudes.

Conclusion

Cole (2012: 95) stated 'in the light of escalating racism in Britain ... measures to undermine institutional racism are more urgent than ever'. In the context of the murders of Stephen Lawrence (1993), Anthony Walker (2005) and BLM, this urgency has not diminished. There is little research data which specifically discusses the issues and opportunities for implementing an organization-wide initiative in small mainly monocultural organizations. As Universities must provide the OfS with an Access and Participation Plan (OfS, 2023), this paper has appraised one possible approach which could be used to demonstrate an active commitment to promote equality and to work to become a capable ally for Black minorities.

Although there are still unresolved discussions on the best and most appropriate way to educate university students and others, there is general agreement that all students will need to have the skills which will enable them to operate effectively in the wider world. This necessarily means both having an understanding of wider communities and the ability to work within them. BHM is a tool which can be used to help develop this understanding and while successive governments have shown different commitment towards multicultural or anti-racist education, all governments seem committed towards the idea of cohesive communities able to contribute to the well-being and wealth of the nation. As the population of the UK continues to diversify, the need to have a better understanding of the groups which make up the population becomes increasingly more important and in areas which have small populations of Black minorities, structural opportunities to develop communities' understanding need to be implemented. By taking these opportunities, universities can support all students and staff to develop the skills they will need to live in a diversifying nation and to better understand the histories and identities of groups within the UK.

While HE in the UK may have been established from a White-centric perspective, to perpetuate a monocultural provision is to deny and ignore the changes happening in the UK and the need to respond positively, moving away from a defensive protection of the past to an affirmative welcome of the future, both embracing opportunities and working to resolve any emergent challenges. Although the culture of Whiteness may have dominated Universities in the past, this need not be the template for the future and BHM is a tool which can be used to interrupt, disrupt and challenge a persistent narrative of domination.

Critical reflective questions

1. There is no requirement for any public organization to support or celebrate BHM and its very existence could be considered tokenistic. How is BHM recognized in your organization and what is the rationale for this choice?
2. BHM may be a tool to help promote White allyship and to challenge inequalities. What is the tension between allyship and saviourship and how might such a tension be navigated?
3. Thinking about your own organization, if BHM is currently celebrated, does the organization intend to carry on promoting BHM? Why has this decision been made? If BHM is not celebrated, what is the institutional rationale for this choice?

References

Bernard, C. (2018). Black history month: A provocation and a timeline. *Critical and Radical Social Work*, 6(3), 391–406.

Bhavnini, R., Mirza, H. S., and Meetoo, V. (2005). *Tackling the Roots of Racism, Lessons for Success*. Bristol: Policy Press.

Braun, V. and Clarke, V. (2006). Using thematic analysis in psychology. *Qualitative Research in Psychology*, 3(2), 77–101.

Cole, M. (2012). Racism in the UK: Change and continuity, in M. Cole (ed.), *Education, Equality and Human Rights – Issues of Gender, 'Race', Sexuality, Disability and Social Class*, 72–102, Abingdon: Routledge.

DeFlaminis, J. A., Abdul-Jabbar, M., and Yoak, E. (2016). *Distributed Leadership in School: A Practical Guide for Learning and Improvement,* New York: Routledge.

DiAngelo, R. (2019). *White Fragility – Why It's so Hard for White People to Talk About Racism.* Allen Lane: Penguin Books.

Diversity UK (2023). *Census 2021 Data Reveals Ethnic Make-Up of UK Population.* Available online: https://diversityuk.org/census-2021-data-reveals-ethnic-make-up-of-uk-population/#:~:text=England%20and%20Wales,-In%20England%20the&text=%22Black%2C%20Black%20British%2C%20Caribbean,was%202.2%25%20(1.2%20million) (accessed 9 September 2023).

Doharty, N. (2019). 'I Felt Dead': applying a racial microaggressions framework to black students' experiences of black history month and black history. *Race and Ethnicity in Education,* 22(1), 110–29.

Equality and Human Rights Commission (2022). *The Public Sector Equality Duty.* Available online: https://www.equalityhumanrights.com/guidance/public-sector-equality-duty?return-url=https%3A%2F%2Fwww.equalityhumanrights.com%2Fsearch%3Fkeys%3Dpsed%26f%255B0%255D%3Dcontent_type%253Aguidance_article (accessed 8 November 2023).

Gov UK (1965). *Race Relations Act.* Available online: https://www.legislation.gov.uk/ukpga/1965/73/pdfs/ukpga_19650073_en.pdf (accessed 16 September 2023).

Gov.UK (2022). *Entry Rates into Higher Education.* Available online: https://www.ethnicity-facts-figures.service.gov.uk/education-skills-and-training/higher-education/entry-rates-into-higher-education/latest (accessed 8 November 2023).

King, L. J. and Brown, K. (2014). Once a year to be black: Fighting against typical black history month pedagogies. *The Negro Educational Review,* 65(1–4), 23–43.

Kotter, J. (2012). *Leading Change.* United States of America: Harvard Business Review Press.

Leonardo, Z. (2009). The color of supremacy beyond the discourse of 'white privilege', in E. R. Taylor, G. Gillborn and G. Ladson-Billings (eds.), *Foundations of Critical Race Theory in Education,* 321–33, Abingdon: Routledge.

Macpherson, W. (1999). *The Stephen Lawrence Inquiry.* London: The Stationery Office.

Mathieu, F. (2018). The failure of state multiculturalism in the UK? An analysis of the UK's multicultural policy for 2000–2015. *Ethnicities,* 18(1), 43–69.

Munby, S. (2019). *Imperfect Leadership: A Book for Leaders Who Know They Don't Know It All.* Carmarthen: Crown House Publishing.

Office for Students (2022). *Our Approach to Equality of Opportunity.* Available online: https://www.officeforstudents.org.uk/advice-and-guidance/promoting-equal-opportunities/our-approach-to-equality-of-opportunity/ (accessed 11 November 2023).

Office for Students (2023). *Regulatory Notice 1: Access and Participation Plan Guidance.* Available online: https://www.officeforstudents.org.uk/media/bfd27f68-7634-4237-8e6c-36bb8e436631/regulatory_notice_1_access_participation_plan_guidance_december_2023.pdf (accessed 14 December 2023).

Opie, C. and Brown, D., eds. (2019). *Getting Started in Your Educational Research: Design, Data Production and Analysis.* London: Sage.

Peart, S. (2018). The significance of further education for black males. *Education + Training,* 60(6), 544–55.

Quraishi, M. and Philburn, R. (2015). *Researching Racism: A Guidebook for Academic and Professional Investigators.* London: Sage.

Ray, V. (2019). *Why So Many Organizations Stay White*. Available online: https://hbr.org/2019/11/why-so-many-organizations-stay-white (accessed 10 December 2023).

Rivas, C. (2012). Coding and analyzing qualitative data, in C. Seale (ed.), *Researching Society and Culture*, 3rd edn, 366–92, London: Sage.

Rollock, N. (2018). The heart of whiteness: Racial gesture politics, equity and higher education, in J. Arday and H. S. Mirza (eds.), *Dismantling Race in Higher Education: Racism, Whiteness and Decolonising the Academy*, 313–30, Switzerland: Palgrave Macmillan.

Singh, S., Pykett, J., Kraftl, P., Guisse, A., Hodgson, E., Humelnicu, U. E., Keen, N., Kéïta, S., McNaney, N., Menzel, A., N'dri, K., N'goran, K. J., Oldknow, G., Tiéné, R., and Weightman, W. (2023). Understanding the 'degree awarding gap' in geography, planning, geology and environmental sciences in UK higher education through peer research. *Journal of Geography in Higher Education*, 47(2), 227–47.

Spencer, K. L. (2020), Black history month jeopardy at PWI: A how-to. *Public Services Quarterly*, 16(4), 265–72.

Tatum, B. D. (2009). Teaching white students about racism, in E. R. Taylor, G. Gillborn and G. Ladson-Billings (eds.), *Foundations of Critical Race Theory in Education*, 277–90, Abingdon: Routledge.

Terzi, L. (2008). *Justice and Equality in Education: A Capability Perspective on Disability and Special Educational Needs*. London: Continuum.

Tikly, L. (2004). Education and the new imperialism. *Comparative Education*, 40(2), 172–98.

Transforming Access and Student Outcomes in Higher Education (2023). *Theory of Change Resources*. Available online: https://taso.org.uk/evidence/evaluation-guidance-resources/toc/ (accessed 14 December 2023).

Universities UK (2020). *Tackling Racial Harassment in Higher Education Executive Summary*. Available online: https://www.universitiesuk.ac.uk/sites/default/files/uploads/Reports/tackling-racial-harassment-in-higher-education-exec.pdf (accessed 12 November 2023).

Van De Mieroop, K. (2016). On the advantage and disadvantage of black history month for life: The creation of the post-racial era. *History and Theory*, 55, 3–24.

von Unger, H. (2021). Ethical reflexivity as research practice. *Historical Social Research*, 46(2), 186–204.

Safe and Accessible Use of Social Media Is a Matter of Social Justice

Katya Bozukova

13

Introduction

Picture this: You have just decided to learn how to drive. You are signed up for theoretical courses and you look forward to your practice session. But your teachers, your family and everyone who considers themselves an expert in driving only ever talk to you about how terrible cars are. How they pollute the environment, how they are congesting our cities, how terrible car accidents are for all those involved. Certain places won't even accept you as a student, saying you're better off not picking this up as a skill. If you do find a driving school that will take you, you will be taught begrudgingly, and everyone involved will make it clear they have no enthusiasm for the task.

At the same time, your town or your county does not have good transport links. You can take the bus or walk to school or to work, but it is going to take longer, the transport links are unreliable, and there are many parts of the route that are unsafe. Everyone tells you cars are bad, but driving is the only reliable option you have if you want to ever leave your house.

Now replace the 'car' with 'social media and the Internet' and you might get an idea about how young people nowadays feel when educators talk to them about the digital sphere. The discussion of digital literacy for children has been mired in the language of moral panics (Clapton, Cree and Smith,

2013) and tragedy (Crawford, 2019), and while the online world carries many risks, that is not the full story. Like a driver's license, digital literacy is fast becoming indispensible.

This chapter presents the findings of a qualitative research project involving eleven families – sixteen adults and twenty-two children in total. Ages of the child participants ranged from four to fifteen years of age, with the majority being between nine and thirteen. Most of the young participants had – at the time of the research project – very limited or no presence on social media. In addition to working with children and their parents, several gatekeepers such as educators, church leaders and librarians were asked about their experiences in using social media and helping young people navigate the digital space.

Although the project explored a variety of questions about risk and trust in family practices and attitudes towards social media technologies, the focus of this chapter is on educational establishments, and the support (or lack thereof) that families received when their children were about to discover digital citizenship.

Digital citizenship and why it matters

Even before the outbreak of the 2019 Covid-19 pandemic, the importance of digital citizenship was becoming increasingly significant in the UK. Various government offices, for example His Majesty's Revenue and Customs (HMRC, 2015), Department of Work and Pensions (DWP, 2015) and the Driver and Vehicle Licensing Agency (DVLA, 2015), offered hybrid services, or had already switched to online-first services before the word 'lockdown' was part of the shared vernacular. Banks, stores and educational providers were allowing customers to access their services online, and digital transformation of these services has only continued to accelerate (Sorbet, 2023).

At the same time, there is limited support for schools to increase children's digital literacy. Before an online safety curriculum was released from the Department for Education in 2023 (Department for Education, 2023), the only official guidance was focused on bullying and cyberbullying (Morgan and Department for Education, 2015; Department for Education, 2018). Before publication of the 2023 guidance, individual schools had to come up with their own curriculums on social media and online safety, or they delegated the responsibility for digital literacy to parents and carers.

Pre-Covid, the importance of social media may have been dismissed as a new and possibly insignificant fad. Social media is a relatively new phenomenon (Facebook was founded in 2004) and the general population appears to not be fully aware of the power and money that can be harnessed through these social networks. However, after acknowledging the role of social media in managing public health during the pandemic, there is now no reasonable excuse for educators to shrink from that responsibility. The new curriculum issued by the Department of Education acknowledges a lot of that complexity, and includes guidance on a number of topics, including: How to evaluate what you see online, How to recognize techniques used for persuasion, Online behaviour, How to identify online risks, How and when to seek support, Online media literacy strategy, and more (Department of Education, 2023).

At the same time, curriculum and official guidance are only part of the challenge for schools and educators. Time, money and the teachers' own confidence in the subject matter have just as much impact as the material being suggested. Indeed, what makes digital citizenship a social justice matter is the impact of this lack of teaching has on people's ability to engage in civic discourse and social life: Families that have the time, education and inclination to engage actively and critically with social media will raise young people who have the tools to engage as digital citizens. Everyone else will be left to figure things out on their own and risk putting themselves in harm's way.

A note about legislation of social media platforms: During the writing of this chapter, several events took place that accelerated the discussion of online safety and the role of Government to legislate and regulate social media platforms. The first is the passing of the Online Safety Bill (2023) which compels social media firms to protect children from 'some legal but harmful material' online (Rahman-Jones and Vallance, 2023). The second is the sentencing of the murderers of Brianna Ghey (Pidd, 2024a), whose trial raised a lot of public discourse around the role of social media in harming children and teenagers. Since the sentencing, Brianna's mother, Esther Ghey, has led calls for stricter controls on social media access for under-16s (Pidd, 2024b).

These are all very important discussions and it is valuable to remember that legislation is a crucial part of ensuring the safety of children online. At the same time, legislation is only part of the puzzle. Digital literacy, critical thinking and equal access remain a crucial factor of digital citizenship. This socio-cultural-financial division between the haves and have-nots is serious and potentially harmful. And, as the rest of this chapter will show, even families who hold the best of intentions and resources can struggle to teach young people on how to positively engage with social media and the Internet.

Parental perspectives

This section of the chapter discusses parental and carer perspectives on the education and support (or lack thereof) available to families as children reached the age where they were interested in social media and entering the digital sphere.

Key themes that emerged from the interviews regarding education and support around social media technologies were as follows:

- Parents and family carers receive unhelpful advice on social media technologies from many different sources;
- Parents and family carers experienced high anxiety around the subject of social media technologies;
- Parents and family carers resort to covert gate-keeping practices to support children.

As a consequence, adults tasked with teaching children and young people about social media and digital citizenship are approaching the task with limited information and low confidence. The success of the adults' intervention is broadly reliant on their relationships with the children and young people, how much credence children and young people give to their carer's advice, and how likely those young people are to stay with that advice when faced with outside challenges. Remaining faithful to family advice was often made complex because of the behaviours of the child's peer groups, as well as the extent to which the school reinforces the same messages as the parents. These themes will be explored in more detail in this section.

Unhelpful advice

Across all eleven group interviews, no child talked about receiving any kind of formalized education or support from schools on social media and digital citizenship. At the same time, adult participants did not feel that the advice they received from schools was helpful in teaching their children about social media technologies. Indeed, interview data indicated that parents were either given no advice at all, or told to limit their children's access to social media and mobile devices as much as possible.

Such an approach was perceived as unhelpful for several reasons. First, the interviewees did not consider themselves informed enough about social media to undertake this teaching themselves. Second, parents and carers felt that they were able to control and contain social media usage only while their children were very young – as they grew older and their friends started using the Internet more, such containment strategies were no longer seen as feasible. Finally, the participants in the study all ascribed to in what Valcke and colleagues described as 'permissive' or 'authoritative' parenting styles (Valcke et al., 2010) – in other words, they valued autonomy and cooperation in their relationships with their children.

Another approach taken by schools which families found unhelpful was the usage of cautionary tales by teachers. Interviewees described these tales about 'other people' being used to discourage children from being online, or to limit their usage of social media. However, when such stories were brought up during the interview, parents and carers expressed disbelief and doubt, suggesting that the story was likely to be false or exaggerated.

Taken together, the advice that families received from educational establishments was deemed to be unhelpful or frustrating. Additionally, it was noted in the interviews that schools sometimes contradicted their own suggestions – telling parents to limit screen time while also assigning homework online and expecting children to use the Internet for assignments.

It is worth noting that interview data collected for this project took place before the pandemic. With the widespread use of Zoom and Microsoft Teams for teaching, it would be interesting to see if the quality of the cybersecurity advice dispensed by schools has improved. It would also be interesting to see whether there are any changes to the advice given by schools following the guidance released by the Department of Education (Department of Education, 2023).

Parental anxiety

While 'anxiety and insecurity become an integral part of the modern condition' (Wilkinson, 2001: 4), there was one particular concern that all parents expressed in the interviews – that their children were growing up online and there was very little they felt like they could do to support them. The parental 'anxiety' was both a response to the uncertainty experienced towards social media and the lack of trust they have in what will happen in the future. Moreover, the perception of moving on other people's timeline resulted in parents feeling rushed and frustrated.

> **Parent 1** *(father): Well that's quite interesting because I've found a little bit with (Child) starting secondary school this year, so they got um, a mobile phone, this year, I sort of set them up with, you know, a Gmail account and that sort of stuff, and really you're not meant to be like looking at the small print, you're not meant to have some of this stuff referred to you, and I kind of ... felt like as a parent, not pressured*

into but kind of all their friends were going to be using social media and I sort of stopped them from using it at that age where they would become like excluded from stuff that was going on lately, so it's sort of interesting really, from a parental perspective.

(...)

Parent 2 *(mother): so it's a really tricky one, as – as a parent because … when (Child) got their phone quite a lot later than a lot of their friends –*

Child *(12): A **lot** later*

Parent 2: *(pause) and, um, that in itself, they felt excluded from social situations at school, like … parties and things*

Excerpt, family group interview.

This anxiety manifested in many different ways, including:

- Hyper-vigilance and monitoring the online activities of young children;
- Actively modifying search/watch histories on YouTube to control what content young children saw;
- Encouraging older children to spend more time outside and actively discouraging screen time;
- Concerns about social media 'materialism' and unrealistic beauty standards.

As stated in the previous section, while monitoring and restricting social media use was seen as feasible while the children were younger, parents felt that was no longer feasible when the children entered secondary school. The commencement of social media usage tended to coincide with the purchase of the first mobile phone, although some parents felt that was still too early.

Indeed, most parents associated their children's entry to digital citizenship with a loss of control – control of the content that the child consumed, control of what the child did online, and control of what information the child might share about their parents or their younger siblings. To some extent, even the family's participation in the project was an extension of the parental anxiety – during some of the interviews, there were times when the parents expected me as an identified expert to give them personalized advice on their social media practices. On one occasion I was even asked to assess and effectively grade parental practices.

While the parental and carer responses were, to a degree, predictable, the lack of avenues that parents felt they had to work through their anxiety is pertinent. As stated earlier, schools were seen as unhelpful, and parents did not report feeling comfortable discussing the topic with other parents. Importantly, the increased usage of social media by young people does not seem to have been accompanied by an increase of support for their parents (by schools, by government, by local communities). In such situations, it is possible that more and more parents will resort to activities to try and control their children's online usage through different, more subtle ways – a hidden gatekeeping of sorts.

Hidden gatekeeping

In addition to imposed formal rules on children's usage of social media, the parents also used more covert gatekeeping activities. Such hidden gatekeeping activities and other covert surveillance included:

- Reviewing the watch history on the iPad and other shared devices once the child had finished using it for the day;
- Changing or erasing the watch history on certain social media technologies (like YouTube) so that the algorithm does not 'lead (the child) astray' (except, family group interview);
- Speaking to the children about risks on social media that the parent had read about or heard on the news;
- Speaking to the children about what they had learned in school about social media technologies;
- Speaking to their children about what the parents perceived to be issues about social media, such as materialism or the ease of committing identity fraud;
- Talking to their children about the content they consumed.

Hidden gatekeeping activities differed from formal rules in several ways. First, they did not involve issuing the child with specific directives (such as not bringing devices into their bedrooms or accepting friend requests from strangers); rather the parents framed the hidden gatekeeping activity as part of an ongoing discussion about social media technologies. Second, the hidden gatekeeping activity was something the parent could connect to another material source – a newspaper chapter, a lesson at school, a child's search or watch history online. Third, the hidden gatekeeping activity focused on shaping behaviours and attitudes, more so than a direct rule – it was not so much about what the child cannot do, but about shaping the future behaviour, tastes and attitudes, and encouraging different future actions.

> **Parent 1** *(mother): Because we've only recently been … having those discussions, and one of, one of the policies we've discussed is that, f-for them (the children) is not to respond, sometimes not to respond, that they don't have to respond to comments*

Child *(14): Mmm*

Parent 1: *Cause I often think that, that escalates, you know, people misinterpret things, or, you might respond in the heat of the moment, and then regret that afterwards.*

Excerpt, family group interview.

The extent to which such hidden gate-keeping activities were effective was difficult to ascertain. While children expressed agreement with a lot of their parents' views, they were also discussing their perspective and point of view as experts in their own experiences. At the same time, as said earlier, most of the families interviewed for this project exhibited what Valcke and colleagues call a 'permissive' or an 'authoritative' style of digital parenting (2010): there was warmth and mutual respect in the family interactions, and as a consequence there was a great deal of time, effort and emotional labour invested in these hidden gatekeeping activities.

In other words, the parents were willing to put in the additional work that went into hidden gatekeeping activities – monitoring their children's social media usage, engaging with children in challenging discussions and keeping themselves informed about new threats. The importance of time, knowledge and effort cannot be overestimated, given the lack of perceived support from the wider community that the parents experienced.

Pause for thought: Families know best?

For many parents and carers, the content children and young people access on social media is also very concerning. Part of the reason why digital literacy used to be delegated to parents and carers is the fact that each family has a different view of what information is considered 'child-appropriate' and what is not. To give one example, LGBTQIA+ topics that are considered controversial by one family might be completely unremarkable to another. As public discourse on topics of social justice becomes more polarized, how should educators and schools approach teaching digital literacy, while remaining impartial about the content that children may access online?

First, it is worth noting that democracy, rule of law, respect and tolerance, and individual liberty are not controversial topics – they are fundamental British values that schools are encouraged to instil in young people through their curriculum. The next time you are asked or challenged about a part of your curriculum, try replacing that topic in a sentence with one of those values. '*I don't want my child to learn about trans rights*' sounds very different when rephased as '*I don't want my child to learn about respect and tolerance.*'

Second, schools are not expected to take a stance on contentious issues, but the curriculum does guide them to teach children and young adults about recognizing misinformation and applying critical thinking to what they find online. In that way, the argument is not about educators taking sides on social justice matters – it is about whether educators will provide students with the tools they need to navigate an increasingly treacherous world of misinformation online. To use the earlier example of driving, we are not asking whether we should teach students to drive manual or automatic; we are asking whether students should take driving courses before they are allowed behind a wheel.

Last but not least, consider the role of trust between educators and students. Trust is difficult to build, easy to lose, and even harder to regain. Children and young people deserve a safe space to discuss controversial topics, and they may not all feel comfortable doing so with their parents or carers. Regardless of the educator's personal perspectives on a subject, they have a responsibility towards their students to provide a trusted environment in which to learn.

Children's perspectives

The previous section examined the perspective of parents and how they responded to the perceived lack of support from their wider community in helping prepare children for digital citizenship. However, children were also influenced by this perceived lack of support. This section will argue that children's actions to protect themselves online are largely influenced by the perceived lack of support from the wider community.

> **Parent 1** (mother): When, when you were doing the one on the piano the other day, you (Child) wanted me to film from an angle because you were doing it in your school uniform
> **Child** (13): I was doing it in my school uniform, I remember saying, make sure you
> **Parent 1:** take it at this angle so that you don't see the [school logo]
> **Child** (13): because that would help identify the school.
>
> Excerpt, family group interview.

Specifically, the way children were found to respond to a perceived lack of support outside of the family unit can be summed up in the following themes:

- Deliberately self-limiting behaviour online to minimize risk.
- General unwillingness to talk about difficult situations while they are happening.

- Taking whatever actions they could to hide personally identifiable information.

Child *(13): I spend a lot of time like making sure that the people I follow online are really nice people (...) it's nice to see um, you know, how different they live to where we live, and the way they live is similar to the way we live (...) these are people who I feel like are good people (...) You know, if anyone I knew or anyone I didn't know said 'oh I'm having a baby' I would say 'oh, congratulations' and I would feel really good; and I think because I had grown to familiarize myself with these people and like ... I wanted to make sure they were okay, and that, their baby, their twins, I wanted to make sure that their babies are gonna ... come out okay (...) that's just why I did it, and like I know some people get really obsessed with YouTubers and say ohmygosh you saved my life, I love you, you're great and, but I would never say I love you, I think that's way too weird, because a relationship has got to be two-sided (...) But I think that er, you know I don't have any form of relationship with them, I just ... I just think that they're inspiring people, just like there's some .... Just like following celebrities on Instagram, or ... going to a concert for a musician, or something like that, it's just kind of ... wanting to support someone. (quietly) And it's good to connect.*

Excerpt, family group interview.

Regarding support and preparation for digital citizenship, children's testimonies demonstrated an understanding that, good or bad, social media technologies are there to stay. Children were more likely to bring up the positive aspects of social media, and how it was helping them stay in touch with friends and family even before the Covid-19 lockdown, too. Additionally, children were more likely to talk about how social media helped them understand and develop empathy for people who were not like them, which is an important and crucial aspect of developing one's critical thinking and ability to engage in thoughtful debate. Unfortunately, children also noted that, aside from their parents, they did not feel like they could count on support from school or from social media platforms themselves.

Self-limiting behaviours

The first aspect of social media usage most child participants referred to was how they voluntarily limited their own interactions online. This was done both as a means of assuaging their parents' anxiety, and to increase their own sense of control of their digital environment. These behaviours varied across the cohort and examples included:

- Having a closed/private profile.
- Only talking to friends and friends-of-friends.
- Limiting how much personal information they disclosed online.
- Allowing their parents to see their social media accounts.
- Only using 'kid' platforms.
- Blocking accounts and content perceived as 'inappropriate'.
- Telling their parents if something was wrong.

What is interesting about some of these rules is their plasticity and the capacity to vary in their interpretation. For example, some of the children considered not using their real names online as sufficient for limiting personal information shared; others went further, not sharing information about their parents or siblings, or editing out their school pictures or school insignia on their uniforms in clips they posted online.

Another example of how those rules were up to interpretation could be seen in what children considered to be 'kids' platforms. Younger children (aged 9–12) perceived platforms and applications like Facebook, Twitter and Instagram to be 'for adults', while other platforms like Snapchat, Minecraft and TikTok (previously Musical.ly) were perceived as being 'for children'. However, platforms like YouTube Kids were considered to be 'for babies', which suggests the distinction is more about which platforms are popular with friends rather than which are 'for adults'. It is worth noting, regardless of how young people chose to engage with those media, that all social media platforms mentioned have a minimum age restriction of 13. Below that age, co-operation guidelines prohibit engagement.

> **Child** *(13): (S)o it's turning off any videos about LGBT content, or um, mental health issues, or they are not on like the safe moderation [...] So of course I'm not going to turn restriction mode on, because it's the content that I want to see, and I want to be supporting these people. They can't get adverts on their things, they don't earn as much money, because YouTube thinks that anything that has the word anxiety, or depression, or bisexual, or anything in the title, that it is mature content. And it's just ... I'm just ... I'm really, really against that, so I'm not going to turn any of them on, that's just cause of my moral reasons, so ...*
>
> Excerpt, family group interview.

However, children did not respond well to what they perceived as censorship by the social media platform moderators. Indeed, participants expressly objected to censorship practices that affected minority and LGBTQIA+ creators on platforms like YouTube. While they wanted platforms to be more decisive in banning bullies or people who were otherwise inappropriate, participants felt that these platforms focused on limiting content that was not advertiser friendly. This demonstrates that children do not trust social media platforms to have their best interest at heart, and that they believe social media platforms do not use their resources in a productive manner.

It is also significant that, outside of conversations with friends and parents, the research interview seemed to be the only other space that young participants had to talk about these topics. Many of these participants had long, thoughtful answers to complicated questions, but there was a sense that they had not had a chance to fully express those opinions in other areas of their lives. To some extent, this was a product of their environment – there were no spaces in schools where they could discuss matters of digital literacy or digital citizenship. It is worth considering whether the children's own self-limiting behaviours had an impact on how much they felt they could discuss with their parents.

Unwillingness to ask for help

Family responses to risk on social media, and especially children's responses, are extremely fragmented and individualized. This fragmentation extends to the children's decision to involve their parents when a situation online became risky or otherwise vexatious.

The research project with families involved a vignette-based scenario that required participants roleplaying various digital scenarios. These scenarios ranged from the benign to more high-risk ones, and were randomized between families. Participants were given the option to 'block' the person reaching out to them, to 'go along' with the interaction, or to put the question to the group to ask for advice.

Out of 122 scenarios, 74 were offered to children. During of those scenarios, children only put a scenario to the group and asked for advice nine times. In contrast, out of the forty-eight scenarios that were put to the adults, five were referred to the group for advice. In other words, while one in eight scenarios put to the children were ones where they asked for advice, nearly one in ten scenarios put to the adults resulted in the players asking for advice, suggesting the reticence could not be explained by age alone. Younger children who did not already have much social media presence did not hesitate to ask their parents for help. Older children, who had some experience with being online, seemed more reticent. In one group, the child used a cyberbullying scenario to talk about what they perceived as an ineffectual response on the part of their school and why they did not have trust in the formal processes to resolve the situation.

Additionally, some of the participants had examples where a direct bystander intervention had resolved the situation online more effectively than trying to get support from outsiders. Indeed, one of the participants expressed frustration at how slow the platforms responded to complaints, even when adults got involved.

> **Child** *(13): Um, I don't enjoy the aspects of having um ... I want to add somebody tried to follow me, and I don't like the aspect of ... without ... like ... the ... if you report something, it doesn't like you don't get a face to face conversation with somebody, you go in and, 'this is what they've done, can you ... help us ... to solve that', and they just take it on, and if so many people have the same thing happening to them, then they do something about it rather than if one person has an issue with their brand of social media, they don't-, they don't take you as your own person, they take you as a group of people rather than*
> **RESEARCHER:** *hmmm*
> **Child** *(13): and also, I'd rather have them have like age categories, kind of like cause I don't want people ... that are not my age, or over my age to follow me or to even ... look at what I'm posting or anything like that, that even if it's just my profile picture, just because (pause) you don't know what people are thinking about you, especially if you ... got all these like filters on you and stuff and you can definitely not look your age and so when people who are like over your age look at you, you don't know what they're thinking and that makes me so, not scared, you know, but ...*

Excerpt, family group interview.

More than anything else, though, children's testimonials demonstrated their desire to carve out a space for themselves, to be present and seen on social media and to participate in digital citizenship. Part of that appeared to be managing their own risk and demonstrating to their parents that they can be self-sufficient online – the implication being that if they asked for help, they would be considered as less capable and thus have their autonomy and digital freedom restricted.

Educators' perspectives

The next section closely examines the perspectives expressed by educators and the challenges schools might face from their perspective when teaching children about social media technologies.

Data from gatekeeper interviews and informal conversations with education professionals on the topic of social media revealed varied opinions. Some professionals appeared to view social media the same way as participants did: as a mixture of benefits and risks that needed to be managed on a case-by-case basis. However, they nonetheless appeared to subscribe to the view that children might be too dependent on social media:

> 'I think that parents do have to exercise a responsibility (…) and there is just more options these days with social media. I know of one parent who ordered their son to remove something from Facebook I think because it was inappropriate (…) so yeah, I think the community have a responsibility'.

Excerpt, interview with the head of a community centre.

This view was supported by other gatekeepers, including teachers, librarians, church leaders, community centre staff and trustees. A common theme was that of social media as a mixed blessing. While education professionals shared the view that children should have the best experiences online, they also felt they were in a position where they could not afford to dedicate a lot of time to nuanced discussions around children's cybersecurity. In other words, while education professionals wanted to support students and their parents in a nuanced discussion about the Internet, a lack of resources and time was one of the major challenges in addressing social media in a meaningful way. This was apparent during the discussion on cyberbullying, which one teacher identified as 'a big problem for their school' in an informal conversation.

None of the gatekeepers seemed aware of cybersecurity resources such as the NSPCC's 'Share Aware' which had resources for schools. It would be interesting to see whether the new guidance issued by the Department for Education (2023) would empower educators to better engage with issues around cybersecurity.

It is important to note that cyberbullying and other types of digitally assisted abuse are just some of the issues that children and their parents face. Digital citizenship is a far more complex, far more nuanced topic and schools can provide a lot of value – not only in teaching young people about safe and effective uses of digital technologies, but also in holding space for difficult conversations that parents may not feel equipped to have at home.

However, it is important to note that the role of schools in a child's education – particularly around topics that might be considered 'family matters' – is a contentious topic, one that schools may feel ill-equipped to handle, raising further challenge for social justice and digital citizenship, and the role of educators in supporting families to navigate a rapidly evolving terrain.

Conclusion

The topic of social media is complicated and contentious for families. Parents expressed anxiety and frustration and what they perceived as unhelpful advice. Both parents and children engaged in covert or self-limiting gatekeeping behaviours to try and exercise some control over their digital environment. However, children still felt unable to talk to their parents about the parts of social media that might be a concern, and parents felt like they didn't have the tools necessary to address the conversation head on.

In such situations, schools could have a vital role to play by helping address the immediate dangers towards children and young adults online, and in educating children and young people about the fundamentals of digital citizenship.

However, teaching safe usage of social media and digital technologies is not an easy task. Educators are already faced with significant constraints of time and of resources. School budgets are stretched, and the rising cost of education creates challenges for educators. The situation is further complicated by the perception of digital literacy being perceived as a 'family matter' and may face pushback from the local community.

However, there is also a demand for level-headed, clear and helpful approaches to social media. Educators are in a unique position where they can hold space for these discussions and deliver helpful advice without singling one parent out or child. Educators can also monitor discussions and support their students with topics their students might find challenging.

Above all else, it is important to remember that social media and digital technologies in general are here to stay. Responsible digital citizenship is no longer an optional extra and therefore needs to be taught widely in education, and receive the support it deserves.

Critical reflective questions

1. When was the last time you considered you own digital footprint? Is the 'self' you present on social media reflective of your true 'self'? Why/why not?
2. When working with students and their families on matters of social media, what tone do you adopt? Do you approach the conversation from a place of fear or a place of understanding?
3. How are you working within your role and within your school to provide children and young people with useful social media skills?

References

Clapton, G., Cree, V., and Smith, M. (2013). Moral panics, claims-making and child protection in the UK. *British Journal of Social Work*. Oxford University Press, *43*(4), 803–12. doi: 10.1093/bjsw/bct061.

Crawford, A. (2019). Instagram "helped kill my daughter" – BBC News, *BBC*. Available at: https://www.bbc.co.uk/news/av/uk-46966009/instagram-helped-kill-my-daughter (accessed 22 December 2023).

Department for Education (2018). *Keeping Children Safe in Education Statutory Guidance for Schools and Colleges*. Available at: https://assets.publishing.service.gov.uk/government/uploads/system/uploads/attachment_data/file/741314/Keeping_Children_Safe_in_Education__3_September_2018_14.09.18.pdf (accessed 22 December 2023).

Department for Education (2023). Teaching online safety in schools, *gov.uk*. Available at: https://www.gov.uk/government/publications/teaching-online-safety-in-schools/teaching-online-safety-in-schools (accessed 22 December 2023).

Department for Work and Pensions (DWP) (2015). DWP actions in response to the government digital strategy, corporate report, *gov.uk*. Available at: https://www.gov.uk/government/publications/department-for-work-and-pensions-government-digital-strategy-actions/dwps-actions-in-response-to-the-government-digital-strategy accessed 22 December 2023.

Driver and Vehicle Licensing Agency (DVLA) (2015). Taking control of our future – we're driving transformation, *Inside the DVLA Blog*. Available at: https://insidedvla.blog.gov.uk/2015/09/29/taking-control-of-our-future-were-driving-transformation/ (accessed 22 December 2023).

His Majesty's Revenue and Customs (HMRC) (2015). Making tax digital, policy paper, *gov.uk*. Available at: https://webarchive.nationalarchives.gov.uk/ukgwa/20161003134753/https://www.gov.uk/government/publications/making-tax-digital (accessed 22 December 2023).

Morgan, N. and Department for Education (2015). *New Measures to Keep Children Safe Online at School and at Home – GOV.UK, UK Government*. Available at: https://www.gov.uk/government/news/new-measures-to-keep-children-safe-online-at-school-and-at-home (accessed 22 December 2023).

Mythen, G. (2004). *Ulrich Beck: A Critical Introduction to the Risk Society*. London: Pluto Press.

NSPCC (2015). *Share Aware: Help Your Child Stay Safe on Social Networks | NSPCC, NSPCC*. Available at: https://www.nspcc.org.uk/preventing-abuse/keeping-children-safe/share-aware/ (accessed 22 December 2023).

Online Safety Act (2023). Available at: https://bills.parliament.uk/bills/3137 (accessed 14 May 2024).

Pidd, H. (2024). "I want to make things better": Esther Ghey on her hopes for online reform, *The Guardian*. Available at: https://www.theguardian.com/media/2024/feb/12/i-want-to-make-things-better-esther-ghey-on-her-hopes-for-online-reform (accessed 14 May 2024).

Pidd, H. (2024). Teenagers jailed for "exceptionally brutal" murder of Brianna Ghey, *The Guardian*. Available at: https://www.theguardian.com/uk-news/2024/feb/02/brianna-ghey-murderers-named-sentenced-to-life-in-prison (accessed 14 May 2024).

Rahman-Jones, I. and Vallance, C. (2023). Online safety bill: Divisive internet rules become law, *BBC*. Available at: https://www.bbc.com/news/technology-67221691 (accessed 14 May 2024).

Sorbet, A. (2023). Digital-first banking transformation: An innovative approach by financial sector, *Finante*. Available at: https://finanteq.com/blog/fintech-trends/digital-first-banking-transformation-an-innovative-approach-by-financial-sector/ (accessed 22 December 2023).

Valcke, M., Valcke, M., Bonte, S., De Wever, B. and Rots, I. (2010). Internet parenting styles and the impact on internet use of primary school children. *Computers and Education,* 55(2), 454–64. doi: 10.1016/j.compedu.2010.02.009.

Wilkinson, I. (2001). *Anxiety in a Risk Society*. London: Routledge.

The Expansion of Digital Technology in the Post-Compulsory Sector and Factors Which Influence Students' Engagement with Using Technologies: Are We Swimming or Sinking in Today's Information Age?

Theresa Marriott

Introduction

The rapid advancement of technology over the last twenty years has revolutionized, and continues to revolutionize, all aspects of society. Education is no outsider to this with devices, digital tools, platforms and software/hardware gradually becoming firmly embedded into learning environments across all educational sectors. As this evolves further, the demand for capable and competent individuals becomes more apparent with the technological trajectory moving so rapidly. Due to this, the gap between the technology and the users is now widening; technology is developing more quickly than we can train individuals to use it creating a sizeable issue for both national and local governments in how to tackle this shortfall.

Governments are being proactive in strategizing and implementing plans to try and minimize the issue but there are several additional factors which stand in the way of this being fully realized. The main two factors are digital poverty and its relationship to digital skills and capabilities. Both Covid and the cost of living crisis in the UK have only served to expand the difficulties of individuals' ability to afford technology and use it proficiently; this provides strong links with individual beliefs about digital abilities as a consequence. Digital beliefs can be so strong in individuals that it can affect individual abilities to engage with technology and develop digital skills; this form of impostership can be attributed to a specific type of Imposter Syndrome which can be defined as Digital Imposter Syndrome. This chapter will review the evolving role of technology in education for workplace digital skills and the implications on individuals as a result of living through a progressive digital age.

The rise in technology and requirement for digital skills

The rise of technology in education represents a transformative shift in pedagogical practices and learning environments, driven by the integration of digital tools, platforms and resources into educational settings. This phenomenon reflects a broader societal trend towards digitalization and technological advancement, with education emerging as a key domain for supplying graduates ready for a more digitized and technologically advanced workforce on a global scale. This combined with places of work being on a much wider scale since the Covid pandemic, and the integration of working and studying from home as a 'new norm' has meant that access to technology and digital skills are now more apparent and in demand than they have ever been previously. UNESCO (2018a: 2) defines these skills as moving from what was previously 'optional' to 'critical' as the majority of workplaces now have the use of technology as a normal part of the job role requirements and for those countries who are digitally poor, this is having an economic impact on employers and employees at a national level (UNESCO, 2018b). In a UK setting, over a million households have no access to the Internet at home; this is set to rise even further as many cannot afford to pay for household Internet access at home due to consistent rising costs of living. This means that millions of individuals in the future will not be able to carry out basic tasks using the Internet thus creating a significant skills gap in the next decade and widening the digital divide even further (Ofcom, 2022; Communications and Digital Committee, 2023).

Baseline digital skills for work and study are no longer considered to be optional by the UK Government, educational institutions and the majority of workplaces (Department for Digital, Culture, Media & Sport, 2019; Department for Education, 2019). Governmental research has highlighted the ever-growing urgency for individuals to be digitally competent and confident at a foundational level to ensure employers have staff in place for national economic stability. The rate of technological growth has outstripped the labour market in terms of individuals having enough digital skills to be able to work proficiently in the majority of sectors. Additionally, prosperity is linked to knowledge, experience and skills across all sectors therefore the current workforce and prospective employees require intervention upskilling to raise aspirations and increase personal income.

Digital skills have become a universal requirement, a passport to greater options and opportunities. In the UK alone, it is predicted that by 2030 there will be 5 million workers who will be severely lacking in digital skills at a cost to the economy of £63 billion per year. If no action is taken, this is set to grow even further (Communications and Digital Committee, 2023). It is also recognized globally as a serious issue with catastrophic consequences, The World Economic Forum (2023) estimates that 85 million jobs could lie vacant by 2030 due to the digital skills shortage.

With the current governmental focus on the year 2030 across the globe, an additional issue has steadily evolved and become recognized; entering and moving from the fourth to the fifth industrial revolution and what this could entail (World Economic Forum, 2016). Due to the rapidity of technological advances, the distance between industrial revolutions is now likely to be much shorter than previous industrial revolutions, particularly with the invention and implementation of Artificial Intelligence (AI) at a momentous pace (Schwab, 2017). A natural consequence of this is an uncertainty of what the workplace and jobs within it will look like; how can we train individuals for jobs that do not yet exist? (Taylor and Rafferty, 2023). Inevitably this is posing a problem across the globe although one universal concept pervades; everyone needs to possess foundational digital skills at the very least by 2030 as no sector will remain untouched by digital innovation (Department for Digital, Culture, Media & Sport, 2019).

Whilst the rise of technology in education presents numerous benefits and opportunities, it also poses challenges related to digital equity, effective integration and pedagogical alignment. As technology continues to evolve and shape the educational landscape, educators, policymakers and stakeholders (including students) must navigate these complexities in order to harness the transformative potential of technology in advancing learning outcomes and preparing individuals for success in the digital age.

Factors which impact digital capabilities

We know how students learn has changed to become more focused upon using technology as a fundamental tool to engage with their learning (Jisc, 2022); Covid amplified this greatly and enforced a new way of learning which may not feel comfortable for those who deliver it or access it. Post pandemic, technology and digital skills have come to be considered the 'new norm' but in some respects this fails to acknowledge the longstanding underlying issue of those who do not have easy access to technology and the Internet which may also impact on digital capabilities (Office for Students, 2020; World Economic Forum, 2021). This particular group within the population, who are digitally excluded, have been recognized as falling into three main categories by Ofcom (2022); the communications regulator in the UK and further revised by the Communications and Digital Committee in 2023. These categories are fluid and can blend into one another.

> **affordability** – those who struggle to afford access to internet packages or suitable devices, and so either go without it or experience other financial strains to retain access; **access** – those who do not have an adequate internet connection at home or elsewhere (for a variety of reasons, not just affordability); and **ability** – those who lack the digital skills and/or confidence to navigate the online environment safely and knowledgeably, or face barriers related to disability. (Communications and Digital Committee, 2023: 8)

The issue of digital poverty and corresponding digital divide, which widens the higher the level of poverty exists, is a growing concern. Affordability, access and ability are all standalone issues within themselves which require targeted interventions. Both nationally and globally developed nations are implementing strategies and releasing funding to ensure that the digital skills gap reduces before 2030 based upon these three key areas. Digital poverty serves to exacerbate existing problems and further reduce an individual's contribution to society; the risk of individuals being left behind as a result of lack of access to technology and resources are sadly increased.

It is surprising that in developed economies, many individuals are unable to afford basic technology and connectivity due to financial limitations or locality (Office for Students, 2020). The issue is further amplified if we consider that more and more devices and systems are now either entirely reliant or partially reliant on having Internet connectivity (World Economic Forum, 2021; Ofcom, 2022). In order to provide a more equitable provision, the preceding UK Conservative Government were working with Internet providers, public services and community organizations to ensure that access to technology and the Internet is available to as many people as possible

(Department for Digital, Culture, Media & Sport, 2022; Communications and Digital Committee, 2023). This forms part of a much wider plan to upskill the nation (Department for Digital, Culture, Media & Sport, 2019).

It is easy to see that individuals can very quickly become part of a digitally poor and excluded micro population as a result which inevitably impacts on their lives. The concern is so great that Article 19 of the Universal Declaration of Human Rights, 'Everyone has the right to freedom of opinion and expression; this right includes freedom to hold opinions without interference and to seek, receive and impart information and ideas through any media and regardless of frontiers'. United Nations (2024: 1) has adopted a resolution for the 'the promotion, protection and enjoyment of human rights on the Internet' (Article 19, 2021: 1). Many nations are now questioning and considering if access to the Internet is a basic human right in response to global issues with technology growth and widespread low digital capabilities.

Digital personalities and categories

In today's education landscape, understanding the diverse digital identities of individuals is crucial for effective teaching, learning and assessment. Since the surge in technological developments post-90s, there has been wide interest in the categorization of individuals in respect of their technological and digital competencies. Initially, Prensky (2001: 1) identified that:

> Today's students have not just changed incrementally from those of the past, nor simply changed their slang, clothes, body adornments, or styles, as has happened between generations previously. A really big discontinuity has taken place. One might even call it a 'singularity' – an event which changes things so fundamentally that there is absolutely no going back. This so-called 'singularity' is the arrival and rapid dissemination of digital technology in the last decades of the 20th century.

The rapid dissemination he discusses, leads him to identify a population split in the way individuals process and comprehend information termed as groups of 'Digital Natives' and 'Digital Immigrants'. Simply, Digital Natives are natural speakers of digital language and born into technology use whereas Digital Immigrants try to adapt to the new digital language and technology due to not being born into it; essentially playing catch up to the digital world.

Following on from this, the most commonly referred to, and popularized in mainstream media, are the widely known Generation X, Y and Z categories covering specific time frames and aligned with digital and technological developments worldwide from the mid-1960s onwards (Wolstencroft and

Table 2 Generation Categories and Digital Capabilities (Prensky, 2001; Wolstencroft and Zhou, 2020)

Digital Generation	Years of Birth	Features
X	1965–1980	Present for the birth of new technologies and developments. Used to ways of working and living without technology and the requirement for digital competence. For this reason there may be a delay in engaging with it and they may be reluctant/sceptical to do so.
Y	1981–2000	There for the development of technology and constant change; resilient and adaptable as they have lived through a proliferation of new technology and its implementation into life.
Z	2001– current	Born into technology and digital literacies; digital natives. Fluently use technology and have high demands in its use but have low attention spans.

Zhou, 2020) (Table 2). These distinct digital identities, or personalities, offer a lens to view an individual's approach to technology and how they interact with it, but what must be considered is that technology has moved at such a monumental pace in the last ten years that the application of categorization to individuals is becoming much more difficult in terms of assuming an individual's digital approaches and capabilities.

Typically, Generation Z are considered to be the generation for whom technology is an embedded part of their lives with an assumption that because of this, their use of technology will be fluid and seamless. What lacks consideration is what specific technology they are fluid and seamless with, as Generation Z were born into the era of advancing mobile phone technology and social media; this does not indicate that they are proficient in the use of all technology, just specific items. Herein lies the problem; we currently have multiple generations using technology either by choice or through enforcement, each having different approaches to how they perceive and use it without being entirely based upon their age. Using a restrictive generational guide to assess an individual's approach, confidence and capabilities in terms of the use of technology can never accurately represent each individual if we also take into consideration their personal circumstances such as financial status, locality, learning abilities and disabilities.

In 2022, a King's College study surveyed almost 3,000 people aged 18+ on how people focus and live in the modern information environment, specifically in terms of using technology. The study suggested more appropriate labels to attribute to users of technology rather than generational labels, such as Generation X, Y and Z or Digital Natives/Digital Immigrants, in light of the rapid advancements of technology over the last ten years (Table 3).

These new digital 'types' discount age and instead focus on individual approaches, grounded in digital beliefs which could be more representative of technology users as a whole. We must remember, that just as personal identities and beliefs are multi-faceted and complex, so too are digital identities. By trying to understand what shapes digital beliefs and identities, there are opportunities to foster a positive navigation through the complexities of a digital world. Additionally, accepting and embracing the diversity of digital identities serves to enrich both educators' and students' experiences in ever-changing learning environments.

Table 3 Generation Categories and Digital Capabilities (King's College London, 2022: 1)

Digital Types	Features
Positive Multi-screeners	Highly engaged users; keen information searchers; relaxed in terms of managing information; some concerns about attention spans but see lots of benefits from the wealth of information available. This is the biggest group in the population, confirming that individuals do not all see technology trends as negative.
Stressed Tech Addicts	Feel overloaded with information; highly engaged users that see benefits in having these information sources, particularly social media; but the greatest concern about what it is doing to attention spans, and believe it is causing the end of deeper thinking.
Overloaded Sceptics	Feel overloaded with information; very concerned about decreasing attention spans and the loss of deeper thinking – but much more negative about the value social media brings, compared with the 'stressed tech addicts'.
Disengaged and Untroubled	Uninterested in searching for information; no concerns expressed about attention spans or the amount of information; and barely notice any signs of an 'attention war'.

Imposter Syndrome and its relationship to Digital Imposter Syndrome

The term 'Imposter Syndrome' is now well recognized and accepted as a behaviour that many people can identify with regardless of knowledge, age and biological sex. Researched heavily in the 1970s by Pauline Rose Clance and Suzanne Imes, the female researchers involved wanted to investigate why high achieving women in particular felt 'fake' and doubted their own abilities which in turn affected their performance and ability to progress in the workplace (Clance and Imes, 1978). As a result of identifying imposter beliefs within the female research participants, Clance and Imes identified key indicators for Imposter Syndrome and suggested a variety of Gestalt based strategies to use to develop confidence in abilities in female individuals. Clance (1985) went on to further develop the Imposter Phenomenon Scale which provided additional characteristics of Imposter Syndrome and indicators of the scale individuals were suffering from it (Table 4).

As we move into the current day, Clance and Imes foundational work has been built upon although the same key indicators of Imposter Syndrome

Table 4 Key Indicators of Imposter Syndrome (Phenomenon) Based on Clance's Imposter Phenomenon (IP) Scale (Clance, 1985: 20–2)

Lacks confidence in abilities despite no evidence of previous failure.
Pretends to be confident despite feeling unconfident.
Avoids evaluations and feedback.
Finds it hard to accept praise and live up to expectations afterwards.
Success is considered a fluke, just luck, or a one off.
Worries that you may be 'found out' for not being capable or lacking knowledge.
Reflects on mistakes rather than successes.
Focuses on perfectionism and is critical of oneself.
Believes success is likely to be a mistake and cannot be repeated.
Struggles with accepting compliments and dismisses praise.
Feels they should have achieved more.
Worries about failure when trying new things.
Compares themselves unfavourably to others.

still remain relevant and applicable. An interesting development over the last twenty years is the expanded inclusion of all sexes, and the recognition that Imposter Syndrome exists outside of the workplace; it can now occur in everyday life and can happen to anyone at any time. Students are a particular area of growth for feelings of impostership. The majority of universities now have specific support pages to reassure and try to combat this, specifically for first year and returning to study students. A recent developing factor for student impostership are those going into higher education post-Covid. Through experiencing online learning for a high level of their studies, and gaining awards from teacher assessed work, these students are more likely to feel fraudulent in their undergraduate studies and pose a high risk of drop out (Henry, 2021; Dickenson, 2023).

How, therefore, do these issues relate to digital poverty and the digital divide? If you are disadvantaged through access to technology and the Internet, then exposure to them is reduced. Reduced exposure and use of technology is far more likely to impact on confidence when using them when the opportunities arise (Communications and Digital Committee, 2023). Digital exclusion based on own beliefs not only impacts on home life but also work life and studies, and the opportunities available to individuals as a result. This lack of confidence suggests that another form of Imposter Syndrome has developed: Digital Imposter Syndrome.

Digital Imposter Syndrome appears to have the same impostership beliefs (Clance and Imes, 1978), but is linked to an individual's perception of their digital capabilities which can hinder engagement and success in the short and long term. This can play out in a number of ways such as: an unwillingness to try out new things, barriers are put in place to circumnavigate what is being asked, there are high chances of activities being abandoned, and individuals distance themselves from others and the work required. If not identified in a timely manner, these behaviours can then go on to severely limit an individual's ability to complete technology based tasks and form relationships with others in the same learning environment which then creates feelings of exclusion and isolation, serving to compound the digital divide even more. In extreme circumstances this could lead to individuals retreating completely and withdrawing from their commitments such as studies or work due to strong feelings of Digital Impostership which sufferers feel that they cannot overcome.

Based upon personal practice from working in several universities, there appears to be some commonalities amongst staff and students in terms of the issues they experience when asked to undertake digital tasks as part of their work and studies (Table 5). These issues and behaviours have been collated below and indicate that both staff and students have similar fears about similar things; these were predictably more evident during Covid.

Table 5 List of Common Issues and Behaviours Arising from Individuals Being Asked to Carry Out Digital Tasks

Feel out of their depth when using technology they are unfamiliar with.

A previous negative experience may impact on engagement and continuity with doing something new/different.

Anxiety is caused when changes to routine processes and methods are required such as asking for a narrated presentation instead of a face-to-face presentation.

A reluctance to try out a different way of doing something when an established method has already been put in place that seems viable.

Unrealistic individual expectations may develop due to comparisons with other individuals' successes and failures.

Individuals may go into complete communication shut down and retreat in order to avoid doing what is asked of them.

Group think may develop – one person can't do it therefore no one can; group behaviour can then be challenging and oppositional, blocking tactics may be deployed.

Feel that usual access to support mechanisms may be out of reach when they need it due to being off campus when studying or distance learning.

External factors may amplify worries about continuation of learning in the current climate e.g.: cost of living, family and caring responsibilities, additional learning needs, disabilities.

Strategies to support individuals with Digital Imposter Syndrome including artificial intelligence (AI)

Initially the approach taken is highly valuable and high stakes when working with those showing signs of Digital Impostership. Humans are complex beings and how the individual got to that point and formed their beliefs is highly personal; no one person is the same when it comes to how their Digital impostership manifests and where it originated from. Further, 'saving face' is key; it is very difficult to admit that you believe you cannot do something or are fearful, which is why a holistic and enabling approach is the most thoughtful, appropriate and empowering (Whitmore, 2017).

It is important to build relationships and instil confidence right at the start through reassurance and clear open communication. The individual should feel confident that you can metaphorically 'catch them if they fall' so that they know it is ok to try, and to make mistakes. Usually making mistakes highlights inadequacies therefore this should be downplayed and the focus should be on the 'trying' part as part of the growth process (Dweck, 2012). Utilizing an empowering method of demonstration first then independent working offers individuals to try out things in a safe space and fosters self-confidence. It is crucial that ego is preserved throughout and to remember that there will be some occasions where you are learning together due to rapid digital advances. In essence, modern coaching and mentoring methods work very well when supporting individuals with Digital Imposter Syndrome.

The rise of artificial intelligence

Artificial Intelligence technologies have become increasingly pervasive across a high level of industries and society, and they show no signs of slowing down. Across the world, nations are setting up AI programs and producing strategies to support AI enabled economies as there is recognition that employers will start to experience technical skills gaps related to AI expertise in the short-term future (HM Government, 2021; Office for Artificial Intelligence, 2021). As well as their use in industry, they have a key role in supporting individuals in education in a variety of ways for both education sector workers and students alike, particularly in reducing workload and supporting individuals to build and develop information.

A key consideration for students is AI's ability to plug and fill gaps in terms of both academic knowledge and digital knowledge, which can suppress feelings of lack of knowledge and digital impostership in students. Although this aspect of using AI is highly beneficial for students, it does come with its own set of issues within education; mainly due to the fine line it holds between originality of individual work produced and accuracy of content (Department for Education, 2023a, b). One of its main benefits is the reduction of workload, which for those who have limited access to technology and the Internet can act as an appealing draw. The recommendations for educators moving forward, and in terms of diversity and inclusion, is to educate and inform students on how to make the most of technology and tools when available, and reinforce the parameters of what is and is not acceptable when using AI for academic work. Just as search engines are used proliferously to find out information, it is likely that AI will be used in the same way too in the future.

Now the initial shock of a new form of knowledge creation and production has settled down, governments, industries and organizations are now investigating how AI will affect the economies and the individuals within it (Office for Artificial Intelligence, 2021). It is crucial to remember that

AI cannot perform the same work as a human in terms of judgement and knowledge expertise but it is now more likely to be used, and eventually embedded, into everyday working practices and education; it is here to stay.

> **Pause for thought: Vignette – Who speaks digital?**

As an educator, teaching theories, models and ideologies form a considerable part of the 'knowledge' toolkit for planning teaching, learning and assessment. There are several theories on how individuals approach and engage with technology, the most prevalent being Prensky's (2001) metaphorical work on Digital Natives (speakers of digital language and its use) and Digital Immigrants (digital language learned later in life) which then developed into the Generation X, Y and Z categories that are familiar today.

Reflection

Consider the two perspectives to view the foundational Digital Natives and Digital Immigrants categories from: as an educator, and as a student. As an educator, there's an expectation that students born into a digital age (Generation Y and Z) possess digital knowledge and capabilities which are naturally inherent; their experiences are built around technology and they feel comfortable with it; they are Digital Natives (Prensky, 2001). As a student born into Generation Y and Z, they mostly have had consistent access to technology and believe they are experienced users of it; again, identifying as Digital Natives. For educators, students born into Generation X and prior to that, are classed as Digital Immigrants; more wary of technology and having to learn a new 'digital' language. It can be argued that this classification of digital personalities falls short in several ways. For instance, many Generation Y and Z (Digital Natives) are proficient in using their phones and tablets for social media but are wholly unprepared and digitally unconfident when using technology for academia; it's an area of work they are unfamiliar with and often feel overwhelmed at having to learn subject knowledge in addition to learning digital skills, particularly for assessments such as PowerPoints. In the case of Generation X (Digital Immigrants), they have chosen to learn or ignore use of technology but often find themselves in the same position as the Digital Natives; overwhelmed in academia at learning subject knowledge and digital competencies at the same time. Inevitably, regardless of age or generation, students struggle with different types of digital skills and competencies; this is before other aspects are taken into consideration such as socio-economic status, learning abilities and existing knowledge and experiences.

Many students will require additional support with their digital skills during studies irrespective of age. A significant number will also require support to develop their digital capabilities for academia. There is a growing recognition that technology and digital skills are becoming firmly embedded into curricula at all levels but not all providers have the ability or resource to be able to support the training or development for this. When designing learning, particularly for assessment, if technology and digital skills are required then a key area to review is how the students will achieve this and who will support it? Expecting students to demonstrate knowledge and understanding using technology and digital skills will require additional scaffolding and support in some form and should be planned for accordingly.

Conclusion

The mass cultivation of personal digital skills is no longer an optional requirement for the majority of society. Digital skills have become indispensable in the technology driven world and are becoming essential for more prosperous life chances. As technology continues to grow, we too must grow with it or be left behind and be excluded from many aspects of a growing digital economy. By equipping individuals with these skills, they are becoming empowered and adaptable to changing technological landscapes. As a nation, investing in building and developing digital competencies fosters economic growth, innovation and social inclusion; bridging the digital divide and unlocking opportunities that may not have been accessible before. Embracing digital change alongside our own digital beliefs can be achieved with the right approach to developing personal digital skills; acknowledging that we are all individuals with our own hopes and fears regarding technological change and how we move within it.

The exponential growth of AI in the last three years provides us with countless opportunities to revolutionize all industry and public sectors; education being one of the key areas to benefit. It is essential to approach it with careful consideration to ensure that it enhances rather than undermines the sector and educational outcomes. AI is currently the biggest revolutionary aspect within all sectors, particularly education, and instigated the chapter title: are we swimming or sinking in today's information age? It would appear that both as a nation and globally we are doing both at the same time as we try to unanimously wade through the water of a technological tidal wave.

Critical reflective questions

1. Consider if age always equates with digital competence, i.e.: if you are young you are good at using technology and if you are old you are not good at using technology. What issues could arise with this way of thinking?
2. Are digital assumptions being made within education and academic practice for both educators and students?
3. Consider if the categories in the King's College study provide an accurate representation of today's population in terms of digital approaches and capabilities?
4. What could be the long-term consequences of ignoring digital poverty on economic development and social mobility?
5. How could Digital Imposter Syndrome be fully mitigated in a learning environment? Is this possible at an individual level in education?
6. Consider if there are specific cultural or societal factors that influence the experience and expression of Digital Imposter Syndrome in individuals.
7. Could AI be a helpful solution or hindrance for those with Digital Imposter Syndrome?

References

Article 19 (2021). *UN: Human Rights Council Adopts Resolution on Human Rights on the Internet*. Available at: https://www.article19.org/resources/un-human-rights-council-adopts-resolution-on-human-rights-on-the-internet/.

Clance, P. R. (1985). *The Imposter Phenomenon: When Success Makes You Feel Like a Fake*. Toronto: Bantam Books.

Clance, P. R. (2013). *Imposter Phenomenon*. Available at: https://www.paulineroseclance.com/impostor_phenomenon.html.

Clance, P. R. and Imes, S. (1978). The imposter phenomenon in high achieving women: Dynamics and therapeutic intervention. *Psychotherapy Theory, Research and Practice*, *15*(3), 241–7.

Communications and Digital Committee (2023). *Digital Exclusion (HL Paper 219)*. Available at: https://publications.parliament.uk/pa/ld5803/ldselect/ldcomm/219/219.pdf.

Department for Digital, Culture, Media & Sport (2019). *No Longer Optional: Employer Demand for Digital Skills*. Available at: https://assets.publishing.service.gov.uk/media/5cfe713fed915d097daca4b5/No_Longer_Optional_Employer_Demand_for_Digital_Skills.pdf.

Department for Digital, Culture, Media & Sport (2022). *Policy Paper: UK's Digital Strategy*. Available at: https://www.gov.uk/government/publications/uks-digital-strategy.

Department for Education (2019). *Guidance: Essential Digital Skills Framework*. Available at: https://www.gov.uk/government/publications/essential-digital-skills-framework/essential-digital-skills-framework#digital-foundation-skills.

Department for Education (2023a). *New Drive to Better Understand the Role of AI in Education*. Available at: https://www.gov.uk/government/news/new-drive-to-better-understand-the-role-of-ai-in-education.

Department for Education (2023b). *Generative Artificial Intelligence (AI) in Education*. Available at: https://www.gov.uk/government/publications/generative-artificial-intelligence-in-education.

Dickenson, J. (2023). *WonkHE: Are Students Dropping Out because Universities Admitted Them to Courses They Can't Do?* Available at: https://wonkhe.com/wonk-corner/are-students-dropping-out-because-universities-admitted-them-to-courses-they-cant-do/.

Dweck, C. S. (2012). *Mindset: How You Can Fulfil Your Potential*. New York: Ballantine Books.

Henry, J. (2021). *The Guardian: Britain's Covid-Era University Students May Suffer 'Impostor Syndrome'*. Available at: https://www.theguardian.com/education/2021/sep/25/britain-covid-era-university-students-impostor-syndrome-a-level-exams-undergraduates.

HM Government (2021). *National AI Strategy*. Available at: https://assets.publishing.service.gov.uk/media/614db4d1e90e077a2cbdf3c4/National_AI_Strategy_-_PDF_version.pdf.

Jisc (2022). *Student Digital Experience Insights Survey 2021/22: UK Higher Education(HE) Survey Findings*. Available at: https://repository.jisc.ac.uk/8850/1/2022-07%20%28iDFltdP024.11%29%20DEI%20HE%20%26%20FE%20Reports%202022%20%28HE%29%20v1-05.pdf.

King's College London (2022). *Are Attention Spans Really Collapsing? Data Shows UK Public Are Worried – But Also See Benefits from Technology*. Available at: https://www.kcl.ac.uk/news/are-attention-spans-really-collapsing-data-shows-uk-public-are-worried-but-also-see-benefits-from-technology.

Ofcom (2022). *Digital Exclusion: A Review of Ofcom's Research on Digital Exclusion among Adults in the UK*. Available at: https://www.ofcom.org.uk/__data/assets/pdf_file/0022/234364/digital-exclusion-review-2022.pdf.

Office for Artificial Intelligence (2021). *Research and Analysis: 9 Key Findings from Understanding the UK AI Labour Market: 2020 Report*. Available at: https://www.gov.uk/government/publications/understanding-the-uk-ai-labour-market-2020/9-key-findings-from-understanding-the-uk-ai-labour-market-2020-report.

Office for Students (2020). *'Digital Poverty' Risks Leaving Students Behind*. Available at: https://www.officeforstudents.org.uk/news-blog-and-events/press-and-media/digital-poverty-risks-leaving-students-behind/#:~:text=The%20ability%20of%20students%20to,teaching%20and%20learning%20is%20launched..

Prensky, M. (2001). Digital natives, digital immigrants. *On the Horizon*, 9(5), 1–6.

Schwab, K. (2017). *The Fourth Industrial Revolution*. London: Penguin Books.

Taylor, A. and Rafferty, V. (2023). *Times Higher Education: Training Students for Jobs That Do Not Exist Yet*. Available at: https://www.timeshighereducation.com/campus/training-students-jobs-do-not-exist-yet.

UNESCO (2018a). *Skills for a Connected World: Concept Note*. Available at: https://en.unesco.org/sites/default/files/unesco-mlw2018-concept-note-en.pdf.

UNESCO (2018b). *A Global Framework of Reference on Digital Literacy Skills for Indicator 4.4.2*. Available at: https://uis.unesco.org/sites/default/files/documents/ip51-global-framework-reference-digital-literacy-skills-2018-en.pdf.

United Nations (2024). *Universal Declaration of Human Rights*. Available at: https://www.un.org/en/about-us/universal-declaration-of-human-rights.

White, D. S. and Le Cornu, A. (2011). Visitors and residents: A new typology for online engagement. *First Monday*, *16*(9).

Whitmore, J. (2017). *Coaching for Performance: The Principles and Practice of Coaching and Leadership*. Boston, MA: Nicholas Brealey Publishing.

Wolstencroft, P. and Zhou, X. (2020). The Digital Literacy Myth: Not All Are Natives. Available at: https://www.advance-he.ac.uk/news-and-views/The-Digital-Literacy-Myth.

World Economic Forum (2016). *The Fourth Industrial Revolution: What It Means, How to Respond*. Available at: https://www.weforum.org/agenda/2016/01/the-fourth-industrial-revolution-what-it-means-and-how-to-respond/.

World Economic Forum (2021). *COVID-19 Exposed the Digital Divide: Here's How We Can Close It*. Available at: https://www.weforum.org/agenda/2021/01/covid-digital-divide-learning-education/.

World Economic Forum (2023). *Forum Institutional: 5 Ways We Can Develop the Digital Skills Our Economy Needs*. Available at: https://www.weforum.org/agenda/2023/01/5-ways-develop-digital-skills-davos2023/.

Conclusions and Key Messages for Educators

Sheine Peart

Introduction

By drawing examples from different sectors, this book has demonstrated how social justice issues matter to all educators and has shown how practitioners are recognizing, confronting and accommodating these issues to continue to provide the best possible educational experience for all in education. As communities accessing education continue to diversify and as practitioners are arriving with skill sets developed in many different settings, new strategies and approaches are demanded to meet these changing needs. This text has provided examples of the various ways in which different settings are creating and developing new methods to work with and through these challenges as well as exploring opportunities to work differently. Education has changed significantly and continues to evolve in a variety of predicted and unpredicted ways. Through examining how theory relates to practise and by encouraging readers to apply their learning to their individual and organizational contexts, the text has tackled engagement with social justice at a more personal level by questioning how practitioners fulfil their responsibilities in their daily working lives. This book has suggested how some of these changes might be managed and how educators can, driven by a commitment to social justice, continue to embed more relevant, responsive practices into their roles and avoid adopting an easy 'one-size-fits-all' model.

Key messages

Education is dynamic and is impacted by broader societal and governmental actions and changing learner populations. Educators are contractually obliged to meet the needs of all learners and are tasked with to making real successive government promises that education will provide a comprehensive service capable of meeting divergent and diverse student needs. Educators need to seize this challenge and through their agency and local knowledge, take the opportunity to shape and form policy, creating solutions and providing options which respond to differing needs. By identifying new approaches and showcasing best practice which promotes equality and challenges negative discrimination, education can make real differences to the lives of individuals, settings and whole communities. Informed by a commitment to social justice and through encouraging the active engagement of the wider learning community, education can change the way it works so that it improves outcomes and enhances the lives and life chances of all.

This means settings need to have a clear understanding of the moral and ethical obligations they have towards learners and for setting staff. In working to achieve social justice, it is important to recognize that:

1. Social justice needs to be part of every education setting and all educators' professional and personal DNA. Social justice is the cornerstone of a fair and equitable education system and the constant challenge for all in education is how to protect, preserve and promote social justice. Social justice practice must be embedded in every aspect of work and provide learners with the opportunities and support needed to become independent learners with a clear understanding of their own agency.

2. Education settings need to encourage staff to think creatively and provide or develop resources which support learners to engage and participate. This requires an acute understanding of inclusion and a commitment to embed inclusive practice throughout the organization. The continuing fragmentation of education where practitioners are confined to isolated silos and lack the opportunity to work and be with others threatens the capacity to remain alert to wider social issues and mindful of the ways we engage with others.

3. In unsettled and unsettling times, which have witnessed policy withdrawals and reversals, coupled with reductions in funding, it is incumbent on individuals to have a clear sense of self, personal values and individual capacity to impact and affect change. By having this understanding educators can map a way forward, within existing constraints, which celebrates social justice.

4. Educators need to, and can, decide to assume responsibility and act with integrity and continue to work for change which embeds and promotes inclusion.

What happens next?

'Education is a key site for struggles over quality and justice' (Benjamin and Emejulu, 2012: 33), therefore educators need to develop strategies which continue to make social justice a priority and reality for all learners in all settings. In cost-conscious environments, where the focus can sometimes be on price rather than quality or equity, it may be challenging for organizations to consistently remember the core values of collaboration and mutuality that underpin education and it may be expedient and simpler to use more easily quantifiable metrics. Educators need to look beyond reductive numerics, which may only provide a partial representation of an educational experience, and work to include the voices of all service-users to gain a fuller, more holistic understanding of the different ways groups perceive, receive and experience education. By incorporating diverse voices settings can show they value and respect wider community views and are genuinely willing to engage with partners to create a fairer, more equal system where everyone can realize their potential.

Social justice is predicated on an acceptance that, given the opportunity, learners and staff are capable of making 'good choices for themselves' (Wolf, 2010: 21). As change brings new opportunities, educators need to be willing to take risks, share decision making and learn from other settings and practitioners. To ensure that all users continue to benefit, social justice must remain as the bedrock of education and educators need to challenge 'the stereotypical view' (Peart, 2013: 120) which may curtail opportunities and to work in a way that opens horizons rather than compelling students and staff 'to make certain typical choices' (Peart, 2013: 121). Social justice does not mean granting special favours to any group, rather it is establishing a culture which enables all to participate and engage on an equal footing with their peers, underpinned by relevant, timely support and is achieved by the combined energies of the whole education community.

To ensure this effort produces optimal outcomes, organizations need to

- Develop systems to dismantle existing discriminatory practice;
- Work to create a supportive institutional culture;
- Enable staff and learners to recognize and utilize their personal agency in a positive fashion;
- Create new, relevant user-responsive support systems.

Education 'is a profession of hope. It involves the formation of each new generation into citizens of tomorrow, for a world that is not yet known. We do not know what the future will look like, but we do know that what happens …

today will help to shape it' (Wrigley, Arshad and Pratt, 2012: 209). Therefore, tutors need to 'stand up for justice and [have] the courage to speak out rather than stay silent' (Arshad, 2012: 15). Educators must recognize their ability to influence situations and to work to drive the changes they can make in themselves and in their settings those and the which in turn 'will make an important difference' (Mitchell, 2012: 19) to learners and will promote social justice for all.

Conclusion

To make real the changes needed to achieve social justice in education requires determination from all members of the learning community from holding the highest official position in the organization to those who are accorded little formal authority. These parties, and all in between, must come together recognizing that each has the capacity to influence outcomes to question and confront systems and search for new ways of working and create a connected, collaborative response. This is principal challenge to achieving social justice and all educators need to commit to 'transform learning' (Alexander and Potter, 2005: 203) so they can build a system characterized by equality and fairness. In the UK, the 2010 Equality Act was introduced to bring together all existing equality legislation into one coherent Act and to directly tackle all forms of discrimination and inequality. This legislation applies equally to organizations and to individuals.

While it is evident that 'social justice is a theory and practice that fosters democratic relations and social solidarity in order to build a society that is based on equality, liberty and respect' (Benjamin and Emejulu, 2012: 43), achieving this justice is complicated, with many different and sometimes apparently contradictory features. These challenges are being faced and worked through in different settings by whole learning communities. Social justice is not to provide an unfair advantage to any one group or individual; it is a commitment and a mechanism to try and enable everyone to participate and to achieve. It is not gifting a particular benefit to a specified group; it is removing barriers and obstacles and needs to be underpinned by an all-encompassing ethos and supported by a set of robust policies, procedures and practices. Achieving social justice requires agility, dedication and creativity and the will to want to improve the educational journey of learners and staff. Because simple, quick-fix solutions are not readily available, it remains incumbent on the education community and others committed to achieving justice to continue to develop new responses and to build a more flexible and caring education system.

References

Alexander, T., and Potter, J. (2005). Manifesto: Education for change, in T. Alexander and J. Potter (eds.), *Education for a Change*, 3–21, London: RoutlegeFalmer.

Arshad, R. (2012). Shaping practice: The impact of personal values and experiences, in R. Arshad, T. Wrigley and L. Pratt (eds.), *Social Justice Re-Examined, Dilemmas and Solutions for the Classroom Teacher*, 196–206, Stoke on Trent: Trentham Books.

Benjamin, S., and Emejulu, A. (2012). Learning about concepts, terminology and theories: From ambiguity to clarity, in R. Arshad, T. Wrigley and L. Pratt (eds.), *Social Justice Re-Examined, Dilemmas and Solutions for the Classroom Teacher*, 33–48, Stoke on Trent: Trentham Books.

Mitchell, L. (2012). Individual teachers making a difference in the classroom and the school, in R. Arshad, T. Wrigley and L. Pratt (eds.), *Social Justice Re-Examined, Dilemmas and Solutions for the Classroom Teacher*, 19–32, Stoke on Trent: Trentham Books.

Peart, S. (2013). *Making Education Work: How Black Men and Boys Navigate the Further Education Sector.* Stoke on Trent: Trentham Books.

Wolf, A. (2010). *Shifting Power to the Learner*, Adults Learning, April, 20–2.

Wrigley, T., Arshad, R., and Pratt, L. (2012). Some final Thoughts, in R. Arshad, T. Wrigley and L. Pratt (eds.), *Social Justice Re-Examined, Dilemmas and Solutions for the Classroom Teacher*, 209–12, Stoke on Trent: Trentham Books.

Index

Abdulrahman, Hadiza Kere vi, viii, 135–6
ableism 106–7, 111
Access and Participation Plan (APP) 55, 145, 150, 158–9
access to digital technology 165, 170, 182, 184–5, 189, 191
access to nature 23–34
accessibility 24, 26, 55, 63–4
adult learners 64, 72
Advance HE 138, 150
advice 166–8, 174, 177
affordability 184
agency 9–11, 19–20, 54, 57–8, 65–6, 69–70, 91, 108, 198
Alexander, Titus 200
Alford, Schevaletta 145
Algraigray, Hatim 123
Allen, Paul 138–9, 145
Andrews, Jack 123
anti-racist 139, 153
antisemitic 78, 82, 85–6, 88
AQA 78
Arday, Jason 137
Armstrong, David 120, 122, 127–8
Arnot, Madeleine 37
Arshad, Rowena 200
artificial intelligence 27, 183, 190–1
assessment 31, 59, 102, 120–2, 125–7, 129, 138, 185, 192–3
Association of Teachers of Mathematics (ATM) 93, 95, 97–8
attainment gap 37, 119, 130, 138
Aylward, Nicola 51

Badiyi, Reza 112
Baker, Sally 50–1, 57, 59
BAME 135–9, 141–6
Bandura, Albert 9
Barkham, Jo 40
Bates, Elizabeth 122
Becker, Fiona 52
Beery, Thomas 29
belonging 6, 19, 25, 51, 136–9, 144, 146, 154
Benhabib, Seyla 11

Benjamin, Shereen 199–200
Bernard, Claudia 154
Bhavnini, Reena 153
Bhopal, Kalwant 135
biophilia 28–9
Bishop, Rudine 105
Black 135–46, 149–54, 157, 159–60
Black History Month (BHM) 149, 151, 153–60
Black Lives Matter (BLM) 153, 159
Blake, William 79
Blatchford, Peter 39
blue spaces 23, 25
Boal, Augusto 95
Bonner, Fred 138
Bourdieu, Pierre 67–8, 73
boys 37–41, 43
boys' failure 39, 43
Bozukova, Katya vi, viii, 163
Braun, Virginia 157
Breach Theatre 91–2, 103
Brill, Frances 123
British Political Speech archive 91
Brownhill, Simon 37, 39–42
Bruce, Anne 11
Brunton, Ginny 14
Buchanan, Rebbecca 19, 11
Bukatko, Danuta 120
Bunce, Louise 138
Burke, Penny 138–9, 146
Burn, Elizabeth 40–1
Burns, Tracey 26
Burton, Karen 52

Cabrera, Nolan 136–8
Cannadine, David 80
care 10, 41, 44–6, 49–53, 56–7, 59
care farming 32
careers 9, 19, 44, 142
care-free 49, 51, 53, 57
care-full 49, 51, 55, 57, 59
Carer's Charter Quality Award (CCQA) 50, 53–7, 59
Carers First 49–50
Carers UK 49, 52, 54

Casalme, Anna 107
Cassen, Flora 81
Chambers, Jane v, ix, 9
Chase, Malcolm 80
Chatzitheochari, Stella 115
Chazan, Robert 81
children's development 15, 119–20, 126–30
children's learning 16, 120–30
Christianity 78–9, 81–3, 87
Christmas Carol 77–9, 82, 84–5, 87–8
church 79–80, 164, 176
Clance, Pauline 188–9
Clandinin, Jean 13
Clapton, Gary 163
cognitive 27, 30, 71, 119–20
Cole, Elizabeth 138
Cole, Mike 151–3, 159
collaboration 102, 152, 199
Collins, Kathleen 112–13, 137
Collyer, Edward v, ix, 77, 106
Communications and Digital Committee 182–5, 189
community 16, 19, 24, 29, 49–59, 77–81, 87, 95, 100, 102, 153, 155–6, 158, 170–1, 176–7, 184, 198–200
confidence 19, 65–6, 68, 165–6, 184, 186, 188–90
Constable, Karen 23, 32
cost of living 182, 190
Costas, Jana 123, 129
Cotton, Tony vi, x, 91
Covid xi, 5, 26, 92, 98–9, 164, 172, 182, 184, 189
Crawford, Angus 164
Crip theory 5, 106
Critical Race Theory (CRT) 136
cultural colour-blindness 143, 150
cultural homogenization 122, 142
culture 27, 37, 39, 92, 123, 130, 136–8, 146, 149–50, 154, 160, 183, 185, 199
curriculum ix–x, xii, xiv, 2–3, 5, 15, 31–2, 37, 40, 77–8, 88, 93–4, 98, 101, 107, 115, 119, 121, 124–5, 138, 145, 153–4, 156, 158–9, 164–5, 170–1
cybersecurity 167, 176

Day, Chantelle 11
Day, Christopher 59
decolonise 92, 105
Deleuze, Gilles 122
delivery 58, 64, 94, 156
Denscombe, Martyn 141
Department for Digital, Culture, Media & Sport 183, 185

Department for Education (DfE) 9, 63–4, 78, 119, 121, 126–9
Department for Environment, Food & Rural Affairs 24
Department for Work and Pensions 164
developmental norms 124
DiAngelo, Robin 151
Dickel, Simon 105
Dickens, Charles 77–88, 113
Dickenson, Jim 189
digital beliefs 182, 187, 193
digital capabilities 184–7, 189, 193
digital citizenship 164–6, 168, 171–2, 174–7
digital competencies 185, 192–3
digital divide 182, 184, 189, 193
digital exclusion/excluded 184, 189
digital identities 185–7
Digital Immigrants 185, 187, 192
Digital Imposter Syndrome 182, 188–91, 194
Digital Natives 185–7, 192
digital poverty 182, 184, 189, 194
digital skills 182–4, 192–3
disability xi, 50, 105–14, 123
Disability Studies 105–6
disabled 5, 105–15
disabled teachers 113–14
disclosure 50–6
discrimination 44, 46, 93, 111–12, 140, 150, 152–3, 198, 200
disparities 4, 23–4, 33–4
diverse xiii, xiv, 1, 3, 30, 42–3, 58, 111, 113–14, 124, 128, 130, 135, 146, 185, 198–9
diversity ix, 23, 42, 51, 57–8, 64, 78, 101, 105, 111, 120, 122, 136, 149–51, 154, 187, 191
Doharty, Nadena 154
Done, Elizabeth 123
drama 5, 91–5, 98
Dressel, Janice 106
Driver and Vehicle Licensing Agency (DVLA) 164
Dweck, Carol 191

Early Childhood Education xii, xvi, 120, 124, 130
Early Learning Goals (ELG) 119, 126, 128–9
Early Years vi, xii–xiii, 2, 5, 30, 40, 46, 68, 94, 119, 121, 125, 128
Early Years Foundation Stage (EYFS) 119, 121, 126–7, 129–30
Ebenezer Scrooge 5, 77–8, 82–5, 87

educators 1–6, 9–11, 13–15, 17, 19–20, 27–9, 33, 40–1, 77–8, 84, 87–8, 91, 93, 99, 123, 152–3, 163–5, 170–1, 175–7, 183, 187, 191–2, 197–200
Egalite, Anna 114
Ekins, Alison 124
Elliott, Victoria 105, 110
employment 10, 20, 24–5, 33, 39–40, 43, 64–5, 125, 152
Emslie, Carol 19
English as an additional language (EAL) 124, 127, 130
English Education 119, 123
English Literature 82, 84
English teaching 79
environment 23–6, 28, 30–2, 34, 51, 55, 57–8, 86, 123–5, 137, 139, 141, 143, 145, 163, 171–2, 174, 177, 184, 187, 189
equality 77, 88, 92, 139, 141, 143–5, 149–50, 152–3, 155, 159, 198, 200
Equality Act 2010 141, 145, 149, 152–3, 200
Equality and Human Rights Commission (EHRC) 78, 150
ethical 1, 51, 87, 120, 122, 127, 156, 198
ethnic 2, 92, 135–40, 145, 149–51
eugenics 109–10
expected level of development (ELD) 123, 126–9

fairness 77, 88, 94, 200
families 15, 17, 25, 27, 29, 45, 92, 100, 155, 164–7, 170, 174, 176–7
family 9, 12, 14, 16, 39–40, 49–50, 52–3, 58, 63–4, 68–71, 80, 91, 109, 113, 163–4, 166, 169–77
Fasheh, Munir 102
Fell-Chambers, Rachael v, vi, x, 23, 32, 149
female 37, 40, 44–6, 65, 140, 188
femininity 38–9
Fields in Trust 24
Fifth industrial revolution 183
Flood, Alison 87
food 25, 32, 121
Foucault, Michel 123
foundation degree 64
Fourth Industrial Revolution 183
Fox, Bonnie 11
Francis, Becky 38, 42, 92
Friends of the Earth 25–6
Freire, Paulo 73–4

Gavron, Hannah 9, 19–20
gender 37–9, 41–6, 144, 157
gender specific 41

gender stereotypes 39
General Certificate of Secondary Education (GCSE) 77–8, 105
generation X, Y, Z 185–7, 192
Georgiou, Michail 23
Gershenson, Seth 114
Gillborn, David 92
Glazzard, Jonathan 121, 126
Gonzalez-Arnal, Stella 51
Gov.co.uk 114, 151–2
Gov.UK 151–2
government 1–2, 24–7, 67–8, 91–2, 121, 127–30, 136, 143, 155, 164–5, 169, 183–4, 191, 198
Gray, William 106
Grbich, Carol 11
green space 23–6, 28–30, 32–4
Greenwood, Davydd 67–8
Grierson, Jamie 26
growth 10, 30, 84, 119–20, 122, 183, 185, 189, 191, 193
The Guardian 92, 99
Guild HE 138

Hauerwas, Stanley 120–1
Hausstatter, Rune 124
health 24–7, 29–30, 32–4, 49–50, 53–4, 56, 99, 119–20, 165, 173
Heleta, Savo 137
Higher Education (HE) 49, 63, 67, 135–40, 145, 150, 154, 158, 189
Hinkley, Trina 26
His Majesty's Revenue and Customs (HMRC) 164
Hokka, Paeivi 10–11, 19
Holland, Dorothy 12
Honig, Alice 120
housing 24–5, 32
Hubble, Sue 63
human functioning 30, 93
Human Rights 150, 185
Hutchings, Merryn 123

IB Learner Profile 94
identity 9–20, 38–9, 46, 51–3, 70–1, 101, 105, 137, 150
Illeris, Knud 68–9, 71–2
impairments 106, 108–9, 111–12
imposter 182, 188–91
inclusion 5, 42, 63, 65, 143–4, 154, 189, 191, 193, 198
inequality 11, 24–6, 34, 37, 77, 80, 138, 150, 154, 200
Inglis, Kenneth 80
International Alliance of Carer Organisations 49

International Baccalaureate (IB) 94
Internet 163, 165, 167, 176, 182, 184–5, 189, 191
ITV News 37

Jew 81
Jewish 77–84, 86–7
Jisc 184
Johnson, Paul 80
Jordan, William 81
Judaism 81–2
justice 2–3, 5–7, 32, 77, 85, 87–8, 91–4, 101, 130, 163, 165, 170–1, 176, 197–200

Kaplan, Stephen 29–30
Kelchtermans, Geert 11
Kettell, Lynn 50
Khan-Shah, Fatima 49
Kim, Jean 19
King, Lagarrett 153–4
Knight, Tim 68
Kotter, John 158

Larkin, Mary 50–1
Lawrence, Clare vi, x, 105
legislation 80, 152, 165, 200
Leland, Christine 119, 123
Leonardo, Zeus 137, 152–3
Leverton, Leanne v, x, 49
Lindt, Nienke 50
loans 63–4, 66
local authority 91, 126, 128, 130
local government 26, 91, 143
Loftis, Sonya 106, 112
Louv, Richard 27
Lovejoy, Meg 12, 19
Lunenberg, Mieke 10
Lyotard, Jean-François 10

Maclaren, Peter 73
Macpherson, William 149
Mahon, Clare xi, 105
male 4, 10, 38, 40–2, 44, 46, 140
Manzo, Ula 106
Marandet, Elodie 52
marginalization 136, 140
marginalized 6, 140, 146, 150, 154
Marriott, Theresa vi, xi, 181
masculine approach 40
masculinity 38–9, 41
Mason, Jessica 106
Mason, Sacha v, xii, 49, 63, 66–7
Mathematics 5, 91–6, 98–100, 102
Mathieu, Felix 154
mature learners 63–8, 72–3
Maxwell, Rachel 57–9

Maykut, Pamela 141
McDonnell, Amy 30
McLean, Dawson 9
McMillan, Margaret 28
McRuer, Robert 106
Mead, George 16
Meijers, Frans 42
Mell, Julie 81
men 4, 11, 37–46
mental health 25, 27, 30, 34, 50, 173
Meredith, Caroline v, xii, 37
Merleau-Ponty, Maurice 13
Mezirow, Jack 70–1
Mice and Men 105–10, 112–14
Mihalakakou, Giouli 29
Milestone, Lewis 112
Miller, Paul xvi
Miller, Tina 10, 12
Milne, Alisoun 51
Mistry, Malini 38
Mitchell, Laura 200
Moore, Robin 26
Moreau, Marie-Pierre 49, 51, 53
Morgan, Kenneth 80
Morgan, Nicky 164
mother, mothers 9–10, 12–20, 52, 69–70, 109, 165
motherhood 9–14, 16–20
mothering 40
motivation 43, 68, 70, 72, 92, 157
MT251 102

Nario-Redmond, Michelle 112
narrative 9, 13, 42–3, 45, 57, 65, 78–9, 83, 108–10, 112, 136, 160
National Association for the Teaching of Drama 93
National Health Service (NHS) 25, 50–1
National Statistics 25–6, 37, 145
National Trust 26
National Union of Students (NUS) 50–1
nature 23–4, 26–34
nature-based 26
Nature-Friendly Schools 27
Neaum, Sally 121
Newlove-Delgado, Tamsin 25
Nicholson, Nyree xii, 119, 122
Nikolajeva, Maria 113
Noddings, Nel 12, 19
normalization 122–3, 126–9
normative 38, 40–1, 44, 119–22, 124, 126–30
NSPCC 176

Ofcom 182, 184
Office for Artificial Intelligence 191
Office for National Statistics (ONS) 26, 145

Office for Students (OfS) 50, 63, 145, 150, 184
Ofsted 27, 123, 126, 129–30
Opie, Clive 156
outdoor learning 27, 31
outdoors 23, 26–9, 31, 33–4
Overgaard, Charlotte 57

Paechter, Carrie 38–9
Palacio, Raquel 105, 108–10, 112
Palaiologou, Ioanna 120–2, 127
parenthood 4
parenting 167, 170
parents 15, 26, 43–4, 69, 109, 124, 130, 164, 166–77
Peart, Sheine v, vi, xiii, 1, 135–6, 149, 159, 197, 199
pedagogy 27, 57, 64–5, 67–8, 73, 77–9, 86, 110
The Pen Green Center 121
Pepperell, Sandy 37
physical activity 26, 30, 33
play 17, 24–6, 29, 32, 95, 101
pollution 29
Postareff, Lisa 70
poverty 24–5, 51, 58, 182, 184, 189
Powell, Martine 106–7
Prensky, Marc 185–6, 192
primary school 37–9, 41, 43–6
primary teachers 44
Pring, Richard 10
Pritchard, Gail 114
professional identities 9–14, 16–20, 39
Public Sector Equality Duty (PSED) 141, 149
pupils 27, 37, 39–40, 78, 82, 87–8, 92, 100, 105–7, 111, 113–15, 151

Quality Assurance Agency 64

race 105, 136, 139, 142–3, 146, 151–3
Race Equality charter 150
race relations 151–2
racial inequality 138, 150, 154
racism 6, 92, 113, 136, 138–9, 145–6, 152–5, 159
Ray, Victor 150
re-cripping 106, 111–13
refugees 97–8
research 1–3, 6, 9–11, 23, 26, 30–4, 38–40, 43, 45, 51, 54, 67–8, 99, 112, 114, 119, 125, 136, 138, 140–2, 144–5, 150–1, 153, 155–9, 164, 174, 183
Right to Roam 24
Rigolon, Alessandro 33

Rivas, Carol 156
Roberts-Holmes, Guy 121, 123
Robinson, Sir Ken 120–1, 123–4
Rogers, Alan 66–7, 73
role model 17, 38, 40–2, 46
Rollock, Nicola 146, 150
Roslund, Marja 23, 30–1, 33
Ruohotie-Lyhty, Marie 11

Saccomanno, Benjamin 69–70
Sandahl, Carrie 106
Savickas, Mark 42
Schensul, Stephen 141
schools 2, 27–8, 31–3, 37–40, 42, 45, 50, 86, 94, 105, 111, 124, 164–71, 174–7
Schwab, Klaus 183
Schwarzfuchs, Simon 81
Scrooge 5, 77–8, 82–5, 87
secondary school 94, 167–8
Seeley, J. Lotus 39
self-efficacy 11, 20, 58, 65–6, 70
sexualized stereotypes 41
Singh, Shivani 154, 158
Sinise, Gary 112
skills 16, 27, 31–2, 64, 68, 78, 93–5, 100, 120, 124, 127, 130, 145, 159–60, 182–4, 191–3
Sleurs, Hanne 30, 33
Smith, George 80
social justice 2–3, 5–7, 13, 15, 77, 85, 87–8, 91–3, 101, 130, 165, 170, 176, 197–200
social media 51, 163–9, 172–7
South Africa 99
Special Educational Needs and Disabilities (SEND) 121, 123–4, 127, 130
Spencer, Katrina 153–4
standardization 123, 125, 128–30
Steinbeck, John 105, 107–10
stereotypes 39–41, 78, 81, 83
sterilization 109
student 2, 4–5, 12, 15–17, 27, 43, 49–52, 54, 56–9, 63–5, 72, 78, 84–8, 92, 94, 100, 114, 124, 135–6, 150, 153–4, 156–60

Tait, Gordon 39
Talbot-Landers, Cait 33
Tarvainen, Merja 108
Tate, Shirley-Anne 135, 145
Tatum, Beverley 153
Tayler, Collette 121
Taylor, Aaron 183
Taylor, Edward 71
teacher education 10, 15, 93
Teaching Assistant (TA) 37–40, 42–3, 45–6

technology 6, 26–7, 57, 64, 181–7, 189, 191–3
Terzi, Lorella 153
Thatcher, Margaret 91
Thiele, Tamara 11
Thompson, Francis 80
Tikly, Leon 154
Tobin, James 27
Toft, Helen vi, xiii, 91
Tollefson, Travis 112
Torre, Margarita 39, 101
traditional 31–2, 63, 65–7, 72, 87, 110, 124
Transforming Access and Student Outcomes in Higher Education (TASO) 150

UK Parliament 38, 80
underachieve 127
United Nations Children's Fund UNICEF 97
United Nations Educational, Scientific and Cultural Organization UNESCO 182
United Nations UN 185
Universities UK 138–9, 145–6, 154–5
unpaid care 49–50, 53
Uprichard, Emma 13

Valcke, Martin 167, 170
Van De Mieroop, Kenan 154
Victorian 77, 79, 82, 84
Vital, David 81, 126
von Unger, Hella 156

Waite, Sue 23, 31
Ware, Hannah 113
Ware, Rhonda 120
Warin, Jo 38, 40
Warwick-Booth, Louise 24
well-being 30, 37, 42, 54
White 5, 105, 113, 135–9, 142–4
White-centric 135, 142
Whiteness 136–8, 141–2, 150, 153, 160
Whitmore, John 190
widening participation 57, 64–5, 68–8, 113
Widrich, Mechtild 81
Wildlife Trusts 33
Wilkins, Chris 136
Wilkinson, Iain 167
Wilson, Edward 28
Wolf, Alison 9–10, 19–20, 199
Wolstencroft, Peter 185–6
women 9–11, 13–16, 18–20, 37–41, 44, 46, 49, 85, 188
Wonder 105–6, 108–13
Wong, Billy 138
workforce 37–9, 42–3, 45–6, 182–3
working 14, 16–17, 27, 29, 32, 39, 41–2, 44–5, 51, 58, 64, 69, 80, 93–4, 99–100, 105, 124–5, 152–3, 155, 159, 164, 182, 184, 190–2, 197, 200
World Economic Forum 183–4
Wright, Cecile 142
Wrigley, Terry 200

Yerushalmi, Yosef 81
Yorknotes 107
Yuhsen 102